Anti-Corruption in International Development provides scholars, policymakers and practitioners with a comprehensive analysis of approaches to combat corruption in the context of international development. International development agencies are constrained in their choice of approaches when engaging governments of countries that face significant corruption challenges. This book contextualises the challenges and opportunities and provides readers with an analysis of potential policy options. The study of the UK's anti-corruption strategies to tackle corruption in developing countries adds important policy and practical perspectives that enhance both the quality of the analysis and the practical value for readers.

Professor Louis de Koker, *La Trobe Law School, College of Arts, Social Sciences and Commerce, La Trobe University, Australia*

Kerusauskaite gives a refreshing overview of the myriad of public sector approaches to combat corruption. Her work emphasises the need for a global response to corruption with close involvement of civil society and the private sector in a 'coalition of the committed'. Development organisations, bilateral and multilateral, can help create such coalitions.

David Johan Kuijper, *Advisor, Financing for Development, World Bank*

Corruption is the cancer at the heart of international development. It infuriates donor nations, whose hard-pressed taxpayers and honest investors are swindled, and denies the poorest people the help we want them to receive. The UK's role in international development and anti-corruption is world leading and is at the heart of making the world safer and more prosperous. I congratulate Ingrida on her work in this field.

Rt. Hon. Andrew Mitchell, *MP, UK, former UK Secretary of State for International Development*

Anti-Corruption in International Development

Corruption is linked to a wide range of developmental issues, including undermining democratic institutions, slowing economic development and contributing to government instability, poverty and inequality. It is estimated that corruption costs more than 5 per cent of global GDP, and that more than one trillion US dollars are paid in bribes each year. This book unpacks the concept of corruption, its political and ethical influences, its measurement, commitments to combat corruption and ways that this is being attempted.

Building on the research on the nature, causes and consequences of corruption, this book analyses international anti-corruption interventions in particular. It discusses approaches to focus efforts to tackle corruption in developing countries on where they are most likely to be successful. The efforts of the UK are considered as a detailed case study, with comparisons brought in as necessary from other countries' and multilateral institutions' anti-corruption efforts.

Bridging a range of disciplines, *Anti-Corruption in International Development* will be of interest to students and scholars of international development, public administration, management, international relations, politics and criminal justice.

Ingrida Kerusauskaite is an Affiliated Lecturer at the Centre of Development Studies at the University of Cambridge and an Advisor on International Development for KPMG.

Routledge Corruption and Anti-Corruption Studies

The series features innovative and original research on the subject of corruption from scholars around the world. As well as documenting and analysing corruption, the series aims to discuss anti-corruption initiatives and endeavours, in an attempt to demonstrate ways forward for countries and institutions where the problem is widespread. The series particularly promotes comparative and interdisciplinary research targeted at a global readership.

In terms of theory and method, rather than basing itself on any one orthodoxy, the series draws broadly on the tool kit of the social sciences in general, emphasizing comparison, the analysis of the structure and processes, and the application of qualitative and quantitative methods.

Anti-Corruption in International Development
Ingrida Kerusauskaite

Corruption Scandals and their Global Impacts
Edited by Omar E. Hawthorne and Stephen Magu

For more information about this series, please visit: https://www.routledge.com/Routledge-Corruption-and-Anti-Corruption-Studies/book-series/RCACS

Anti-Corruption in International Development

Ingrida Kerusauskaite

LONDON AND NEW YORK

First published 2018
by Routledge
2 Park Square, Milton Park, Abingdon, Oxon OX14 4RN

and by Routledge
711 Third Avenue, New York, NY 10017

Routledge is an imprint of the Taylor & Francis Group, an informa business

© 2018 Ingrida Kerusauskaite

The right of Ingrida Kerusauskaite to be identified as author of this work has been asserted by her in accordance with sections 77 and 78 of the Copyright, Designs and Patents Act 1988.

All rights reserved. No part of this book may be reprinted or reproduced or utilised in any form or by any electronic, mechanical, or other means, now known or hereafter invented, including photocopying and recording, or in any information storage or retrieval system, without permission in writing from the publishers.

Trademark notice: Product or corporate names may be trademarks or registered trademarks, and are used only for identification and explanation without intent to infringe.

British Library Cataloguing in Publication Data
A catalogue record for this book is available from the British Library

Library of Congress Cataloging in Publication Data
A catalog record for this book has been requested

ISBN: 978-1-138-57534-9 (hbk)
ISBN: 978-1-351-27204-9 (ebk)

Typeset in Times New Roman
by Wearset Ltd, Boldon, Tyne and Wear

Contents

List of figures ix
List of tables x
Foreword xi
Acknowledgements xvi
List of acronyms and abbreviations xviii
List of treaties and acts xxi
Table of cases xxii

1 **Introduction** 1

   International development and the global fight against corruption 2
   Case study 5
   Methodology 7
   Structure of the book 8

2 **Conceptual framework: definitions and the nature of corruption** 12

   2.1 Definitions of corruption 12
   2.2 Offences of corruption 18
   2.3 Cultural and historic differences 24
   2.4 Summary 32

3 **Theoretical approach to anti-corruption interventions in international development** 38

   3.1 Moral foundations of the anti-corruption debate 38
   3.2 Measurement of corruption 48
   3.3 Nature and causes of corruption 50
   3.4 Consequences of corruption 63
   3.5 The nuances 72
   3.6 Summary 77

4 The UK's anti-corruption work in developing countries   86

    4.1 UK's approach to anti-corruption programming 87
    4.2 Programme foci 102
    4.3 Issues with anti-corruption programming 123
    4.4 Summary 131

5 International law and development: where anti-corruption interventions fit in   139

    5.1 Law and development 139
    5.2 International law 146
    5.3 International anti-corruption treaties and agreements 153
    5.4 Summary 164

6 The UK government's use of multilateral and bilateral approaches to tackle corruption in developing countries   171

    6.1 Multilateral approaches 172
    6.2 Bilateral approaches 180
    6.3 Key strengths and weaknesses of different implementation channels 190
    6.4 Combining the key strengths of different approaches 199
    6.5 Summary 204

7 Conclusions and wider implications   211

    Index   220

Figures

1.1	Top 5 OECD DAC members' ODA contributions (US$ millions)	5
3.1	An illustration of short-term versus long-term approaches	47
3.2	Types of corruption based on the nature of the state and business	54
3.3	Theoretical approaches to corruption	60
3.4	Corruption and state institutions	67
3.5	The influence on and of corruption	71
4.1	UK net ODA levels 1970–2014 (£ millions)	87
4.2	DFID spending in priority countries, 2014–2015 (£ millions)	88
4.3	UK bilateral aid spending in 2014 by sector (£ thousands)	90
4.4	DFID's anti-corruption expenditure, 2007–2018 (£ millions)	95
4.5	DFID spending on anti-corruption, 2004–2020	97
4.6	CPI ratings	98
4.7	DFID's approach to anti-corruption	99
4.8	Key factors in anti-corruption programming	103
4.9	Stages of corruption interventions	104
4.10	Interdependencies between different institutions in the legal sector in achieving results	109
4.11	Interdependencies between different institutions in achieving results from national audits	110
6.1	Breakdown of UK bilateral aid in 2014	180
6.2	2014 bilateral spending by regions	185
6.3	Donors' marginal gains as a function of the recipient country's wealth	186
7.1	The requirements of various policy alignments for successful programmes	215

Tables

2.1	Definitions of corruption used by multilateral agencies	15
2.2	Forms of corporate corruption or misconduct that may be damaging to states' economies	17
2.3	Categories of corruption as relevant in the context of criminalisation and law enforcement	19
2.4	Reforms in Sweden leading to impartiality and combatting corruption	31
3.1	Summary of anti-corruption programme foundations	62
4.1	Percentage of people who identify themselves as religious in countries, by income levels	115
4.2	Attitudes to corruption and bribery in different traditions	116
4.3	The evidence on the effectiveness of various anti-corruption interventions	128
6.1	UK ODA by delivery channel	173
6.2	DFID's contributions to multilateral organisations' core activities	174
6.3	Non-DFID core multilateral contributions	175
6.4	ODA spending by UK government departments other than DFID	184
6.5	Breakdown of UK bilateral net ODA by income group in 2014	185
6.6	Attributes of multilateral, bilateral and multi-bi channels	201

Foreword

We are often told and, indeed, may well agree, that corruption like poverty is inherent to the human condition. The poor and the corrupt will always be with us! No doubt we can, with some value, debate this, but at least in our lifetimes nothing is set or for that matter anticipated, which is likely to change this. Having been accorded the privilege to write a foreword to Dr Ingrida Kerusauskaite's excellent book, I hesitate to moralise, let alone preach, a particular condemnation of corruption even in its most simplistic form of bribery. As a lawyer who, in common with his kin, admires clear lines of demarcation between good and bad, I am forced to recognise that any meaningful debate on corruption cannot be so readily structured. Dr Kerusauskaite's new study certainly does not risk this criticism. She recognises the complexity at all levels and in all dimensions of her topic. Of course, we can properly avow that corruption, when it taints leadership and undermines the respect and confidence that give strength to the fabric of governance, is inimical to the very values and aspirations we cherish. It also weakens stability and security, and therefore the ability of an economy to prosper. It is consequently of real and pressing concern to those who seek development of some of our most vulnerable communities.

Commitment to integrity should be a non-negotiable element in the manifold structures of governance in any constituency and, while we have them in the form we have today, nation-states. Of course we can, with some intellectual confidence at the margin, debate exactly what is conjured up by the notion of integrity. We must also recognise that attitudes, and in particular, the acceptability of certain manifestations of conduct, are dynamic. This is not to give encouragement to those who look, with certain preconceptions, on the political history of developing and especially postcolonial societies, but to recognise the way in which, in particular, social issues are addressed at a point in time can well be specific and relevant to the circumstances of that day. In the USA and UK we have recently witnessed the impact on so many institutions, and not least the government, of controversy centred on what is properly characterised as unacceptable conduct, in a sexual context, between non-consenting adults. What might well have been regarded – by those who formed or at least guided opinion – as socially acceptable in the relatively recent past, today attracts high condemnation, even the threat of prison! An example of conduct not overly dissimilar to corruption, which has journeyed along a somewhat pragmatic path to damnation, is that of insider dealing. Not so long ago there were people in the financial sector – some in positions of great authority – who argued that to fail to utilise material price-sensitive information, albeit having been obtained by virtue of some privileged position, was plain daft and where you acted on behalf of others, arguably a failure to promote their best interests. To utter such sentiments today would be wholly unacceptable. In the case of corruption, debate has centred not so much on whether the taking of a bribe is objectionable, but rather whether it is worth seeking to inhibit and control such conduct, and upon what terms. Dr Ingrida Kerusauskaite skilfully addresses and navigates such intellectually charged viable concerns.

These issues are of practical importance, not such in framing law – particularly where such is going to be intrusive of existing practices, but in its administration. There has been debate on the acceptability of 'mere' facilitation payments and other incentives and countries do take differing approaches, which is reflected in their legislation. Even in the relatively established jurisprudence of the common law on such matters, the superior English courts have recently disagreed as to the basis upon which those who pay and receive bribes and other secret benefits should be rendered liable and held to account.

Dr Kerusauskaite has found a rich and fertile terrain to explore the various characteristics and consequences of corruption. She does so, however, very much from the perspective of a scholar and, indeed, practitioner interested in assisting those who, one way or another, find themselves with the responsibility of discouraging abuse in the broader context of development. While to many, including myself, the implications and consequences of corruption unarguably impede and inhibit development, agencies and organisations concerned with promoting stability and development have – until relatively recently, been hesitant to engage in any meaningful condemnation let alone action. In part, this may be justified because of the intimacy of serious – grand corruption, with those who can express and manipulate issues of national sovereignty and even seek sanctuary in the ideology of empowerment and liberation. This caution, particularly in an era of postcolonialism and stark international political division, was also justified within inter-governmental organisations on the basis that to achieve a measurable result, affirmative action within the domestic legal context would be required and intervention and enforcement were properly beyond their proper concern, let alone mandates. So while, for example, Commonwealth governments as early as 1976 recognised the dangers that economically motivated crime had for development and applauded proposals from the UK, to foster a degree of collaboration that, even today, would be considered optimistic, it was not for another 15 years that corruption was roundly condemned and then only addressed once the apparatus that had been set up to foster more meaningful intervention on a transnational basis against economic crime had been dismantled. Attitudes within bodies such as the World Bank and IMF did start to change in the late 1980s and some were bold, possibly prematurely so, in addressing the issues within, as well as without, legal systems that needed to be mended. Many of the more developed and thus, powerful jurisdictions, including the UK, comfortable in their self-assessed 'absence' of easily identifiable (that is to say egregious) corruption at home and their sensitivity to handicapping the entrepreneurial zeal of their businessmen, were equally coy. Things did, of course, change – as this book so well recounts. The notion that there was some deep and seamless commitment to promoting integrity both at home and abroad as almost intrinsic to our Western democratic traditions was, and sadly remains, a convenient myth.

This book is not, however, another philosophical or historical account of how we have come to do more than worry about corruption and its impact on development and, thus, us all, in the interdependent world in which we exist. This book is a resource in that it analyses the various ways in which corruption can be, and is, addressed and provides an informed appraisal allowing those who have to make decisions on intervention, whether by aid, advice or in more robust ways, to achieve a more sensible and possibly sensitive prioritisation. Now that almost everyone has signed up to fighting the 'war on corruption', we see a plethora of both bodies and actions – a commonality of their condition, being their insatiable appetite for resources and, consequently, the uncertainties surrounding their longevity and efficiency – further compounding any proper assessment of their effectiveness, being the mismatch in objectives between donors and those at the 'coal face' inevitably confronted on a daily basis by the ambiguity of the political system within which they operate. Of course, there are those among us who are still haunted by the scepticism that attached itself to other crusades – such as that against illicit drugs – and even terror! The jaundiced among us might see a lot of what is being advocated, particularly in terms of transparency and accountability of other people's wealth, as being rather more a priority of the taxman and the financial demands of 'Western' social institutions than in protecting the integrity of developing economies and facilitating restitution. Dr Kerusauskaite charts a careful and pensive course through such waters and consequently provides even those of an otherwise cautious stance, with useful tools for evaluating the efficacy of the laws, initiatives and institutions that are being so enthusiastically promoted.

This book addresses, in a practical and, given the author's experience, authoritative way, the effectiveness of the various international development assistance delivery mechanisms that have emerged over the last decade, and, in particular, the anti-corruption programmes that have been developed by the UK. Albeit that the UK has not, until relatively recently, been at the forefront of international initiatives preferring to support almost by stealth, things have changed – perhaps most noticeably due to then Prime Minister David Cameron's commitment and international conference in May 2016. Although surprisingly slow, perhaps even inept in developing its legislation, Britain now has, arguably, in the Bribery Act 2010, one of the best sets of legal provisions in the world. As the author points out, however, specific anti-corruption laws need to be evaluated in the wider context of both the legal system and its administration. In the UK, of equal significance has been the reform of the law relating to fraud (in the Fraud Act 2006) and the development of a comprehensive, albeit costly, anti-money laundering regime. Developing countries do not generally have the resources and ability to have such legal makeovers. The UK law on bribery, while refreshing in the clarity of its drafting, is still complex, difficult and expensive to police. The tapestry of measures and interventions that are currently being implemented or planned at bi- and multilateral levels is also impressive and timely. The author's involvement as a consultant in the design, implementation and monitoring of some of these affords an insight which is, in the academy, unique.

Her discussion and evaluation is not, however, confined to the UK. The author has had considerable international experience and commendably alludes throughout to the experience of other countries and international organisations. She points, in particular, to the efficacy of partnerships and especially those that build upon and incorporate existing resources and programmes within country. It is often the empowering of those who are closest to the problem and most exposed to the consequences, that achieves the best and enduring results.

Those of us who work, in one way or another, in corruption and economic crime control, can be reassured that the worldwide appetite for addressing the threat of corruption in its various forms, will not lessen. The outrage that has been stoked by publication, albeit in circumstances that raise other issues of propriety, of the so-called Panama and more recently the Paradise papers revealing almost the wholesale use of offshore facilities to hide wealth and its handling, attests to the vitality of our concern about such issues. Of course, in the main what is at stake is the desire for discretion on the part of the already wealthy and the moderation of tax, rather than the laundering of ill-gotten gains, let alone bribes. Nonetheless, corruption and its control have relevance not least in the context of those jurisdictions that have been prepared to prostitute their sovereignty and become launderettes for organised criminals and kleptomaniacs. We have also witnessed the tremendous impact of anti-corruption campaigns not least in China. While China has a long, and in fact honourable, history of attempting to address, at least, some aspects of corruption and related abuse, the recent campaign has, in some quarters, been seen as providing an opportunity for wider political changes. That criticism and the legal process is a two-edged sword which can be used to quieten and discourage those who oppose abuse as much as those who take advantage of their position, is well documented. This experience in many countries argues in favour of much more thorough care being taken as to how we address corruption and whether our objectives are relevant, desirable and attainable. This book candidly addresses these questions and is therefore of value beyond the practitioner and specialised researcher. It is, in my view, a significant contribution to the discussion and analysis of a series of issues that are of immense importance, not only to the management and delivery of development, but thereby to us all. Those involved in international relations, diplomacy, public policy and the better management of governance need to carefully consider Dr Kerusauskaite's work and its implications. For far too long the level and degree of thought that has been given in any discipline to protecting our societies from those who, primarily out of greed, undermine the integrity, with all that this risks, of our institutions and societies has been derisory. This book goes a long way in addressing this deficit.

Professor Barry Rider OBE
Professorial Fellow, Centre of Development Studies
University of Cambridge

Acknowledgements

This book draws upon my work and studies of international development – from my PhD and MPhil research at the University of Cambridge, to undergraduate level at the School of Oriental and African Studies (SOAS), University of London and the various professional programmes and projects on which I have worked. It explores in greater detail questions that I have been mulling over for at least a decade: International legal agreements and conventions do not seem to be stopping or very effective at bringing to account all those who committed atrocities and morally wrong behaviour, but why is so much importance attached to those agreements and conventions and funds invested in them? How and do international development interventions contribute to ensuring justice for the most vulnerable people in developing countries? What are the unintended consequences of various international development interventions and what makes them work for the benefit of those they are meant to help? To what extent do international development interventions have the ability to meaningfully alleviate injustices and burdens of lack of development? And when and how are these interventions most likely to achieve their intended outcomes?

This work would not have been done without the support of a number of people. First of all, I would like to thank my PhD supervisor Professor Barry Rider, for his invaluable guidance and support over the three years of my PhD work, for introducing me to various aspects of the complex world of fighting economic crime and for giving me unique and incredible opportunities in teaching, publications and conferences.

Professor Christopher Cramer, at SOAS, University of London, also played a key role in supporting and guiding my academic work from an early stage.

My parents and grandmas gave tremendous support all throughout my work and studies and I am immensely grateful for all they have done to encourage my work.

Matthew Glanville, John Burton, Matthew Smith, Kru Desai and Gil Gorev, thank you for giving me numerous opportunities to work on international development programming on anti-corruption and to combine my academic pursuits with my professional work. This gave me unique insights into the practical aspects of anti-corruption programming.

Staff and students at the Centre of Development Studies, POLIS, the Law Faculty, the Economics Department and at Jesus College created a unique academic atmosphere of debate and scholarship from which I benefited enormously.

Jesus College and everyone involved in the Cambridge International Symposium on Economic Crime played a significant role in my work during the PhD, providing intellectual stimulus and introducing me to various different projects and disciplines that have made me consider a wide variety of approaches to my topic. I am very grateful to Jesus College for facilitating my participation in a number of conferences in the UK and internationally, which helped me refine and discuss my work with my peers and leading experts globally.

I would like to thank all those who endured and entertained discussions with me on corruption and development – in Cambridge, London and the various conferences around the UK, in Hong Kong and Jamaica. Matthew, since you complained about this the most, a special mention goes to you here.

My Cambridge PhD writing buddies, Melisa Bintoro and Ivo Jose Pinto De Macedo Timoteo, made the weekend writing marathons considerably more enjoyable (and/or often substituted them with almost related activities...). Carolin Mester brightened the London weekend writing sessions (similarly, when these were not replaced by trips to the cat cafe or the meerkat farm).

Dan kept things interesting.

This book is based on my PhD submitted to the University of Cambridge in 2016–2017 and a chapter I have published on 'Corruption and International Development Assistance' in the Research Handbook of International Financial Crime *edited by Professor Barry Rider, published by Edward Elgar. That chapter draws directly on some of the chapters of this book, mostly Chapters 2–4.*

Acronyms and abbreviations

AC	Anti-Corruption
ACE	DFID's Anti-Corruption Evidence Programme
ADB	Asian Development Bank
AfDB	African Development Bank
AG	Auditor General
AIIB	Asian Infrastructure Investment Bank
AsDF	Asian Development Fund
AU	African Union
AUCPCC	African Union Convention on Preventing and Combating Corruption
BVI	British Virgin Islands
CDHRI	Cairo Declaration of Human Rights in Islam
CERF	Central Emergency Response Fund
CoE	Council of Europe
COST	Construction Centre Transparency Initiative
CPI	Corruption Perception Index
CPS	Crown Prosecution Services
CW	Corruption Watch
DANIDA	Danish International Development Agency
DFID	United Kingdom's Department for International Development
DOJ	US Department of Justice
EBRD	European Bank for Reconstruction and Development
EITI	Extractive Industries' Transparency Initiative
EU	European Union
FATF	Financial Action Task Force
FCA	Financial Crime Authority
FCO	Foreign and Commonwealth Office
FCPA	Foreign Corrupt Practices Act
FLEGT	Forest Law Enforcement, Governance and Trade
GATFM	Global Fund to Fight Aids, Tuberculosis and Malaria
GDP	Gross Domestic Product
GNI	Gross National Income
HL	House of Lords

Acronyms and abbreviations xix

HMRC	Her Majesty's Revenue and Customs
HRW	Human Rights Watch
IACAC	Inter-American Convention against Corruption
IATI	International Aid Transparency Initiative
IBRD	International Bank for Reconstruction and Development
ICAI	Independent Commission on Aid Impact
ICAR	International Centre for Asset Recovery
ICC	International Criminal Court
ICCom	International Chamber of Commerce
ICCPR	International Covenant on Civil and Political Rights
ICIJ	International Consortium of Investigative Journalists
ICJ	International Court of Justice
ICMT	International Conference on Military Trials
ICU	UK National Crime Agency's International Corruption Unit
IDC	International Development Committee
ILO	International Liaison Officer
IMF	International Monetary Fund
IMT	International Military Tribunal
iNGO	International Non-Governmental Organisation
JMLIT	Joint Money Laundering Intelligence Task Force
MNC	Multinational Corporation
MSF	Médecins Sans Frontières
NAO	National Audit Office
NCA	National Crime Agency
NDB	New Development Bank
NGO	Non-Governmental Organisation
NIE	New Institutional Economics
NORAD	Norwegian Agency for Development Cooperation
OAG	Office of the Auditor General
OCCRP	Organised Crime and Corruption Reporting Project
ODA	Official Development Assistance
OECD	Organisation for Economic Cooperation and Development
OECD – DAC	OECD Development Assistance Committee
PAC	Public Accounts Committee
PBR	Payment by Results
PCT	Public Choice Theory
PEA	Political Economy Analysis
PFM	Public Financial Management
PIDG	Private Infrastructure Development Group
PM	Prime Minister
R2P	Responsibility to Protect
SAP	Structural Adjustment Programme
SEC	US Securities and Exchange Commission
SFO	Serious Fraud Office
SIDA	Swedish International Development Cooperation Agency

SMEs	Small and Medium Enterprises
SOE	State-owned Enterprise
StAR	Stolen Asset Recovery Initiative
TA	Technical Assistance
TI	Transparency International
TNC	Transnational Corporation
UDHR	Universal Declaration of Human Rights
UIDHR	Universal Islamic Declaration of Human Rights
UK	United Kingdom
UN	United Nations
UNCAC	United Nations Convention Against Corruption
UNCAT	United Nations Convention Against Torture
UNDP	United Nations Development Programme
UNGC	United Nations Global Compact
UNODC	United Nations Office on Drugs and Crime
UNWGAD	United Nations Working Group on Arbitrary Detention
USAID	United States Agency for International Development
VCLT	Vienna Convention on the Law of Treaties
WB	World Bank
WDR	World Development Report
WfD	Westminster Foundation for Democracy
WTO	World Trade Organization

Treaties and acts

African Union's Convention on Preventing and Combating Corruption 2003
BVI Companies Act 2004
CoE's Civil Law Convention on Corruption 1999 (CoE, European Treaty Series, No. 174)
CoE's Criminal Law Convention on Corruption 1999 (CoE, European Treaty Series, No. 173)
Convention for the Fight against Corruption involving Officials of the European Communities or Officials of Member States of the European Union 1997
European Savings Directive 2005
Inter-American Convention against Corruption 1996 (E/1996/99)
OECD Convention on Combating Bribery of Foreign Public Officials in International Business Transactions 1997
Pendleton Civil Service Act, United States 1883
Rome Statute of the International Criminal Court, adopted in 1998
Statute of the International Court of Justice
Uganda Anti-Corruption Act of 2009
Uganda The Public Finance and Accountability Act of 2003
Uganda The Public Procurement and Disposal of Public Acts of 2003
Uganda The Whistleblowers Protection Act of 2010
UK Bribery Act 2010
UK International Development Act 2002
UK International Development (Official Development Assistance Target) Act 2015
UK International Development (Reporting and Transparency) Act of 2006
United Nations Charter
United Nations Convention against Corruption (UNCAC) 2004
US Dodd-Frank Wall Street Reform and Consumer Protection Act 2010
US Foreign and Corrupt Practices Act (FCPA) 1977
US International Anti-Bribery and Fair Competition Act 1998
US Omnibus Trade and Competitiveness Act 1988
Vienna Convention on the Law of Treaties (VCLT)
World Bank's Articles of Agreement

Table of cases

Case Concerning the Gabčikovo-Nagymaros Project (Hungary/Slovakia), 1997 ICJ Rep. 7, separate opinion of Vice-President Weeramantry, at para. C(c)
Derby & Co Ltd v. Weldon (Nos 3 and 4) [1989] 2 WLR 412
Hatch v. Baez (1876) 7 Hun. 596
R v. Jones [2006] UKHL 16
R (on the application of Gentle and another) v. Prime Minister [2006] EWCA Civ 1689
Regina v. Bartle and the Commissioner of Police for the Metropolis and Others Ex Parte Pinochet Regina v. Evans and Another and the Commissioner of Police for the Metropolis and Others Ex Parte Pinochet (On Appeal from a Divisional Court of the Queen's Bench Division) (1999), opinion of Lord Lloyd of Berwick
S v. Shaik and Others [2007] (1) SA 240 (SCA)
United States of America v. Noriega 92–4687, (1990) Nos. 96–4471
Underhill v. Hernandez (1897) 168 US 250

US Congress hearings

United States. Congress. Senate. Committee on Foreign Relations. Subcommittee on Multinational Corporations. Multinational Corporations and United States Foreign Policy: Hearings Before the Subcommittee On Multinational Corporations of the Committee On Foreign Relations, United States Senate, Ninety-third – [Ninety-fourth] Congress. Washington: US Govt. Print. Office, 1973–1976.

United States. Congress. House. Committee on International Relations. Subcommittee on International Economic Policy. The Activities of American Multinational Corporations Abroad: Hearings Before the Subcommittee On International Economic Policy of the Committee On International Relations, House of Representatives, Ninety-fourth Congress, First Session ... Washington: US Govt. Print. Office, 1975.

1 Introduction

Corruption has long been a concern of the public. The Christian tradition depicts the start of pervasiveness of corruption with Eve's act of taking a bite of the forbidden apple. As put by Professor Barry Rider, however,

> [t]he fact that corruption is within us all, like the potential for violence, deceit and no doubt lust, does nothing to mitigate our responsibility as a matter of morality, good governance or even self-interest in survival, to control and curb it.
>
> (Rider, 1997, p. 1)

The OECD (2014a, p. 2) quotes that corruption costs more than 5 per cent of global GDP (or US$2.6 trillion) and that more than US$1 trillion is paid in bribes each year, adding that '[i]t is not only a question of ethics; we simply cannot afford such waste'. Most recently, corruption has risen very prominently to the top of the public's concerns. A 2013 WIN/Gallup survey identified corruption as the world's number one problem, having surveyed almost 70,000 people in 69 countries; and surveys commissioned by the BBC in 2010 and 2011, having consulted with more than 24,000 people, reported that corruption was the most heavily discussed topic, ahead of financial issues, unemployment and poverty (Holmes, 2015).

There are numerous reasons why corruption is now featuring higher on governments', international organisations' and academics' agendas. First of all, the global economic slowdown has proven to be, as noted by Warren Buffet, the tide that went down and exposed those who have been 'swimming naked', that is, engaging in corrupt activities (Mendilow and Peleg, 2014, p. 1). Mendilow and Peleg (ibid.) suggest not only a growing distrust of the middle classes in their governments' ability to adequately represent them, but also corruption-related unrest in countries involved in the Arab Spring, as well as Thailand and Turkey.

Accordingly, a wide range of people have called and continue to call for societies to challenge corruption, from government figures to the civil society and businesses.[1] The international development community has naturally also stepped up its efforts to combat corruption.

International development and the global fight against corruption

The foreword to the text of the United Nations Convention against Corruption (UNCAC, 2004) refers to corruption as 'an insidious plague that has a wide range of corrosive effects on societies', further stating that corruption 'is a key element in economic underperformance and a major obstacle to poverty alleviation and development'. As such, corruption has become not only an issue dealt with by justice and law enforcement institutions, but also organisations delivering development assistance as well as government departments for international development.

Corruption is now being linked to a wide range of other developmental issues, including undermining democratic institutions, slowing economic development, contributing to government instability, poverty and inequality, among others. These are explored in detail in section 3.4. The concept of corruption being closely interlinked with other measures of well-being and states' development, and with it the international community's significant engagement in fighting corruption, however, is relatively recent. At the annual meeting of the World Bank (WB) and the International Monetary Fund (IMF) in 1996, James Wolfensohn, the President of the World Bank at the time, declared:

> we need to deal with the cancer of corruption. In country after country, it is the people who are demanding action on this issue. They know that corruption diverts resources from the poor to the rich, increases the cost of running businesses, distorts public expenditures, and deters foreign investors. They also know that it erodes the constituency for aid programs and humanitarian relief. And we all know that it is a major barrier to sound and equitable development.
>
> (World Bank, 1996)

Prior to this, however, corruption was not a topic high on development organisations' agendas. Georg Cremer, who had been working in the international development industry for decades, notes that 'for a long time corruption has been a taboo subject among institutions of development cooperation' (Cremer, 2008, p. 1) and gives the following account of his personal experience of how issues of corruption were dealt with in international development:

> the corruption-related reports I submitted to my dispatching organization were considered more a bother than anything else. Corruption was a taboo subject in project work, left off the record as a matter of course. The reaction of my dispatching organization was completely normal back in the mid-1980s.
>
> (Cremer, 2008, p. xiii)

Since then, a lot has changed and corruption has become a clear priority of international development organisations, including the UK's Department for

International Development (DFID) (see HMT and DFID, 2015). International development organisations globally have been increasingly focusing on anti-corruption work as a key pillar for durable development. For example, the Swedish International Development Cooperation Agency (SIDA) has stated in its 2013/2014 aid policy framework that 'aid must intensify the fight against corruption' as one of its principles for effective and results-oriented aid (Government Offices of Sweden, 2014, p. 44). DFID is taking a similar approach, funding an increasing amount of anti-corruption programmes worldwide. Accordingly, DFID has stated that it

> cannot deliver [its] mission without tackling corruption. Corruption is an inescapable issue in DFID's priority countries, and it is an important part of the problems – poverty and inequality, conflict and violence, low investment and low growth – that we [DFID] are committed to tackling.
> (DFID, 2015, p. 4)

Anti-corruption interventions have been largely based on considerations of individuals' behaviour or institutional and legislative structures within a state. The principal–agent theory, which stresses the incentives that people might have to engage in corruption, shaped the anti-corruption approaches in the earlier period of anti-corruption interventions. Subsequently, the collective action theory, situating individuals' behaviour patterns within the broader social, political, economic and institutional context that they operate in, was largely incorporated into institutions' approaches to anti-corruption. These theories are discussed in Chapter 3.

The context within which corrupt officials, businesses and individuals operate, however, is global. Money syphoned away from developing countries and the proceeds of corrupt payments often pass via numerous jurisdictions and is ultimately invested or laundered within financial centres. This requires a wider, transnational approach to combatting corruption and coordination between different countries and institutions.

As found within any system, the weakest links will usually annul the progress that has been made within other segments of a system. When considering judicial reform, for example, for results to be achieved – for corrupt people to receive sentences and have their illicitly obtained assets to be confiscated and returned, for example – a number of institutions need to function well: the law needs to be adequate, the investigatory and prosecutorial bodies should be strong, the judiciary should be independent and the agencies responsible for recovering the assets and enforcing the judgement should have the resources to do so. One weak link can render the entire system ineffective.

In a globalised world there is an added complication of some of these agencies being based in different countries – as large-scale crimes of corruption occur in various jurisdictions, this often requires the cooperation of various investigatory and prosecutorial bodies to put together a strong case. Information and evidence needs to be passed across borders to the authorities that are prosecuting for offences. For example, Ibori was prosecuted in the UK for crimes he committed in

Nigeria, having diverted the gains from these crimes to the UK (StAR, 2016). For the UK to successfully convict Ibori, the court relied on evidence supplied by the Nigerian authorities. These institutions should therefore not only work well on their own, but also collaborate effectively for the desired reforms to be achieved.

Similar interdependencies can be noted in other systems that can work against corruption, such as the checks and balances on states' activities, which require whistleblowers' protection legislations and guidelines, and the institutions to enforce those, in addition to independent civil society groups and media.

Corruption has been gaining prominence in domestic and international governmental fora. Recently there has been an increased recourse to international approaches to combat corruption, as a means to achieve development aims. This is marked by a proliferation of international legal agreements – conventions, treaties and declarations – which are implemented to varying degrees (see Chapter 5). The very concept of international law and related instruments, however, is a contentious one, due to its fragmented nature, varying levels of input from different countries into its development and often lack of clear enforcement and monitoring mechanisms, as discussed in Chapter 5. Nevertheless, multilateral approaches are an increasingly prominent feature in international development work, especially in the case of government initiatives.

In this context, this book will also examine to what extent bilateral and multilateral legal approaches to tackle corruption in developing countries are achieving their intended purpose, which factors facilitate or inhibit the process, and how a Western government such as the UK could most effectively contribute to combatting corruption in developing countries. The analysis of the UK's anti-corruption work in Chapter 4 presents the broad range of the types of interventions that the UK undertakes in an attempt to tackle corruption in developing countries, and situates the interventions relating to international law in that context.

Furthermore, while corruption clearly exists all around the world, the degree to which it is engrained in society, its depth and its effect on various other aspects of development vary. While numerous theories about corruption have been presented in academia, often what is lacking is a model to prioritise one or one set of interventions over others. It is particularly important to keep in mind the limited set of resources that international development agencies and organisations have at hand and therefore the need to make difficult choices to tackle one set of problems instead of others, depending on which seems to offer the most promising results. This is discussed in further detail in Chapter 4.

The role of political leaders and an active civil society will be considered, as well as whether enshrining a nation's, a region's or 'universal' values in law has an effect on their uniform upholding. The question of ownership of the anti-corruption efforts will run throughout the book, in an attempt to establish which actors' involvement (and the nature of their involvement) in anti-corruption work appears to lead to the best results.

There is an increasing body of literature produced on corruption, its causes and effects on various measures of development. Building on that research, this book contributes to the much smaller body of literature on anti-corruption interventions. This book looks at international development assistance in particular, and contributes to the debates on how countries could ensure that their efforts to tackle corruption in developing countries are focused on where they are most likely to be successful. As pointed out by Zaum *et al.* (2012, p. 7), 'donor evaluations ... often reveal little about how and why an intervention has succeeded or failed' and '[a]cademic studies are also rarely focused on question of effectiveness or impact'.

Case study

This book considers the UK's work, and that of its Department for International Development (DFID) in particular, on anti-corruption in developing countries. DFID is a dynamic organisation that constantly adapts its approach to development assistance in response to emerging theories, debates, changing political climates and evidence from programming. The mapping of the UK's anti-corruption work and the analysis of the comparative benefits of different UK institutions delivering anti-corruption support and programmes in developing countries will be invaluable not only as an academic contribution but also for policy programming analysis. It is particularly relevant as the UK is evolving its approach to international development, for example, by reducing the amount of overseas official development assistance[2] it spends through DFID in favour of channelling more through its other government departments, to draw 'on their complementary skills' (Her Majesty's Government (HMG), 2015).

The UK is one of the largest overseas Official Development Assistance (ODA) donors in the world (see Figure 1.1), and was the first OECD member state to achieve the UN target of 0.7 per cent of the country's Gross National Income (GNI) spending on ODA.

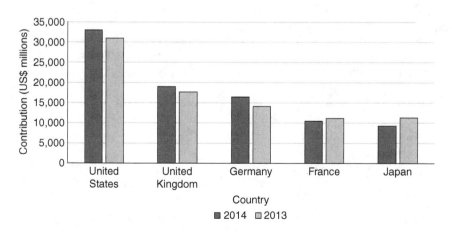

Figure 1.1 Top 5 OECD DAC members' ODA contributions (US$ millions).
Source: compiled with data retrieved from OECD (2016b).

6   Introduction

The UK channels most of its ODA through DFID. DFID is increasing its current funding for a wide variety of programmes and projects to address corruption in developing countries, both directly and indirectly (ICAI, 2014). Direct programme support is given to government anti-corruption agencies and NGOs that work directly with anti-corruption issues. Indirect programmes attempt to address corruption by, among others, improving public procurement mechanisms or generally strengthening civil society organisations so that they would subsequently be able to demand accountability from the government. While the aims of a wide range of anti-corruption programmes are desirable and commendable, the practicalities of achieving the intended results are complex. DFID's support to multilateral initiatives and developing countries' implementation of the United Nations Convention against Corruption (UNCAC) will be reviewed in greater detail, as will anti-corruption support to developing countries delivered by other UK government departments and institutions (this includes Her Majesty's Revenue and Customs (HMRC), the Foreign and Commonwealth Office (FCO) and the National Crime Agency (NCA)).

The UK is a particularly good example to take due to its transparency commitments. The OECD peer review of the UK's international development assistance noted that the 'UK is a top performer on transparency ... It is widely viewed as a leader in providing comprehensive data' (OECD, 2014b, p. 20). DFID publishes extensive data about its programmes, including the business cases for its programmes, annual, mid-term and project completion reviews, information about the recipient and implementing organisations as well as predicted versus actual spending on its devtracker.dfid.gov.uk website (DFID, 2016a). DFID has also committed to ensuring that its suppliers publish broken down details of what they spend money on, under DFID's contracts, according to International Aid Transparency Initiative (IATI) standards (DFID, 2016b, p. 33; IATI, 2014, pp. 124–125). Suppliers that implement programmes in consortia are responsible for ensuring that their sub-contractors also publish their spending with the same amount of detail, to enable both the public and DFID to trace all the funds it commits down to the beneficiaries. IATI has noted that 'DFID has established itself as a leader on international aid transparency' (IATI, 2014, p. 124); and other UK government departments, albeit having lower scores currently, have been given the target of attaining 'good' or 'very good' ratings within a maximum of five years, which parliament is suggesting changing to two years (IDC, 2016, p. 15). DFID is also seen as a model international development agency both among international development organisations and within academic research (Barder, 2005).

Working with DFID's suppliers on DFID-funded programmes as well as participating in conducting two reviews of DFID's work for the Independent Commission on Aid Impact (ICAI) has permitted the author to gain an insight not only into DFID's programming and procurement cycles, but also to question and challenge DFID's and UK government departments' other than DFID, that spend the UK's ODA funds, approaches to development assistance. This is in addition to getting to grips with the process from some of the organisations that implement DFID's programmes side. This includes insight into the commercial and technical considerations of putting together a proposal, negotiating milestones and ultimately delivering an anti-corruption programme. Bringing practical experience to the book means incorporating first-hand knowledge of how some actions, which would seem logical from a theoretical analysis, are in reality complicated by a number of individual, political or commercial factors and might impact the effectiveness of interventions. Incorporating the awareness of such factors contributes to this book's aim to be a practically relevant piece of academic research.

The UK's global standing also makes it a good case study. The UK is a member of a number of significant international bodies, such as the G7, G20, the OECD and, until recently, was a key member of the European Union. Its ability to leverage global networks and influence other donors is therefore considerable. A 2014 peer review of UK's development assistance by the OECD's Development Assistance Committee (OECD DAC) noted that '[i]ts peers value the UK's leadership in driving the development agenda' (OECD, 2014b, p. 15).

The UK has been taking a position of global leadership on anti-corruption, most recently to organise the Corruption Summit in May 2016, which resulted in a number of countries committing to concrete action (the summit is discussed in more detail in Chapter 6). Furthermore, anti-corruption efforts feature significantly within these governmental ODA aims. This includes the UK's increasing focus on stability, security, governance and prosperity in its latest aid strategy (discussed in Chapter 4) and two interdepartmental funds, each worth more than £1 billion over 5 years, that it has set up (see Chapter 6). Anti-corruption is a key element of these efforts.

The considerations of the respective benefits of delivering international development assistance using multilateral and bilateral mechanisms have been underexplored. DFID, however, is being asked by various government accountability bodies, such as the Committee for Public Accounts and the Independent Commission on Aid Impact (ICAI), to demonstrate the reasoning behind choosing multilateral over bilateral aid delivery channels (Comptroller and Auditor General, 2015, p. 12; IDC, 2016, p. 12). This book will contribute to the debate on the effectiveness of the various international development assistance delivery channels.

Methodology

The book examines the underlying assumptions and structural issues that influence the effectiveness of global initiatives to fight corruption, and considers in detail two major ways of combatting corruption in developing countries – using multilateral initiatives and instruments of international law and bilateral aid agency undertakings.

Having unpacked the concept of corruption (Chapter 2), this book considers its political and ethical influences, its measurement (section 3.2), commitments to combat corruption and ways that this is being attempted. Corruption is often treated as a uniform phenomenon, affecting all states in the same way. It is important, however, to disaggregate the types of corruption (systemic-sporadic, grand-petty, predatory-taxationary, etc.); the differing effects of different types of corruption on the economy, institutions and people's lives; as well as the readiness and receptiveness of countries and specific segments of society and government to change.

A wide range of academic literature in different academic fields is drawn upon. This includes law, politics, international relations, economics, development, sociology, anthropology and history, in addition to the extensive literature and data produced and compiled by international organisations (such as the World Bank, agencies of the United Nations and the European Union), DFID and the research centres funded by DFID (such as U4), non-governmental organisations (NGOs) such as Transparency International and Global Witness, aid oversight bodies and other organisations.

The analysis will build upon the anti-corruption study approach elaborated upon by Johnson (2014), which distinguishes between corruption at theoretical and implementation levels. Academic literature in the aforementioned fields will be used as a basis for analysis. For the analysis of international development interventions, however, this book relies more significantly on grey literature from international development organisations (such as the UN agencies and the OECD), and DFID in particular. This is due to the fact that transnational interventions on corruption in foreign states are a relatively new phenomenon, and research on the topic is still comparatively scarce. This is discussed in Chapter 5. Furthermore, recent developments within the UK's approaches to anti-corruption globally, such as the Corruption Summit that was held in 2016, offer new approaches to tackling corruption transnationally and are examined in this book.

Discussions with practitioners working in the field of anti-corruption within international development, government officials (both in the UK and those working in countries that receive international aid to combat corruption) and staff of international development agencies and other UK government departments have helped inform the research with insights into the decision-making processes when programmes are designed and commissioned, particular issues that international development organisations are faced with when carrying out anti-corruption programming, as well as wider structural issues that may influence the efficiency of anti-corruption programmes within international development. These discussions also helped triangulate the information from agencies' publications and research findings and form a more rounded approach and understanding of the practical workings of international development programming, from the perspective of people representing donor agencies, NGOs, private sector representatives that implement the programmes and governments that work and benefit from international development programmes. This was in addition to the author's own advisory work in international development and anti-corruption.

Structure of the book

Chapter 2 analyses the conceptual framework for studying corruption, including its definitions, causes and rationalisation.

Chapter 3 discusses the philosophical bases that have been used to justify anti-corruption interventions in international development. This chapter also reviews the effects of corruption on various aspects of states' development that have been put forward in the literature.

Chapter 4 analyses the UK's approaches to development and corruption. The chapter maps the UK's current efforts, assessing the strengths and weaknesses of different approaches. As such, the chapter identifies DFID's comparative advantages in the sphere of anti-corruption interventions and assesses to what extent the organisation does and could use it.

Chapter 5 reviews the existing trends in the academic literature on international law and development. The concept of legal pluralism is explored, namely the relationship between domestic, regional, transnational and international laws in the context of development and ensuring substantive justice. The chapter further considers the role of indigenous laws that are based on philosophies and practices differing from those that developed in the West. The historic evolution of international and transnational law is also analysed, as is the extent to which it can be a useful tool to address corruption in developing countries.

Chapter 6 analyses in more detail the UK government's use of multilateral and bilateral instruments to combat corruption and its support to other countries to implement and get the most out of such agreements. The chapter evaluates the strengths and weaknesses of bilateral and multilateral approaches to combatting corruption, and suggests ways of combining these to increase the effectiveness of anti-corruption efforts.

Chapter 7 concludes, suggesting that DFID could more effectively work with other partners and direct its anti-corruption efforts towards initiatives of international law.

Notes

1 For example, in May 2016 the Prime Minister (PM) of the United Kingdom (UK) held a high-level summit on anti-corruption, which was attended by a number of heads of state and international organisations. Similar business and civil society events took place prior to the PM's conference. The summit is discussed in more detail in section 6.4.
2 ODA is the official category of development assistance spending as defined by the OECD DAC. Expenditure has to fulfil the following criteria to qualify as ODA (as outlined in OECD (2008, p. 1):

   1 Recipients should be countries and territories on the DAC List of ODA Recipients (which includes most low- and middle-income countries) and is available in OECD (2016a) and multilateral development institutions.
   2 Funds should be 'provided by official agencies, including state and local governments, or by their executive agencies'; and each transaction of which:
      a is administered with the promotion of the economic development and welfare of developing countries as its main objective; and
      b is concessional in character and conveys a grant element of at least 25 per cent (calculated at a rate of discount of 10 per cent).

Bibliography

Barder, O.M., 2005. Reforming Development Assistance: Lessons from the UK Experience. Center for Global Development, Working Paper No. 70. Available at: https://ssrn.com/abstract=984062 or http://dx.doi.org/10.2139/ssrn.984062.

Comptroller and Auditor General, 2015. *Managing the Official Development Assistance Target*. January.

Cremer, G., 2008. *Corruption and Development Aid: Confronting the Challenges*, translated by Elisabeth Schuth. Lynne Rienner Publishers, Boulder, CO.

DFID, 2016a. Development Tracker. Available at: https://devtracker.dfid.gov.uk/ (accessed 8 September 2016).

DFID, 2016b. Department for International Development: Annual Report and Accounts 2015–16. Williams Lea Group on behalf of the Controller of Her Majesty's Stationery Office, UK.

DFID, 2015. Anti Corruption Evidence 'ACE' Programme Business Case and Summary. DevTracker Project. Available at: https://devtracker.dfid.gov.uk/projects/GB-1-203752/documents (accessed 3 September 2016).

Government Offices of Sweden, 2014. Aid Policy Framework: The Direction of Swedish Aid. Government Communication 2013/14:131.

HMG, 2015. Policy Paper: Official Development Assistance. Her Majesty's Government, London.

HMT, DFID, 2015. UK Aid: Tackling Global Challenges in the National Interest. Paper. Her Majesty's Treasury. Available at: www.gov.uk/government/uploads/system/uploads/attachment_data/file/478834/ODA_strategy_final_web_0905.pdf.

Holmes, L., 2015. *Corruption: A Very Short Introduction*. Oxford University Press, Oxford.

IATI, 2014. *IATI Annual Report 2014*. International Aid Transparency Initiative.

ICAI, 2014. *DFID's Approach to Anti-Corruption and its Impact on the Poor*. Report.

IDC, 2016. UK Aid: Allocation of Resources: Interim Report, Third Report of Session 2015–2016.

Johnson, J., 2014. Corruption and Stabilisation: Aid Agencies' Anti-corruption Strategies in Fragile States. Thesis. University of Cambridge.

Mendilow, J., Peleg, I., 2014. *Corruption in the Contemporary World: Theory, Practice, and Hotspots*. Lexington Books, Lanham, MD.

OECD, 2016a. DAC List of ODA Recipients Effective for Reporting on 2014, 2015 and 2016 Flows. Available at: www.esrc.ac.uk/files/funding/funding-opportunities/esrc-dfid/degrp-call-3/countries-of-focus-dac-list-of-oda-recipients-oecd/ (accessed 4 January 2016).

OECD, 2016b. Development Finance Data. Available at: www.oecd.org/dac/financing-sustainable-development/development-finance-data/ (accessed 8 September 2016).

OECD, 2014a. OECD CleanGovBiz Background Brief: The Rationale for Fighting Corruption. Available at: www.oecd.org/cleangovbiz/49693613.pdf.

OECD, 2014b. OECD Development Co-operation Peer Reviews: United Kingdom. OECD Publishing.

OECD, 2008. Is it ODA? Factsheet. ISBN: 978-90-411-0712-1.

Osborne, D., 1997. Corruption as Counter-Culture: Attitudes to Bribery in Local and Global Society, in: Rider, B.A.K. (Ed.), *Corruption: The Enemy Within*. Kluwer Law International, Boston; The Hague, pp. 9–34.

StAR, 2016. StAR – Stolen Asset Recovery Initiative – Corruption Cases – James Ibori (United States). Available at: https://star.worldbank.org/corruption-cases/node/19584.

UNCAC, 2004. United Nations Convention against Corruption. Available at: www.unodc.org/documents/brussels/UN_Convention_Against_Corruption.pdf.
World Bank, 1996. Annual Meetings. Address by James D. Wolfensohn, President, The World Bank, 1 October. Available at: http://web.worldbank.org/WBSITE/EXTERNAL/EXTABOUTUS/ORGANIZATION/EXTPRESIDENT/EXTPASTPRESIDENTS/PRESIDENTEXTERNAL/0,,contentMDK:20025269~menuPK:232083~pagePK:159837~piPK:159808~theSitePK:227585,00.html (accessed 3 September 2016).
Zaum, D., Taxell, N., Johnson, J., 2012. Mapping Evidence Gaps in Anti-corruption: Assessing the State of the Operationally Relevant Evidence on Donors' Actions and Approaches to Reducing Corruption. U4 Anti-Corruption Resource Centre. Available at: https://assets.publishing.service.gov.uk/media/57a08a9ae5274a27b2000699/U4Issue-2012-07-mapping-evidence-web.pdf.

2 Conceptual framework
Definitions and the nature of corruption

> At the one end of the spectrum is the broad interpretation that corruption, like beauty, lies in the eyes of the beholder. At the other end is a legalistic approach, according to which an act or omission is corrupt only if explicitly identified as such in legislation.
>
> (Holmes, 2015, p. 2)

Corruption is an inherently complex phenomenon, often defined, understood, measured and prosecuted according to differing standards, as illustrated by Holmes' analogy (see Holmes, 2015, p. 2). This section will unpack what different organisations and entities refer to as 'corruption', its causes, as well as the varying understandings of the effects of the phenomenon on societies under distinct circumstances. This will be useful in assessing whether international organisations' as well as countries' international development departments' anti-corruption efforts are focused where they are likely to have the highest potential to translate into meaningful and long-term improvements in societies.

Categorisation of corruption is particularly important as it will determine not only the type of behaviour to be criminalised, but also who has primary responsibility to act to address it. Most countries have anti-corruption agencies that are charged with addressing crimes of corruption. These are discussed in more detail in Chapter 4.

2.1 Definitions of corruption

Corruption has been defined in different manners by the various scholars, governments and international organisations that attempt to combat it (see, for example, Heidenheimer *et al.*, 1970; Heywood, 1997; Philp, 1997). As put by Rider (1997, p. 1), '[c]orruption is and can be many things to many people, and is chameleon in its forms'. Three main groups that address corruption within the literature – academia, legal and policy – approach the definition of corruption in rather distinct manners. These will be presented individually in this section.

It is also worth keeping in mind, however, the inherently moralistic and emotional reaction that many people will have to the very term 'corruption'. The term 'corruption' itself has acquired the connotations of 'sin' and 'evil'; and elicits strong reactions from the public, thereby making the fight against corruption susceptible to capture by political groups for their own purposes. This has also been the case historically. Brooks (1970, p. 56) notes:

> [p]arty orators and writers, journalists, 'muck rakers', and reformers all use it with the utmost freedom, and it occurs not uncommonly in the less ephemeral pages of political philosophers and historians. Transactions and conditions of very different kinds are stigmatised in this way, in many cases doubtless with entire justice; but apparently there is little disposition to inquire into the essential nature of corruption itself and to discriminate in the use of the word.

This notion will be explored in more detail in subsequent chapters.

While corruption has been a prominent concept within society and politics for a very long time, its definitions and meanings have been abundant. Heidenheimer *et al.* (1970, p. 3) note that the 'only connotation that many usages of the work *corruption* has in common in this period [the 1900s] was that it was somehow the antithesis of *reform, rationality* and the demands of the public weal'. Some academics, such as Leff (1964), however, have argued for an overall positive effect of corruption on economies, which would contradict the connotations referred to by Heidenheimer. This is explored in detail in Chapter 3.

Most definitions of corruption centre around the concepts of fulfilling one's official duties: compliance with the law or putting one's personal interests above the interests of the public (Mulgan, 2012). Academic definitions of corruption have evolved over time, perhaps the most important change being removing the requirement for there to be public officials' involvement for an action to be considered corrupt. For example, Nye (1970, pp. 566–567) defined corruption as 'behaviour which deviates from the normal duties of a public role because of private-regarding (family, close private clique), pecuniary or status gains; or violates rules against the exercise of certain types of private-regarding influence'.

Bayley (1970, p. 522) defined corruption as follows: 'while being tied particularly to the act of bribery, [corruption] is a general term covering the misuse of authority as a result of considerations of personal gain, which need not be monetary'. While this definition does not explicitly mention the public sphere, in his article, however, Bayley continues to consider corruption within the civil service and the differences between what is expected from civil servants in Western Europe as opposed to developing states:

> in both Africa and India the man who uses his official position to obtain jobs for his relatives is not considered immoral: in traditional terms, he is only doing what every loyal member of an extended family is expected to do.
> (Bayley, 1970, p. 523)

Political theorists such as Philp (1997) argue that corruption needs to be considered in relation to its opposite – the lack of corruption or a situation of good government and 'healthy' society.[1] A definition of corruption in politics would accordingly suggest that corruption occurs where one allows his private interests to illegitimately interfere with public interests.

Due to the complex nature of the phenomenon, corruption itself is most often not directly referred to in criminal law; and in the cases where it is explicitly defined, these definitions are often too precise or too obscure and therefore result in few prosecutions and convictions (OECD, 2008, p. 22). Instead, various offences that can be classified as corrupt behaviour are referred to – these include bribery, embezzlement and fraud. The OECD, the Council of Europe, the African Union and the UN conventions do not define the term 'corruption' either, but establish a range of corrupt offences (OECD Observer, 2007; U4, 2010). This is presented in detail in section 2.2.

In the policy sphere, clearly defining the issues to be addressed, as well as the different types of manifestations of corruption, is integral for organisations and states to be able to effectively direct their efforts and resources (a) in a coherent and complementary manner and (b) to where they can have the most significant effect. As such, for policy purposes most international organisations' and states' international development departments do define corruption, as can be seen from Table 2.1.

Different definitions of corruption will clearly impact the focus of organisations' anti-corruption efforts. It is therefore important to consider what is included in, and what is excluded from, these definitions.

The early definitions presented in Table 2.1 clearly centre around the notion of misuse and abuse of public office, and the later ones – abuse of office or power for private gains.[2] These can be both material and immaterial (this would include prestige and power). This definition, however, is problematic for several reasons. First of all, 'misuse' of power is a subjective term. There may, in fact, be multiple opinions as to what would be the primary subject (beneficiary) that public officials should primarily consider – such as the state's institutions, citizens in general or a particular group of citizens. For example, Huntington (1968, p. 25) argued that public interest is

> not something which exists a priori in natural law or the will of the people. Nor is it simply whatever results from the political process. Rather it is whatever strengthens governmental institutions. The public interest is the interest of public institutions.

Johnson (2014) also points out that one should consider who is responsible for setting the standard as to what constitutes proper use of office; the definition may become meaningless in cases where the government is aware and supportive of acts that may, by others, be perceived as corrupt. Therefore, the notion of acting against the public interest should also be included in the definition of corruption.

Table 2.1 Definitions of corruption used by multilateral agencies

Organisation	Definition
World Bank (WB)	'A corrupt practice is the offering, giving, receiving or soliciting, directly or indirectly, anything of value to influence improperly the actions of another party' (World Bank, 2017) 'the abuse of public office for private gain' (World Bank, 1997, p. 8)
European Commission (EC)	'abuse of public office for private gain' (European Commission, 2014, p. 37)
OECD	'active or passive misuse of the powers of Public officials (appointed or elected) for private financial or other benefits' (OECD, 2013)
Transparency International (TI)	'The abuse of entrusted power for private gain. Corruption can be classified as grand, petty and political, depending on the amounts of money lost and the sector where it occurs' Private gain means 'both financial or material gain and non-material gain, such as the furtherance of political or professional ambitions' (TI, 2009, 2007, p. xxi)
DFID	Uses TI's definition – 'abuse of entrusted power for private gain' (ICAI, 2014, p. 2)
SIDA	'an abuse of trust, power or position for improper gain. Corruption includes e.g. offering and receiving bribes – including bribery of foreign public officials – embezzlement, conflict of interest and nepotism' (SIDA, 2015)
NORAD	Cites the Norwegian Penal Code's main provision against corruption and applies to both public and private sectors and states: 'Any person who a) for himself or other persons, requests or receives an improper advantage or accepts an offer of an improper advantage in connection with a position, office or assignment, or b) gives or offers anyone an improper advantage in connection with a position, office or assignment, shall be liable to a penalty for corruption' (NORAD, 2015)
UNDP	'misuse of entrusted power for private gain' (UNDP, 2008, p. 7)
USAID	'the abuse of entrusted authority for private gain' (USAID, 2005, p. 8)

It is worth considering, however, that politicians are mandated to represent their constituencies, in addition to considering the interests of the entire public. If we are to consider a politician faced with a choice between the better policy option for the constituency that he represents or the one that would more significantly benefit more people in his country, and having chosen the former, it could be interpreted as both (a) that the politician 'misused' his position to benefit his own constituency; as well as (b) that the politician was carrying out his mandate and keeping his electoral promises to his constituency. Given that authoritative distribution of resources will inevitably create winners and losers, Mendilow and Peleg (2014, p. 4) ask a pertinent question: 'Where and how are we to draw the line between policy and corruption, the representation of particular interests and sleaze?'

Instead of the term 'misuse' it may therefore be more appropriate to consider the issue of transparency. A useful aspect of a definition of corruption would be to stress the issues of disclosure and transparency (which, for example in the case of cabinet officials' financial support of political parties in many states already makes the distinction between legal and illegal activities). Organisations working on combatting corruption could define corruption as 'the unauthorised and undisclosed use of one's status and power for private gains at the expense of the public interest'. This book, however, will mainly focus on the definitions of corruption that are currently being used, in order to present a more accurate situation of anti-corruption initiatives within international development activities.

The issue of transparency is recognised by international development organisations which attempt to tackle corruption indirectly, by focusing on civil society, advocacy and transparency, in addition to working to tackle corruption directly by, for example, strengthening the capacity of anti-corruption agencies or reforming legal systems (see, for example, DFID, 2016; SIDA, 2015). Explicitly including it in the definition of the phenomenon that the organisations are attempting to tackle would seem to be both natural and imperative.

As Transparency International (TI) and other institutions working in the sphere have now recognised, it is not viable to restrict the understanding and focus of anti-corruption activities to those involving the public sector. It may, at times, be difficult to strictly separate the public sector from the private sector. For example, state-owned enterprises (SOEs) are still prevalent in many countries. To illustrate this point, Cremer (2008, p. 9) suggests the example of an NGO manager who, in a position of power and trust, could also divert funds intended for public purposes for his own personal use.

Furthermore, a lot of corruption that occurs within the private sphere also severely impacts the general public, by, for example, minimising the level of tax revenues collected by the government or limiting market competition. This would apply to behaviour such as insider dealing or price collusion. Table 2.2 presents a number of 'new forms' of corporate corruption that, for the most part, would not be captured under most of the definitions in the table, but nevertheless can have a significant impact on states' economies and broader development (the table presents examples from Bracking (2013)). The evolving nature of law, however, means that these and other offences that are currently not illegal could be outlawed in the future.

Table 2.2 Forms of corporate corruption or misconduct that may be damaging to states' economies

Activity	Description
Deliberate bankruptcy	'Practices in which the owners and/or managers of a company knowingly take excessive remuneration, strip the firm's assets, or otherwise conduct corporate affairs for short-term private gain at the expense of the firm's continued operational viability. This sometimes also occurs in the context of avoiding future financial obligations of the operating entity, such as pension funds.'
Illicit financial flows	'Money that is illegally earned, transferred, or utilised.'
Jurisdiction shopping	'In the corporate context, the active selection of a particular jurisdiction in which to domicile part or all of an economic entity away from its material operations in order to avoid or evade tax (see Palan, 2002, p. 172). This often involves the fictional fragmentation of a firm into a complex and opaque set of distinct legal entities located in different jurisdictions.'
Tax evasion	'Criminal non-payment of tax. Tax avoidance is a related practice that also leads to non-payment but is technically legal.'
Thin capitalisation	'Underinvestment of a domestic company relative to its offshore parent in order to evade or avoid tax. It is often accompanied by an inverted company structure in which the bulk of the assets are kept offshore, with an onshore shell (see Heggstad and Fjeldstad, 2010). This is an established term, and some countries have "thin-cap" regulations.'
Trade mispricing	'Abuse of pricing in trade between apparently unrelated parties, such as through the deliberate over-invoicing of imports or under-invoicing of exports, usually for the purpose of tax evasion.'
Transfer pricing	'A transfer price is a price, adopted for book-keeping purposes, which is used to value transactions between affiliated enterprises integrated under the same management at artificially high or low levels in order to effect an unspecified income payment or capital transfer between those enterprises.'
Cover quoting	'The collusion of firms in a procurement bidding process where all parties agree on who will tender the most competitive price, allowing the bidders to artificially raise their bids and misrepresent their costs. The 'winner' is chosen in rotation. The actual work is often reapportioned under memorandums of understanding between the parties after the result is announced by the public authority.'
Fronting	'The use of an individual or firm belonging to a historically disadvantaged group (black, Indian, or coloured) to act as the lead bidder in a procurement process in order to raise the chances of a firm or individual that would otherwise be characterized as white. Once the contract is awarded to the front person or firm, the work is often carried out by another entity.'
Javelin throwing	'Practice in which a public employee uses insider or advance information about an economic opportunity that will arise in the future in order to become the eventual beneficiary of the tender or bid. Metaphorically, they throw the 'javelin', or opportunity, into the future, then move into the private sector or set up a firm which includes their disguised participation or ownership in order to catch the javelin later.'

Source: Bracking (2013).

18 *Conceptual framework*

It is noteworthy that international development agencies and organisations do acknowledge the importance of tackling corruption within the private sector, despite some of these practices not directly falling under the definitions in Table 2.1. In 2000, the World Bank did start investigating the extent to which corporations could exert undue influence over governments, what can in more severe cases be called 'state capture' manifested by practices such as 'purchase' of decrees and legislation (Hellman *et al.*, 2000). This work, however, has not been integrated centrally in policy debates (Bracking, 2013).

DFID acknowledges the importance of corruption in the private sector, as well as the general lack of research on a number of topics within anti-corruption interventions. In early 2015, it announced a business case to invest £9.6 million over 5 years in supporting new anti-corruption research (DFID, 2015), much of which is to focus on private sector development and economic growth. In particular, the programme attempts to fill the research gap in the sphere of the interaction between the private sector and the government as well as relationships between private actors. The former sphere includes public procurement, allocation of land and utilities as well as licensing in areas such as minerals and telecommunications; and the latter, inter alia, the interaction between private firms in manufacturing and infrastructure delivery chains.

Furthermore, it is notable that most definitions of corruption refer to 'entrusted' power. Corruption, however, can also occur in the case of coerced rather than entrusted power. It is debatable whether non-democratic leaders such as Ben Ali or Mubarak who personally appropriated large sums of money themselves or facilitated their family members and associates to do so (see Lynch, 2011) were abusing 'entrusted' power.

2.2 Offences of corruption

The United Nations Convention against Corruption (UNCAC) clearly outlines how corruption is damaging to societies and the importance of international cooperation in the eradication of corruption. When addressing the issue of criminalisation and law enforcement, however, it does not give a clear definition of corruption, instead outlining the different offences that fall under the umbrella of corruption. This is necessary to address the issues from a criminal law perspective, as the crimes are more clearly defined and attributable. Table 2.3 outlines the categories of corruption and their definitions referred to by UNCAC.

UNCAC signatory countries are responsible for incorporating these offences into their domestic legislation (UNODC, 2012). It is worth noting, however, that in cases involving multiple jurisdictions harmonised definitions of corruption offences are needed for the requirement of dual criminality to be met.

Clearly identifying the acts makes it significantly easier for law enforcement organisations to bring to justice people engaging in illicit activities. The OECD, however, points out that there is no consensus about which acts in particular should be included or excluded from the definition of corruption (OECD, 2008, p. 22).

Table 2.3 Categories of corruption as relevant in the context of criminalisation and law enforcement

Offence	Definition	Source
Bribery of national public officials	'When committed intentionally: (a) The promise, offering or giving, to a public official, directly or indirectly, of an undue advantage, for the official himself or herself or another person or entity, in order that the official act or refrain from acting in the exercise of his or her official duties; (b) The solicitation or acceptance by a public official, directly or indirectly, of an undue advantage, for the official himself or herself or another person or entity, in order that the official act or refrain from acting in the exercise of his or her official duties.'	UNCAC Article 15
Bribery of foreign public officials	'When committed intentionally, the promise, offering or giving to a foreign public official or an official of a public international organization, directly or indirectly, of an undue advantage, for the official himself or herself or another person or entity, in order that the official act or refrain from acting in the exercise of his or her official duties, in order to obtain or retain business or other undue advantage in relation to the conduct of international business.'	UNCAC Article 16.1
Bribery in the private sector	'When committed intentionally in the course of economic, financial or commercial activities: (a) The promise, offering or giving, directly or indirectly, of an undue advantage to any person who directs or works, in any capacity, for a private sector entity, for the person himself or herself or for another person, in order that he or she, in breach of his or her duties, act or refrain from acting; (b) The solicitation or acceptance, directly or indirectly, of an undue advantage by any person who directs or works, in any capacity, for a private sector entity, for the person himself or herself or for another person, in order that he or she, in breach of his or her duties, act or refrain from acting.'	UNCAC Article 21

continued

Table 2.3 Continued

Offence	Definition	Source
Embezzlement	'The fraudulent conversion of another's property by a person who is in a position of trust, such as an agent or employee.'	Legal Dictionary (2016a) Referred to in Article 17 of UNCAC in the case of the public sector; and Article 22 in the private sector.
Trading in influence	'When committed intentionally: (a) The promise, offering or giving to a public official or any other person, directly or indirectly, of an undue advantage in order that the public official or the person abuse his or her real or supposed influence with a view to obtaining from an administration or public authority of the State Party an undue advantage for the original instigator of the act or for any other person; (b) The solicitation or acceptance by a public official or any other person, directly or indirectly, of an undue advantage for himself or herself or for another person in order that the public official or the person abuse his or her real or supposed influence with a view to obtaining from an administration or public authority of the State Party an undue advantage.'	UNCAC Article 18
Misappropriation	'the intentional, illegal use of the property or funds of another person for one's own use or other unauthorized purpose, particularly by a public official, a trustee of a trust, an executor or administrator of a dead person's estate, or by any person with a responsibility to care for and protect another's assets (a fiduciary duty).'	Legal Dictionary (2016b) Referred to in Article 17 of UNCAC
Diversion of property by a public official	'Diversion by a public official for his or her benefit or for the benefit of another person or entity, of any property, public or private funds or securities or any other thing of value entrusted to the public official by virtue of his or her position.'	Referred to in Article 17 of UNCAC

Laundering of proceeds of crime	'When committed intentionally: (a) (i) The conversion or transfer of property, knowing that such property is the proceeds of crime, for the purpose of concealing or disguising the illicit origin of the property or of helping any person who is involved in the commission of the predicate offence to evade the legal consequences of his or her action; (ii) The concealment or disguise of the true nature, source, location, disposition, movement or ownership of or rights with respect to property, knowing that such property is the proceeds of crime; (b) Subject to the basic concepts of [a country's] legal system: (i) The acquisition, possession or use of property, knowing, at the time of receipt, that such property is the proceeds of crime; (ii) Participation in, association with or conspiracy to commit, attempts to commit and aiding, abetting, facilitating and counselling the commission of any of the offences established in accordance with this article.'	UNCAC Article 23
Abuse of functions	'The performance of or failure to perform an act, in violation of laws, by a public official in the discharge of his or her functions, for the purpose of obtaining an undue advantage for himself or herself or for another person or entity.'	UNCAC Article 19
Illicit enrichment	'A significant increase in the assets of a public official that he or she cannot reasonably explain in relation to his or her lawful income.'	UNCAC Article 20
Concealment	'The concealment or continued retention of property when the person involved knows that such property is the result of any of the offences established in accordance with [UNCAC].'	UNCAC Article 24
Obstruction of Justice	'When committed intentionally: (a) The use of physical force, threats or intimidation or the promise, offering or giving of an undue advantage to induce false testimony or to interfere in the giving of testimony or the production of evidence in a proceeding in relation to the commission of offences established in accordance with this Convention; (b) The use of physical force, threats or intimidation to interfere with the exercise of official duties by a justice or law enforcement official in relation to the commission of offences established in accordance with this Convention. Nothing in this subparagraph shall prejudice the right of States Parties to have legislation that protects other categories of public official.'	UNCAC Article 25

22 Conceptual framework

It is also important to stress that not all bribes or corrupt activities will involve monetary exchange or gain; bribes can take the form of unmerited appointments (including admission of family members to university programmes or awards of honorary degrees) or sexual favours.

The definitions of corruption employed by different agencies (Table 2.1) as well as the various offences of corruption (Table 2.3) also illustrate that the activities that fall under the broader definition of corruption, in the eyes of the law, can be considered as both legal and illegal. Most of the aforementioned activities will be considered as illegal. Others, however, may fall into a grey area. These can relate to significant influence on policymaking processes, monopolies and general state capture. State capture refers to 'shaping the formation of basic rules of the game' – laws, rules, decrees and regulations – through private payments to public officials (Hellman *et al.*, 2000). Kaufmann discussed the 'soft' forms of corruption in more detail:

> the reality of corruption is two-fold: first, it most often involves collusion between at least two parties, typically from the public and private sectors, for a corrupt act to take place; second, where the rules of the game, laws and institutions have been shaped, at least in part, to benefit certain vested interests, some forms of corruption may be legal in some countries.
>
> For instance, soft forms of political funding are legally permitted in some countries, through the creative use of legal loopholes, and may exert enormous influence in shaping institutions and policies benefiting the contributing private interests, and at the expense of the broader public welfare. A similar problem is seen in favoritism in procurement, where, as we mentioned earlier, a transparent and level playing field may be absent, without necessarily involving illegal bribery.
>
> (Kaufmann, 2004, p. 90)

Transparency is therefore a key feature that could make the fight against corruption a lot easier. As put by Rider (1997, p. 3), '[w]hilst the badge of fraud is secrecy, in cases of corruption, the crime will generally be committed between consenting adults in the privacy of their chambers, both having no interest in their activity coming to light'. Giving the policymakers and the public access to up-to-date information on the financing issues in business and politics, among other things, will make it easier to discover, articulate and address the loopholes that are allowing corrupt practices that are damaging to society to persist. This will also, in turn, play a role in keeping the law more up to date with the current situation to criminalise novel corrupt practices that would not have been noticed and outlawed previously.

'Softer' and perhaps not always illegal forms of corruption can include undue influence exerted by corporations over policymakers and politicians, including support to political parties and nepotism. Legalisation on lobbying could be a way to introduce transparency and therefore curb any undue influence of corporations over politicians in return for financial and other support to political parties. However, the result of legal lobbying versus illegal and undue influence may be the same – policies that benefit a minority (for example a particular industry) at the expense of the public. A similar distinction can be made between tax evasion, which is defined by various tax authorities as 'an activity that a person or a business may undertake to reduce their tax in a way that runs counter to the spirit and the purpose of the law, without being strictly illegal', and tax avoidance, which is illegal (Fuest and Riedel, 2009, p. 4). It is worth noting, however, that the scale and severity of tax avoidance might be what makes the difference to most people's perception of what constitutes corruption in relation to tax avoidance. To take a simple example, most people would have no moral reservations shopping in duty free stores at airports, though some of those people might consider the use of trusts and other legal methods to pay no or significantly lower amounts of tax as a form of corruption.

Jordan (2009, p. 205) notes the difficulties in drawing a clear line between what constitutes corruption, and what does not, for researchers of virtually any discipline:

> It is hard for historians now, looking back at the middle ages, as it is for sociologists and political scientists looking at present-day society, to distinguish the bribe, which was in theory illicit and morally tainted, from the gift, which was allegedly licit and morally virtuous, in a world in which the exchange of oaths, of tokens of wealth and of tokens of power was ubiquitous.

Heidenheimer *et al.* (1970, pp. 26–28) categorise corruption into three types: black, white and grey, based on the acceptance within society of those types of corruption. Accordingly, 'black' corruption refers to actions that would be considered by both the mass public and the elite as condemnable and punishable; 'grey' corruption would refer to actions that some would see as punishable, usually the elites, whereas others would be less certain when categorising such actions as acceptable or non-acceptable; and 'white' corruption would refer to actions that the majority of both the elite and the general public would tolerate and not strongly argue to be punished. Heidenheimer *et al.* (1970, p. 27) suggest that classifying actions into the 'white corruption' category would imply that people 'attach less value to the maintenance of the values involved than they do to the costs that might be generated as the result of a change in rule enforcement'.

Furthermore, it is important to distinguish between facilitative and substantive crime. This distinction translates into differences in terms of the motivation (discussed in further detail in Chapter 3) and subsequently the control of crime. Facilitative crimes would include corruption and money laundering – crimes that are not stand-alone crimes or ends in themselves. Looking at attitudes to corruption as a monolithic activity obscures what corruption is seeking to achieve. For example, in some cases corruption might be a means to achieve efficiency in business conduct or to entice officials to create an enabling environment and foster organised crime; and money laundering can be used to avoid state monitoring of one's income or to launder the proceeds of crime and drugs. As such, traditional and the most popular tools to measure corruption, discussed in section 3.2, do not capture these nuances.

It is important to consider not only the different types of activities that the term 'corruption' encompasses, but also the interaction between those activities, as well as other crimes. Chaikin (2008, p. 269) notes that the 'recursive links between corruption and money laundering suggest that policies which are addressed to fighting both corruption and money laundering may have a mutually reinforcing effect'. This could be useful in addressing, for example, bribery to refrain from reporting suspicious activities that facilitate money laundering.

2.3 Cultural and historic differences

A distinction has often been made in the literature between the nature of corruption in developed and developing countries. Bayley (1970, p. 523), for example, suggests the following:

> It not infrequently happens ... in developing non-Western societies that existing moral codes do not agree with Western norms as to what kinds of behaviour by public servants should be condemned. The Western observer is faced with an uncomfortable choice. He can adhere to the Western definition, in which case he lays himself open to the charge of being censorious and he finds that he is condemning not aberrant behaviour but normal, acceptable operating procedure. On the other hand, he may face up to the fact that corruption, if it requires moral censure, is culturally conditioned.

Accordingly, cultural differences are being referred to in order to explain variations in levels of corruption in different states and societies (see, for example, Brunelle-Quraishi, 2011, pp. 91–110; or Rose-Ackerman, 1999, p. 102).

Such suggestions, however, have several flaws. As put by Widmalm (2008, p. 122):

> the view that corruption is rampant where it is culturally accepted is an explanation which easily turns into a circular argument. When the claim is made that corruption is prevalent in a particular area, or even a whole state, the 'proof' of the cultural acceptance is the existence of corruption.

Furthermore, this line of argument assumes homogeneity between both developed or 'Western' states and developing countries. Holmes (2015, p. 5) notes that there is a big difference between people's understanding of what constitutes corruption between different 'developed' or 'Western' countries. The author refers to diagnostic studies, carried out by the World Bank in the late 1990s and the early 2000s, which asked respondents in different countries to rate whether certain scenarios constituted corruption or not, revealing that often respondents' views in neighbouring countries were very different.

There is also often a perception of stark differences between white-collar and blue-collar crimes. The former, being more detached from the victims themselves, is often perceived as somewhat more benign as victims cannot be identified as clearly as with other crimes, such as stealing a car. The damage that can be done to society and victims, however, is no smaller from white-collar crimes. Arguably, few lawyers would store bags of heroin or cocaine in their safes for their clients, but do end up facilitating the laundering of proceeds of drug trades (for example, as in the cases revealed by the Panama Papers, discussed in more detail in section 6.1). Programmes, such as media and education campaigns, stressing how close such lawyers are to the crimes that their clients might be committing, in addition to generally discussing the consequences of various types of corruption, would help bridge such gaps.

Another point to note is that the Western understanding of concepts such as 'rule of law' and corruption is usually based on the unit of a nation-state, as opposed to for example an ethnic group or family.[3] An interesting different approach to consider is China's long tradition of state governance and philosophers' legacies. Among the most notable is the Confucian doctrine, based on the *Li* (礼) principle of ritual, propriety and etiquette; *Yi* (义) of righteousness; and *Ren* (仁) – of altruism and humanity (Muhlemann, 2011). The Confucian doctrine was the basis of the Qing dynasty legal code. Confucianism regarded family relations and obligations as more important than state relations. Consequently, Qing dynasty laws included regulations such as:

> If a son reports his father's crime and the accusation is proven wrong, that is, if the father has not committed the crime, the son shall be executed. If a son reports his father's crime and it is found out that it is true and the father has indeed committed the crime, the son shall receive 100 blows with a stick and shall be incarcerated for three years.
>
> (Yan, 2008)[4]

Such laws are in no sense compatible with the Western definition of the 'rule of law' and right behaviour. Punishing a boy for reporting his father's crimes would be considered a serious infringement on his human, civil and political rights and liberties, as the state is construed as the unit of society to be considered first and foremost. Putting one's family above the state using a system of concealment among relatives ('亲亲相隐') is just another way of organising the society, which in the Confucian analysis was believed to be conducive to a more harmonious society.

The rationale for protecting one's own citizens above others is in fact the same as protecting and prioritising one's family over strangers. The political, economic and ideological dominance of the West in the current global structure has in fact resulted in the perceived supremacy of the Western conception of a nation-state and Weberian bureaucratic governance; it is nevertheless not the only possible structure for a functioning social and legal organisation.

In fact, it is worth noting that this 'Western' conception of the nation-state as the principal unit of social organisation does not appear to be uniformly supported by all in Western Europe, Italy being a notable exception. Some authors have documented mafia-type social relations, where people first and foremost use their own social networks to access services and build businesses. For example, Wrong (2009, p. 53) notes that her Italian mother, having grown up in Italy under a government that made a pact with Hitler and destroyed its economy in unnecessary wars, had little faith in government institutions and 'would happily have lied and cheated in any encounter with the state had she believed she could get away with it'. She nevertheless engaged in one-on-one charitable activities and helped her needy and lonely acquaintances. Wrong (2009, p. 54) argues that her mother was 'not alone in her ability to get things done without the state's involvement. "*Il mio istema*" Italians call it: "my system". Italy is, after all, the birthplace of the Mafia, the ultimate of personal "*sisteme*"'.

Also, if we consider corruption in its more historic sense of 'moral decay' rather than the abuse of one's power or position in office, some people's actions that undermine state institutions where these were artificially introduced by colonial powers in favour of more traditional, perhaps kin relations or tribal customs, would no longer necessarily be classed as 'corrupt'. This would be the case if, for example, people considered their moral obligations as being primarily towards their family or tribe and regarded paying taxes to a state, which may not be very competent or honest in allocating its budget, as a duty imposed on them by power. This nuance highlights the importance of stakeholder engagement and consultation in designing anti-corruption interventions. Unless such legacies and conceptions of state institutions are understood and worked with, anti-corruption interventions have little chance of succeeding. This will be further explored in subsequent sections of this chapter.

Geographical variations

Certain societies have a different understanding of what constitutes corruption. For example, some may consider gift-giving as a perfectly morally acceptable everyday phenomenon, while for others the exact same action may be considered as corrupt (see Kaufmann, 1997, pp. 115–116). A lack of cultural understanding may therefore lead to misguided interpretations of the extent and effect of various types of corruption in different parts of the world.

Concepts that appear to endorse corruption have often been quite explicitly stated by various actors of high status within some developing countries. For example, the Nigerian constitution has been quoted as having included, at one point, a definition of political power as 'the opportunity to acquire riches and prestige, to be in a position to hand out benefits in the form of jobs, contracts, gifts of money etc. to relations and political allies' ('Report of the Constitution Drafting Committee', Lagos, 1976, 1:V, cited by Williams and Turner (1978, p. 133)).

Bayart (1996) notes the particular terminology related to food and meeting one's basic needs that is used in some contexts of national and local politics. The author cites Cameroonians who talk of the 'politics of the belly' and argue that 'the goat eats where it is tethered' and that the people in power intend to 'eat', as well as Nigerians who refer to 'sharing the national cake' (Bayart, 1996, p. xvii). In addition to expressions, the author gives examples of words that have entered some languages that illustrate the same concept. For example, in Yaounde, the word 'credit' (which the author argues is often granted by banks on the basis of political considerations) has become 'kel di' which literally means 'go and eat' (ibid.).

Statements that certain societies are inherently more corrupt that others, however, seem to be misguided and, most significantly, taken out of context. An analysis of the institutional and governance history of the developing states considered is necessary in order to assess the validity of a 'cultural differences' argument to explain the prevalence of corruption. In Africa, states were largely formed artificially in the last century by colonial powers. The institutions created by these colonial powers were designed to serve the interests of the colonisers, namely to facilitate effective rule rather than ensure the rights and maximum benefits for the people of the colonies. Consequently, a small cooperative minority in the colonies was often the colonising power's preferred choice of local allies to assist in the smooth running of the colonies and to ensure the obedience of others. Managerial posts within the bureaucracies were accordingly not filled by the most capable candidates, but rather, those who demonstrated the desired political (and at times ethnic or religious) affiliations. Nelson Mandela is said to have made the following remark: 'Little did we suspect, that our own people, when they get that chance, would be as corrupt as the apartheid regime. That is one of the things that has really hurt us' (see Snider and Kidane, 2007, p. 692). Such a statement illustrates the perception in South Africa, at the time of the fall of apartheid, of corruption being a foreign behaviour bestowed upon their society by the colonisers.

Furthermore, Widmalm (2008, p. 166), having completed survey fieldwork in two provinces in India, states that '[i]n general, corruption is not accepted by most people and most respondents in the survey favour a rule-governed bureaucracy within a democratic setting regardless of whether the context is plagued by corruption or not'.

Bayart (1996, p. 2) discusses in detail a general 'reluctance to recognise African societies as historical and political entities in their own right' by Western scholars. Bayart (1996) argues that the phenomenon has been taking place since at least Aristotle, who had concluded that the Greeks had the right to rule over the 'barbarians'; and persisted throughout the centuries. For example, in the eighteenth century Montesquieu (1951, p. 602) stated that '[m]ost people on the coast of Africa are savage or barbarian'. Writing from the Congo rainforest in 1900, Captain Vallier reported that 'We find here nothing but anarchy and ill-will, in other words, a society in its infancy, without any organisation, a scattering of humanity, who escape from contact with us and paralyse our most generous efforts with inertia' (cited in Bayart, 1996, p. 3). Bayart (1996) suggests that such European observers' disregard of African societies' social and political arrangements is partially influenced by the historically unequal relations between Africa and Europe.

As Sub-Saharan Africa never posed a military threat to European states similar to that of some Asian empires (for example, the Ottoman or Mongolian empires), the historicity of numerous African societies is often overlooked. Hegel (1965, p. 247) has particularly poignantly illustrated such a view by claiming:

> [Africa] is not interesting from the point of view of its own history, but because we see man in a state of barbarism and savagery which is preventing him from being an integral part of civilisation. Africa, as far back as history goes, has remained closed and without links with the rest of the world. It is the country of god which is closed in on itself, the country of infancy, beyond the daylight of conscious history, wrapped in the blackness of night.

Bayart (1996, p. 4) suggests that it wasn't until 'anthropology came of age that the sub-Saharan societies were fully integrated into political analysis'. As such, some important distinctions in our analysis of corruption within certain developing country contexts can be missed. These are, nevertheless, crucial for an approach to tackling corruption to have the desired effect. Failing that, laws would be drafted (or, even worse, transplanted), programmes designed and institutions set up that may duplicate, undermine or be undermined by existing structures.

Temporal variations

The most important change in the understanding of corruption was probably the shift from viewing corruption as 'moral decay' to an emphasis on the adherence to rules, considering the 'abuse of public office for private gain', to widening the definition to include private sector actors.

In *The Republic*, Plato sets out the differences between 'ideal' states which were ruled by wise and virtuous philosophers and politicians that were 'inferior', possessing qualities of 'decay' (Plato, 2000).[5] Plato used the word 'pthora' for the latter; a Greek term which was later latinised as 'corruptio' (Mulgan, 2012). Plato sets out the various stages of decay of a state, from an 'ideal' and aristocratic state descending to timocracy, oligarchy, democracy and ultimately to tyranny. The ultimate pursuit of the rulers of the state accordingly shifts from wisdom to honour, to wealth, to diffused and undisciplined power under a democracy that is susceptible to capture by a clever tyrannical group. While the moral standing of democracy has clearly changed nowadays, the key feature that distinguishes the 'decaying' or corrupt societies from the ideal ones is the rulers acting with their private versus public interest in mind. The stages of decay of society in *The Republic* therefore gradually represent rulers acting increasingly in their own private interests rather than for the public good:

> The correct forms of government are those in which the one, the few or the many govern with a view to the common interest: but the governments

which rule with a view to the private interest whether of the one, or of the few or of the many are deviations.

(Quoted in Mulgan, 2012, p. 30)

There is therefore no place for private interests in Plato's ideal government. Mulgan (2012) notes that Plato's 'ideal' government is an ideal also in the sense of a standard of government that is, though achievable in principle, not a realistic prospect. It serves the function of showing the contrast between the different types of governance. Mulgan (2012, p. 27), however, argues that current understandings of corruption do allow for a balance between public and private interests, as long as the private do not overshadow the public:

> politicians (and citizens) cannot reasonably be expected to be motivated solely by concern for the common good or public interest. … A condition of … non-corrupt politics is not a polity where everyone pursues the public interest but one where the pursuit of private interests is not allowed to transgress certain minimal public-interest limits.

Accordingly, the author continues to elaborate upon a concept of corruption as a matter of striking an adequate balance between the pursuit of personal interests and the common good (the boundaries of which are blurred and contested):

> corruption is not so much a festering disease in the body politic as a possibly minor imbalance between two legitimate forces in the community. 'Corruption' has connotations of moral absolutism (compare with 'swear off the demon drink') whereas, in practice, it seems to refer to striking the right balance ('drink but not to excess').
>
> (Mulgan, 2012, p. 28)

Earlier authors' understanding of avoiding corruption as acting in the public interest and thereby avoiding 'moral decay' did in fact at times correspond to the currently prevalent definition of abuse of power or public office for private gain. This has led to some authors arguing that our understanding of corruption has not changed very much over the years. For example, Osborne (1997, pp. 12–14) quotes Queen Elizabeth I, 1588, when appointing Sir William Cecil to be a senior official as having said to him: 'This judgement I have of you, that you will not be corrupted by any manner of gift, and that without respect to my private will, you will give me that counsel that you think best.'

Grindle (2012), however, argues that patronage has been the prevailing method for selecting government officials in a wide variety of countries for centuries and has only recently been replaced by Weberian merit-based civil services in some countries, particularly in the Global North. As recently as the twentieth century, however, it was not uncommon to acknowledge the systems of patronage within Western government bureaucracies, such as the United States. For example, the *Syracuse Herald* on 23 October 1913 stated that 'Party government isn't organized for efficiency, nor to serve the people. It is organized to provide jobs for the boys' (quoted in Grindle, 2012, p. 1). This is despite the Pendleton Civil Service Act, which legislated the requirement for permanent federal employment to be based on merit rather than political affiliation, having been passed by the US Congress in 1883. This illustrates the length of time that may be required (and has been required historically) for legislative changes in the sphere of governance to be translated into widespread practices.

Rothstein (2011, pp. 114–119) discusses the reforms that Sweden undertook in the nineteenth century to establish a meritocratic and accountable civil service, free from practices that would now be regarded as 'corrupt'. Table 2.4 picks out some of these reforms.

This table illustrates some of the numerous reforms undertaken by Sweden in the last 200 years, to both directly and indirectly address corruption. The timeframes also show that numerous reforms might be necessary and these can take a long time to implement. This, in turn, has consequences in terms of measuring progress and results within the scope of international development interventions, as will be discussed in Chapter 4.

Also, even nowadays the numbers of corruption, patronage and other scandals in Western developed democracies point to the fact that such a Weberian ideal is far from achieved. For example, recent scandals in the UK include Tower Hamlets election fraud (*BBC News*, 2015), ministerial lobbying on behalf of commercial interest groups (*BBC News*, 2010) or a government secretary admitting to blurring lines between 'professional responsibilities and ... personal loyalties to a friend' (*BBC News*, 2011).

Nuances within the literature

A difference in the terminology used to describe taking advantage of social connections can also be noted between the Global North and the Global South. In the professional world in the Global North, for example, networking forms an integral part of one's professional career, both in the private and public sector. Private sector firms stress the importance of, and organise various training courses on, growing one's networks and making 'clients for life'. Public sector officials often invest in conferences and other events to meet officials from other agencies and jurisdictions, which can then significantly speed up or even enable them to perform their duties. The individuals who excel at this are seen as using good 'soft skills' to discharge their duties more effectively rather than engaging in morally questionable activities. Certain non-democratic governmental arrangements such as those prevalent within the UK's House of Lords are considered as 'tradition' in the UK, but may not be so when observing other societies.

An extensive vocabulary is used to refer to corrupt practices in developing countries, painting practices similar to those described above in a much more negative light. This includes 'nepotism' in the Arab world (Hayajenh *et al.*, 1994); or 'clan politics' in Tajikistan (Collins, 2004); 'neopatrimonialism'

Table 2.4 Reforms in Sweden leading to impartiality and combatting corruption

Year	Reform
1845	The government's right to confiscate newspapers is abolished (which led to the establishment of a newspaper-driven debate about public affairs from the 1850s).
1855–1860	Major revisions are made to the wage system in the civil service to create a Weberian system of pay.
1862	A new general criminal code includes a law on misconduct in public office.
1868	Parliament starts abolishing direct payments for services to individual civil servants. The fees citizens pay for services are state property rather than belonging to individual civil servants.
1869	Parliament requires taxes to be paid in money instead of goods.
1876	National bureaucracies are reorganised from collegial decision-making (the court model) to the modern bureau system with a hierarchical structure.
1878	The 'accord system' is dismantled and a working pension system for civil servants is introduced. The 'accord system' is essentially a position-buying system, which 'allowed civil servants who wanted to advance in their careers to persuade higher-ranking civil servants to resign their offices by paying them an accord in the form of a certain sum of money', the money could then either be used for retirement or towards the purchase of higher-up positions (Rothstein, 1998, p. 294).
1886	Approximately the year when the 'accord system' is abolished.

Source: table based on Rothstein (2011, pp. 115–116).

('straddling between the public and private domains' (Sindzingre and Milelli, 2010, p. 15; Van de Walle, 2007)) or 'prebendalism' ('decentralised patrimonial rule') in Nigeria (Lewis, 1996). Certain authors discuss 'clan politics' in Central Asia (see, for example, Collins, 2004; Starr, 2006) as if it were a phenomenon completely foreign to 'developed' countries. However, some social networks and connections prevalent in developed countries, discussed earlier, may function in the same ways as 'clans' in Central Asia.

It has also been argued that informal networks and institutions can provide alternative methods of governance and management, which will not necessarily be less efficient than the Western model of formal bureaucracy (Helmke and Levitsky, 2003). This may be particularly true in the case of fragile states (see, for example, Glanville, 2015), where an abrupt introduction of Western types and standards of institutional governance systems could have a further destabilising effect and hinder a state's post-conflict recovery.

Bayart (1996, p. 12) further notes that dichotomic categories that researchers often delineate do not accurately reflect the complexities of African societies. This applies to divides between, for example, rural and urban or the traditional and the modern. Bayart (1996, p. 12) states that, in the case of the Ivory Coast '[s]omeone who is ill will consult, one after another, the doctor in Abidjan hospital, the faith healer in the suburbs and the witch doctor in his village because he simultaneously inhabits these different worlds'. Similar 'itineraries' can occur in other aspects of one's social and political engagements, in relation to, for example, nepotism and political leadership. Cultural awareness and flexibility are therefore necessary in the study of social relations and structures of governance in different societies.

2.4 Summary

This chapter has discussed the conceptual approaches to corruption, including the definitions used by the international agencies that attempt to combat it globally, noting the inadequacy of the definitions for the complexity of the phenomenon in question, such as the sometimes blurry distinction between activities that are mostly only frowned upon and those that are illegal. Organisations working on combatting corruption should perhaps adopt a definition that would stress the importance of disclosure and transparency, as well as acting against the public interest. Subsequent chapters of this book, however, will mainly focus on the definitions of corruption that are currently being used, in order to present a more accurate situation of anti-corruption initiatives within international development activities.

Various influences on what is or can be considered as corrupt behaviour, as well as determinants of it, were also discussed. The phenomenon that is often alluded to as monolithic and definable, with measurable effects, is in fact complex and may even be, to some extent, 'in the eye of the beholder'. The vagueness of the term is a key reason why most legal approaches to corruption do not consider corruption per se, rather creating legislation and building cases to address specific offences of corruption, such as bribery, embezzlement or fraud.

A clear understanding of the historical and cultural practices and processes in different environments is required for organisations to effectively tackle corruption, and to identify all the stakeholders who should be engaged if the efforts were to have a long-lasting effect. This refers to identifying the lobbies and their historical, personal and industrial connections to those in power; politicians' voting bases; or the prevailing customs regarding the treatment of friends, family and superiors, just to name a few. Failure to engage all the relevant stakeholders and practices associated may not yield the desired results.

Having set out the conceptual approach to anti-corruption and the complexities involved in defining the phenomenon that is to be addressed, this book will consider in detail the theoretical approaches to anti-corruption interventions in international development.

Notes

1 Mulgan (2012), referring to Austin's (1947) conceptualisation of the terms 'real-word' and 'trouser-word', suggests that corruption should be understood as a trouser-word, 'filled and shaped by its complementary counterpart'.
2 This definition was used by the NGO Transparency International (TI) until 2012 to compile the Corruption Perception Index (CPI), a tool that is very commonly used as a measure of corruption. The definition of corruption that is currently being propagated by TI is 'the abuse of entrusted power for private gain' (TI, 2009). This allows for the incorporation of corruption within the private sector (such as insider trading) under the definition.
3 The system of a Western 'rule of law' in fact does not grant equal rights to all people, as it excludes non-citizens from accessing the justice systems in developed countries on the same terms as nationals, such as 'illegal' immigrants – those who are not explicitly permitted to stay in the country. This section builds on my MPhil work, as mentioned in the preface.
4 Translated by author from 《大清律例》: '子告父,若所告不实, 即父无子所告之罪行, 子当处绞刑;若所 告属实,即父确有子所告之罪行, 子亦须受杖一百,徒三年之罚' (Yan, 2008).
5 An even stronger distrust of politicians can be noted in another historic work, Arthasastra by Kautilya, from around 300 BCE:

> Just as fish moving inside water cannot be known when drinking water, even so officers appointed for carrying out works cannot be known when appropriating money.... It is possible to know even the path of a bird flying in the sky, but not the ways of officers moving with their intentions concealed.
>
> (Quoted in Widmalm, 2008, pp. 117–118)

Bibliography

Austin, J., 1947. *Sense and Sensibilia*. Oxford University Press, Oxford.
Bayart, J.-F., 1996. *The State in Africa*. Longman Singapore Publishers (Pte) Ltd, Singapore.
Bayley, D., 1970. The Effects of Corruption in a Developing Nation, in: Heidenheimer, A.J., Johnston, M., LeVine, V.T. (Eds), *Political Corruption: Readings in Comparative Analysis*. Transaction Books, New Brunswick, New Jersey, pp. 521–533.
BBC News, 2015. Tower Hamlets Election Fraud Mayor Lutfur Rahman Removed from Office. *BBC News*. April. Available at: www.bbc.co.uk/news/uk-england-london-32428648.

Conceptual framework

BBC News, 2011. Liam Fox Sorry over Relationship with Adam Werritty. *BBC News*. Available at: www.bbc.co.uk/news/uk-15234897.

BBC News, 2010. BBC News – Ex-ministers in 'Cash for Influence' Row under Fire. *BBC News*. Available at: http://news.bbc.co.uk/1/hi/uk_politics/8578597.stm (accessed 16 September 2016).

Bracking, S., 2013. A Qualitative Reframing of Private Sector Corruption: Considerations from the Natural Resource Sectors in South Africa. U4. Available at: www.u4.no/publications/a-qualitative-reframing-of-private-sector-corruption-considerations-from-the-natural-resource-sectors-in-south-africa/.

Brooks, R.C., 1970. The Nature of Political Corruption, in: Heidenheimer, A.J., Johnston, M., LeVine, V.T. (Eds), *Political Corruption: Readings in Comparative Analysis*. Transaction Books, New Brunswick, New Jersey, pp. 56–61.

Brunelle-Quraishi, O., 2011. Assessing the Relevancy and Efficacy of the United Nations Convention against Corruption: A Comparative Analysis. Notre Dame *Journal of International and Comparative Law* 2(1), 101–166.

Chaikin, D., 2008. Commercial Corruption and Money Laundering: A Preliminary Analysis. *Journal of Financial Crime* 15(3), 269–281. doi:10.1108/13590790810882865.

Collins, K., 2004. The Logic of Clan Politics: Evidence from the Central Asian Trajectories. *World Politics* 56(2), 224–261.

Cremer, G., 2008. *Corruption and Development Aid Confronting the Challenges*, translated by Elisabeth Schuth. Lynne Rienner Publishers, Boulder, Colorado.

DFID, 2016. Department for International Development: Annual Report and Accounts 2015–16. Williams Lea Group on behalf of the Controller of Her Majesty's Stationery Office, UK.

DFID, 2015. Anti Corruption Evidence 'ACE' Programme Business Case and Summary. DevTracker Project GB-1-203752 Doc. Available at: https://devtracker.dfid.gov.uk/projects/GB-1-203752/documents (accessed 3 September 2016).

European Commission, 2014. Report from the Commission to the Council and the European Parliament: EU Anti-Corruption Report. European Commission, Brussels.

Fuest, C., Riedel, N., 2009. Tax Evasion, Tax Avoidance and Tax Expenditures in Developing Countries: A Review of the Literature. Report prepared for the UK Department for International Development (DFID).

Glanville, M., 2015. Corruption and Public Policy in Post-Conflict States, in: Rider, B. (Ed.), *Research Handbook on International Financial Crime*. Edward Elgar Publishing, Cheltenham, UK, pp. 435–447.

Grindle, M.S., 2012. *Jobs for the Boys: Patronage and the State in Comparative Perspective*. Harvard University Press, Cambridge, MA.

Hayajenh, A.F., Maghrabi, A.S., Al-Dabbagh, T.H., 1994. Research Note: Assessing the Effect of Nepotism on Human Resource Managers. *International Journal of Manpower* 15(1), 60–67. doi:10.1108/EUM0000000003933.

Hegel, G.W.F., 1965. *La Raison dans l'histoire, Introduction a la philosophie de l'Histoire*. U.G.E., Paris.

Heggstad, K., Fjeldstad, O.-H., 2010. *How Banks Assist Capital Flight from Africa: A Literature Review*. Chr. Michelsen Institute (CMI).

Heidenheimer, A.J., Johnston, M., LeVine, V.T., 1970. *Political Corruption*. Holt Rinehart and Winston, New York.

Hellman, J.S., Jones, G., Kaufmann, D., 2000. Seize the State, Seize the Day: State Capture, Corruption, and Influence in Transition, Policy Research Working Papers. The World Bank, Washington, DC.

Helmke, G., Levitsky, S., 2003. *Informal Institutions and Comparative Politics: A Research Agenda*. Cambridge University Press, Cambridge.
Heywood, P., 1997. Political Corruption: Problems and Perspectives. *Political Studies* 45(3), 417–435.
Holmes, L., 2015. *Corruption: A Very Short Introduction*. Oxford University Press, Oxford.
Huntington, S., 1968. *Political Order in Changing Societies*. Yale University Press, New Haven, CT.
ICAI, 2014. DFID's Approach to Anti-Corruption and its Impact on the Poor. Report.
Johnson, J., 2014. *Corruption and Stabilisation – Aid Agencies' Anti-corruption Strategies in Fragile States*. University of Cambridge, Cambridge.
Jordan, W.C., 2009. Anti-corruption Campaigns in Thirteenth-century Europe. *Journal of Medieval History* 35(2), 204–219. doi:10.1016/j.jmedhist.2009.03.004.
Kaufmann, D., 2004. *Corruption, Governance and Security: Challenges for the Rich Countries and the World*. Available SSRN 605801.
Kaufmann, D., 1997. Corruption: The Facts. *Foreign Policy* 107(Summer), 114–131.
Leff, N.H., 1964. Economic Development through Bureaucratic Corruption. *American Behavioural Science* 8(3), 8–14.
Legal Dictionary, 2016a. Embezzlement. *Legal Dictionary*. Available at: http://legal-dictionary.thefreedictionary.com/embezzlement (accessed 15 September 2016).
Legal Dictionary, 2016b. Misappropriation. Available at: http://legal-dictionary.thefreedictionary.com/misappropriation (accessed 15 September 2016).
Lewis, P., 1996. From Prebendalism to Predation: The Political Economy of Decline in Nigeria. *Journal of Modern African Studies* 34(March), 79–103.
Lynch, M., 2011. The Big Think Behind the Arab Spring: Do the Middle East's Revolutions Have a Unifying Ideology? *Foreign Policy*. Available at: http://medicine.tufts.edu/sitecore/content/Fletcher/Home/Alumni/Talloires-Symposium-2012/~/media/28BA6B7DFBAD4C18B066DD1DBF6484C8.pdf.
Mendilow, J., Peleg, I., 2014. *Corruption in the Contemporary World: Theory, Practice, and Hotspots*. Lexington Books, Lanham, MD.
Montesquieu, 1951. De l'esprit des lois, XXI, 2, in: *Oeuvres Completes*. Gallimard, Paris.
Muhlemann, G., 2011. China's Multiple Legal Traditions: An Overview, in: Tomasek, M., Muhlemann, G. (Eds), *Interpretation of Law in China – Roots and Perspectives*. Karolinum Press, Charles University in Prague.
Mulgan, R., 2012. Aristotle on Legality and Corruption, in: Barcham, M., Hindess, B., Evans, P. (Eds), *Corruption: Expanding the Focus*. ANU E Press, Canberra, Australia.
NORAD, 2015. Combating Corruption. NoradDev. Available at: http://norad.no/en/front/thematic-areas/democracy-and-good-governance/combating-corruption/ (accessed 10 September 2016).
Nye, J.S., 1970. Corruption and Political Development: A Cost–Benefit Analysis, in: Heidenheimer, A.J., Johnston, M., LeVine, V.T. (Eds), *Political Corruption: Readings in Comparative Analysis*. Transaction Books, New Brunswick, NJ, pp. 564–578.
OECD, 2013. *OECD Glossary of Statistical Terms: Corruption*. OECD, Paris, France.
OECD, 2008. *OECD Glossaries: Corruption: A Glossary of International Standards in Criminal Law*. OECD, Paris, France.
OECD Observer, 2007. Defining Corruption. *OECD Observer*, March. Available at: http://oecdobserver.org/news/archivestory.php/aid/2163/Defining_corruption.html#sthash.47lgUgOj.dpuf.
Osborne, D., 1997. Corruption as Counter-culture: Attitudes to Bribery in Local and Global Society, in: Rider, B.A.K. (Ed.), *Corruption: The Enemy Within*. Kluwer Law International, The Hague; Boston, pp. 9–34.

36 Conceptual framework

Palan, R., 2002. Tax Havens and the Commercialization of State Sovereignty. *International Organization* 56(1), 151–176.

Philp, M., 1997. Defining Political Corruption. Special Issue, *Political Studies* 45(3), 436–462.

Plato, 2000. *The Republic*. Cambridge University Press, Cambridge.

Rider, B.A.K. (Ed.), 1997. *Corruption : The Enemy Within*. Kluwer Law International, The Hague; Boston.

Rose-Ackerman, S., 1999. *Corruption and Government: Causes, Consequences and Reform*. Cambridge University Press, Cambridge.

Rothstein, B., 2011. *The Quality of Government: Corruption, Social Trust, and Inequality in International Perspective*. University of Chicago Press, Chicago, IL.

Rothstein, B., 1998. State Building and Capitalism: The Rise of the Swedish Bureaucracy. *Scandinavian Political Studies* 21(2): 287–306.

SIDA, 2015. Approaches and Methods: Our Work against Corruption. Available at: www.sida.se/English/how-we-work/approaches-and-methods/our-work-against-corruption/ (accessed 10 September 2016).

Sindzingre, A.N., Milelli, C., 2010. *The Uncertain Relationship between Corruption and Growth in Developing Countries: Threshold Effects and State Effectiveness*. University of Paris West-Nanterre la Défense, EconomiX.

Snider, T.R., Kidane, W., 2007. Combating Corruption through International Law in Africa: A Comparative Analysis. *Cornell International Law Journal* 40(3), 691–748.

Starr, S.F., 2006. Clans, Authoritarian Rulers, and Parliaments in Central Asia. Central Asia-Caucasus Institute & Silk Road Studies Program. Available at: http://isdp.eu/content/uploads/publications/2006_starr_clans-authoritarian-rulers-and-parliaments-in-central-asia.PDF.

TI, 2009. TI Publication – The Anti-Corruption Plain Language Guide, TI. Available at: www.transparency.org/whatwedo/publication/the_anti_corruption_plain_language_guide.

TI, 2007. Global Corruption Report 2007: Corruption in Judicial Systems, TI. Available at: http://issuu.com/transparencyinternational/docs/global_corruption_report_2007_english?mode=window&backgroundColor=%23222222.

U4, 2010. UNCAC in a Nutshell: A Quick Guide to the United Nations Convention against Corruption for Embassy and Donor Agency Staff. U4. Available at: www.cmi.no/publications/file/3769-uncac-in-a-nutshell.pdf.

UNDP, 2008. *Primer on Corruption and Development; Corruption and Development: Anti-Corruption Interventions for Poverty Reduction, Realization of the MDGs and Promoting Sustainable Development*. United Nations Development Programme, New York.

UNODC, 2012. *Legislative Guide for the Implementation of the United Nations Convention against Corruption, 2nd revised edition*. United Nations Publications.

USAID, 2005. *USAID Anticorruption Strategy (No. PD-ACA-557)*. USAID: Washington, DC.

Van de Walle, N., 2007. The Path from Neopatrimonialism: Democracy and Clientelism in Africa Today. Cornell University Centre of International Studies, Working Paper.

Widmalm, S., 2008. *Decentralisation, Corruption and Social Capital: From India to the West*. Sage Publications, India.

Williams, G., Turner, T., 1978. Nigeria, in: Dunn, J. (Ed.), *West African States: Failure and Promise. A Study in Comparative Politics*. Cambridge University Press, Cambridge.

World Bank, 2017. What is Fraud and Corruption? Available at: www.worldbank.org/en/about/unit/integrity-vice-presidency/what-is-fraud-and-corruption (accessed 28 August 2017).

World Bank, 1997. *Helping Countries Combat Corruption: The Role of the World Bank*. The World Bank, Washington, DC.

Wrong, M., 2009. *It's Our Turn To Eat: The Story of a Kenyan Whistle Blower*. Fourth Estate, London.

Yan, Q. 闫清华, 2008. 'Concealment' and the Construction of Harmonious Society – translated from '亲亲相隐'与和谐社会的构建. *Journal of Railway Police College* 铁道警官高等专科学校学报 18(5), 25–65.

3 Theoretical approach to anti-corruption interventions in international development

Johnston (2006, p. 809) has noted that 'American political science as an institutionalized discipline has remained steadfastly uninterested in corruption for generations'. Rothstein (2011, p. 99) examined a number of recent handbooks in political science and public administration (such as Dryzek *et al.*, 2006; Moran *et al.*, 2006; Peters and Pierre, 2002; Rhodes *et al.*, 2006) and concluded that 'corruption is hardly ever mentioned'. Nevertheless, the foundations of the anti-corruption debate can be traced back to more historic debates about rights and justice.

More recently, corruption has been increasingly addressed in political science and international development – by both anti-corruption interventions by various agencies working in international development; and also development, politics and international relations scholarship, as will be elaborated in this chapter.

3.1 Moral foundations of the anti-corruption debate

This section considers the philosophical basis for anti-corruption interventions, looking at various approaches to justice, the nature of the debate on justice itself as well as the motivations for individuals to engage in corruption.

Philosophical basis

One of the main issues with the definitions of corruption used and described in Table 3.1 is the fact that there is no consensus about a comprehensive list of activities to be included in the concept. Some of the practices mentioned in Table 2.2 are not necessarily illegal (such as jurisdiction shopping, transfer pricing or tax evasion). These can, however, fundamentally affect the distribution of resources within a society, thus having a profound impact upon equity, access to opportunities and inequalities within the society. This leads authors such as Bracking (2013, p. 2) to argue that 'the mainstream anti-corruption literature has failed to establish a philosophical basis for the field that incorporates underlying assumptions about morality and ethics'.

Whereas the mainstream academic literature is not abundant in philosophical analyses of morality and ethics in relation to anti-corruption specifically, a large and growing number of academics and philosophers has addressed the broader issue of justice and rights, which is significant for the notion of corruption. This section explores the most relevant approaches to justice, which are incorporated within and influence the more specific theoretical approaches to corruption and the resulting denial of justice (see section 3.3).

Two major types of justice can be differentiated in the literature – criminal justice, which is primarily concerned with prevention, punishment and remediation; and distributive justice, which refers to the distribution of benefits and burdens among different actors (see Jones, 1995; Rawls, 1999). Distributive justice will be directly affected by the levels of corruption in a society.[1]

It is also important to define the concept of 'justice'. Many authors link justice to rights, as argued by Jones (1995, p. 50):

> when we are denied our rights, we typically respond with indignation or outrage, rather than with mere disappointment; we conceive ourselves as the victims of an injustice rather than as mere unfortunates who have been denied the milk of human kindness.

Will Kymlicka (1989, p. 234) refers to justice as 'the system of entitlements on the basis of which people can demand social recognition of their legitimate claims (e.g. for resources, freedoms, etc.)'. For the discussion and definition of 'justice' to be rendered meaningful, it is important to establish the type of rights justice refers to (in terms of economic, social, political rights, issues of equity and equality); who determines what these rights are to be; and upon whom the rights will be conferred.

The question of the principles according to how different rights and privileges bestowed upon different people would be balanced has been engaged with by numerous authors. Practically defining an idea of justice requires weighing up the importance of different rights of different social groups in a country, such as accepting refugees or asylum seekers into a country and granting them welfare and employment rights versus considering the impact on the well-being of the current citizens and inhabitants of the country and the effect that influxes of refugees may have on social cohesion, taxes, employment opportunities and other factors. As put by Rawls (1999, p. 9), a 'complete conception defining principles for all the virtues of the basic structure, together with their respective weights when they conflict, is more than a conception of justice; it is a social ideal'.

Sen (1999) distinguishes three major schools of thought as addressing the notion of justice – utilitarians, libertarians and a 'capability' approach to justice.

Utilitarian approach

Utilitarianism expands the notion of the well-being of an individual as a sum of all of his experiences to the unit of society, thus measuring the well-being of society by the total net sum of positive and negative experiences and the

40 Theoretical approach

extent of fulfilment of the desires of its individuals (Bentham, 1948, pp. 151–154). Hutcheson (1725, sec. 111, par 8) argues, 'that action is best, which procures the greatest happiness for the greatest numbers; and that, worst, which, in like manner, occasions misery'. The aim of society from a utilitarian perspective is therefore to achieve the greatest net satisfaction of all the members of that society, regardless of the distribution of satisfaction among the individuals. Consecutively, any injustices incurred by a minority of individuals would be justified if that would mean that the majority would be better off as a result of the sacrifice of the rights or liberties of the minority. As put by Rawls (1999, p. 25), while the social contract doctrine, as well as the proponents of the conception of 'justice as fairness', would accept the arguments 'about the priority of justice as on the whole sound, utilitarianism seeks to account for them as a socially useful illusion'. Rawls (1999, p. 26) suggests that, while it is common to consider utilitarianism as an individualistic theory, as numerous utilitarians also strongly argued for individual liberties and freedom of thought, 'by conflating the all systems of desires, it applies to society the principles of choice for one man'.

Sen (1999), while rejecting the more direct arguments presented by utilitarianism, suggests that the theory brings an important element to consider in international development programming relating to justice – the consequences of implementing certain types of institutions, programmes or legislations. Namely, utilitarianism urges policymakers to consider whether particular policies result in a better situation for citizens. The results and well-being of people are two key insights highlighted by utilitarians, 'rather than looking only at some abstract and alienated characteristics of states of affairs' (Sen, 1999, p. 61).

Libertarian approach

Libertarian approaches to justice stress the importance of liberty, which includes political liberties, property rights, freedom of choice and association and generally the freedom for individuals to make their own choices. In contrast to utilitarianism, the procedures for guaranteeing rights are deemed to be more important than the outcomes and consequences of following the procedures; as put by Sen (1999, p. 63), 'the issue, then, ... is not the comparative importance of rights, but their absolute priority'.

There are, however, significant variations to this argument within the libertarian tradition. A particularly interesting debate to consider is Harvard academics' Rawls' (1999) and Nozick's (1974) take on distributive justice. Sen (1999, p. 64) calls Rawls' stance an example of 'less demanding formulations of "priority of liberty" presented in liberal theories' while Nozick represents the 'more demanding' version of libertarian theory. These approaches are discussed in further detail in this section. The debate also illustrates that the definition of justice is disputed among not only philosophers, academics and practitioners that come from and live in completely different environments, but also those working under the same roof.

Rawls (1999, p. 7) puts forward the notion of 'justice as fairness',[2] where one of the main functions of justice would be to redress undeserved inequalities within societies. Rawls (1999, p. 6) focuses on social justice, which he regards as 'the way in which the major social institutions [i.e. the political constitution and the principal economic and social arrangements] distribute fundamental rights and duties and determine the division of advantages from social cooperation'. As examples of 'major social institutions' Rawls cites 'the legal protection of freedom of thought and liberty of conscience, competitive markets, private property in the means of production, and the monogamous family' (ibid.). Particular attention is given to the differences in starting points in life that the fact of being born into different socio-economic classes creates. Rawls (1999, p. 88) argues:

> [t]he social system is not an unchangeable order beyond human control but a pattern of human action. In justice as fairness men agree to avail themselves of the accidents of nature and social circumstance only when doing so is for the common benefit. The two principles are a fair way of meeting the arbitrariness of fortune; and while no doubt imperfect in other ways, the institutions which satisfy these principles are just.

Rawls' views on social justice were famously challenged by his fellow faculty-member at Harvard, Robert Nozick. Nozick (1974) argued for a minimal state, which did not get involved in rectifying injustices incurred from being born into lower social classes, or less endowed with marketable talents or skills. Nozick (1974, p. 149) claimed that a more extensive than minimal state would violate people's rights; as a state that takes it upon itself to carry out distributive justice inevitably bases its criteria for an adequate supply and distribution of goods and privileges upon subjective principles that are not necessarily supported by everyone. He disagrees with Rawls' rejection of a system of natural reasoning, and in particular dismisses Rawls' arguments that not only the initial endowments of natural capacity and material assets that people are given are arbitrary, but people's personal character and choice to further develop their skills will also be very much dependent on the arbitrary circumstances and the environment they are born into.[3] Nozick (1974, p. 214) claims that such an argument disregards human agency and 'can also succeed in blocking the introduction of a person's autonomous choices and actions (and their results) only by attributing everything noteworthy about the person completely to certain sorts of "external" factors'.

Nozick (1974, p. 151) argues that '[t]he complete principle of distributive justice would say simply that a distribution is just if everyone is entitled to the holdings they possess under the distribution', that is, 'if it arises from another just distribution by legitimate means'. Such a distribution, according to entitlement, is not 'patterned', as noted by Nozick (1974, p. 157). In other words, it does not rely on a single or combined criteria such as IQ, hard work or need to determine patterns of distribution (as these can be influenced by one-off factors such as luck in gambling, competitions or financial support from foundations or philanthropists). The theory of 'entitlement', however, and the just nature of the distribution of resources poses several issues, such as how far back one should go when rectifying past injustices. Arguably, Europe's colonial history has played a significant role in its current economic prosperity. Questions arise about the legitimacy of the means by which the holdings or wealth were acquired by the colonised states; and to what extent decedents are liable for their ancestors' actions. Furthermore, it is important to keep in mind that the notions of what is just or legitimate (in relation to, for example, slavery or women's right to an inheritance) changes over time, and is different in different societies, which makes balancing the different notions of justice a particularly challenging task.

Sen (1999) provides useful insights into the possible consequences of the supremacy of procedural entitlements. Specifically, Sen (1999, p. 66) points out that deprivation of various kinds (such as lack of access to medical care for curable diseases) can exist even while all the rights that are advocated for by libertarians are fully satisfied. This can be because of the inherent differences in the characteristics and needs of different people:

> At the practical level, perhaps the biggest difficulty in the real-income approach to well-being lies in the diversity of human beings. Differences in age, gender, special talents, disability, proneness to illness, and so on can make two different persons have quite divergent opportunities of quality of life *even when* they share exactly the same commodity bundle.
> (Sen, 1999, p. 69)

Sen (1999, pp. 70–71) further notes that these differences broadly fall under five categories: personal heterogeneities, environmental diversities, variations in social climate, differences in relational perspectives and distribution within the family. These are important to keep in mind when analysing the effects of corruption on different social groups and minorities, and, crucially, when designing policies to help combat corruption and redress the consequences of corruption.

'Capability' approach

Sen (1999) proposes combining the key messages of both utilitarianism (in particular, its focus on the outcomes of different policies and interventions and their effect on human well-being) and libertarianism (and its message of the fundamental importance of individual freedoms and procedural matters) in the 'capability approach'. Sen (1999, p. 85) notes that this approach 'concentrates on the capabilities of people to do things – and the freedom to lead lives – that they have reason to value'.

As such, the capability approach incorporates considerations of both the process and the outcomes, as well as the primary goods and capabilities in one's possession, with his ability to use them as means to achieve their goals and utilities. Sen (1999, p. 74) offers the example of an older or disabled person, who 'can be more disadvantaged in a generally accepted sense even with a larger bundle of primary goods' to stress the importance of this 'translation' or 'conversion' process.

A key element in the capability approach is the freedom to choose one's lifestyle, as similar outcomes can be achieved by people who do not have a choice in the matter as well as those who choose to follow a certain path. Sen (1999, p. 75) evokes the example of two people starving – one affluent person who decides to go on a diet and another who is starving because he cannot afford food. The former has made a choice to forego food, therefore his substantive freedoms and capabilities are unaffected; whereas the latter does not have the capability to lead a life that he 'has reason to value' (i.e. being free from hunger).

Corruption, at all levels of government and various institutions, can infringe on people's access to basic necessities and thus their capabilities. This can be via high-level officials syphoning off money that was meant for healthcare and education into their private bank accounts, leaving fewer or no resources to be sent to deprived areas; or low-level administrative staff demanding extortionate bribes for people to access basic services such as healthcare, education and sanitation, that are supposed to be free or cheaper to access. Sen's capability approach is useful in considering the effects of corruption in the sense that it highlights both the process (of resources being diverted for personal gain rather than public benefit) and the results of corruption (those who lose out on the resources and opportunities that they would otherwise have had access to).

The nature of the debate on justice

To date the debates on justice and access to rights have remained largely state-centred. Theories departing from the premise of a social contract, as discussed by Nussbaum (2007, p. 228), take the nation-state as the basis for their analysis. Such theories depart from considering the state of nature, and whether or not individuals choose a cooperative life under laws they consent to. Transnational aspects of foreign states, international organisations and NGOs intervening in what has traditionally been considered states' domestic affairs has therefore, until relatively recently, not been considered in much detail.

Some, however, have begun emphasising global inequalities and the 'transnational social contract' (Nussbaum, 2007). Nussbaum (2007, p. 225) argues that today,

> [a]ny theory of justice that aims to provide a basis for decent life chances and opportunities for all human beings must take cognizance both of inequalities internal to each nation and of inequalities between nations, and must be prepared to address the complex intersections of these inequalities in a world of increased and increasing global interconnection.

The author evokes the rising power and influence of multinational corporations and the global market and economic system in general, in addition to international NGOs and social movements, international treaties and multinational agencies and institutions, which 'have considerably eroded the power and autonomy of nations' (ibid.).

The question therefore arises as to who should be responsible for ensuring the principles of justice and that people's rights are being upheld. Jones (2001, p. 8) points out that the institutions limiting or increasing people's access to goods, resources and opportunities in life are increasingly international organisations, such as international financial institutions, transnational corporations (TNCs), the WTO, the G8, G20 etc. Most of these international institutions that have an effect on people's access to justice, though, are comprised of states, who tend to consider their own citizens' and corporations first; and TNCs arguably have other priorities than distributive justice.

Buchanan (1990) differentiates between 'justice as self-interested reciprocity' and 'subject-centred justice', which distinguishes between the understanding of justice being 'owed' only to those who could potentially reciprocate in the future, or to everyone who demonstrates certain characteristics such as the capacity for rational agency or to share similar experiences (Jones, 2001, p. 6). The distinction between the two concepts is also found in Barry's (1989) writings on 'justice as mutual exchange' and 'justice as impartiality'. This analysis will be further developed in Chapter 5 on the nature of international law, which is shifting from a largely predominant bilateral nature to a more general one, especially with the development of human rights law.

As pointed out by Jones (2001, p. 9), advocating for the importance of international distributive justice implies the ability to take effective action to address the issue: '"ought" implies "can" and in the current circumstances we cannot, so it is pointless to say that we ought'. Adam Smith (1969 [1759], p. 238), writing 260 years ago, argued that it was pointless to take much interest in the misfortunes of those who are geographically remote, as there was not much that could have been done to improve their situation:

> Whatever interest we take in the fortune of those with whom we have no acquaintance or connection, and who are placed altogether out of the sphere of our activity, can produce only anxiety to ourselves, without any manner of advantage to them. (...) That we should be but little interested, therefore, in the fortune of those whom we can neither serve nor hurt, and who are in every respect so very remote from us, seems wisely ordered by Nature; and if it were possible to alter in this respect the original construction of our frame, we could yet gain nothing by the change.

Modern technology, transport and trade, however, have resulted in an interconnected world where interventions to ensure that principles of justice are upheld globally are not only possible but increasingly common (Hehir, 2013; Wheeler, 2000). It is in this context that anti-corruption interventions are analysed in this book.

Summary

Different approaches to what can be considered as 'just', or the principles according to which it would be desirable for individuals to act, clearly shows disagreement, even among people from the same backgrounds – a Rawlsian understanding of 'justice as fairness', Nozick's theory of entitlement and a utilitarian conception of measuring people's well-being as the sum of the intensity and the number of occurrences of negative and positive experiences of individuals would suggest very different foci for anti-corruption interventions. A collaborative and deliberative approach to programming in the sphere of justice and anti-corruption is therefore necessary to ensure that interventions are welcomed by the population of where the interventions would be carried out (and the different groups within that population) and subsequently are more likely to have and sustain their desired impact.

Motivation for corruption

It is worth considering the motives of individuals engaging in corruption. Pisani (2014) presents the views and experience of a number of interviewees in Indonesia, on corruption and acceding to the seat of the bupati, or the head of a regency, which is the equivalent position of a mayor:

> It's expensive to become bupati. First, you have to pay a political party to back you. Then you have to pick up all the costs of campaigning; costs I heard about but didn't really believe until I spent a few weeks in a campaign office a bit later in the trip. Unless you are massively wealthy, paying for all the electioneering will mean borrowing money. And that means payback. ... The winner, now the bupati, can't pay his debts out of his salary of US$600 a month ... Instead, he repays with a permit to mine, an appointment to this post or that, a contract to build a new hospital or a blue-roofed passenger terminal. 'By the time they get elected they've got so many debts that they can't *not* be corrupt', people would explain, over and over again.

Similar accounts of political party processes were also noted in Kenya, where following decentralisation in 2013, 47 new county governance systems and administrations were set up. Pisani (ibid.), however, notes that not all of this 'payback' is illegal and the actions can be likened to those of a congressman in the United States pushing through fracking-friendly policies that will benefit the sponsors of his elections campaign.

Jordan (2009) analyses the attempts to curb corruption in medieval Europe and suggests that the disadvantaged groups that engaged in bribery and corruption may have broken the laws of the time as they perceived the system to be unjust and morally unjustifiable:

> in medieval Europe many of the tempters (those who resorted to trying to bribe officials to betray their office) were legally disadvantaged, indeed

46 *Theoretical approach*

> disenfranchised groups, Jews and immigrants (like Flemings in London and Bretons in Paris, say). A Jewish or immigrant tempter wanted to induce a breach of trust in the temptee. He wanted to 'corrupt' the royal or local official in order to achieve what was for the former (the Jew or immigrant) an equitable end, that is to say, the decent livelihood being denied to Jews and immigrants by means of much restrictive legislation or social practices then in place. In the case of a Jew, his self-perceived moral right to induce a breach of trust in a royal agent would have been founded on an implicit or explicit theory of unjust laws. Disenfranchised in every meaningful sense, Jews had not formally or tacitly given counsel or consent to the laws. 'What touches all must be approved by all' applied to all Christians, not Jews.
>
> (Jordan, 2009, p. 218)

Therefore, from a moral point of view, in such cases it would be difficult to strictly class bribery by the disadvantaged groups as morally wrong. Today, however, mechanisms to challenge legal injustices exist – domestically within most countries – and within supranational institutions in some circumstances (such as the European Court of Human Rights) (Tomuschat, 2014).

Nevertheless, there could be a number of motives for abusing one's official role or bribing those who are doing so: greed or self-centred motives or, alternatively, considerations of the benefits for the society as a whole or the most vulnerable members of it. This will have important consequences regarding the choice of approaches to addressing corruption, which are discussed in subsequent chapters. For example, we could consider the case where an official of a UN agency would pay an 'under the table fee' in order to ensure that all the required permits and documents were arranged for refugees who had been accepted for resettlement in third countries to be able to leave the country to which they had initially fled. A non-detailed 'expenses' budget could account for such expenditure. The international organisation's staff consenting to such a facilitation payment would surely have considered the needs of the individuals who were granted assistance and the possibility to restart their lives in a different context as the highest priority. Refusing the payment would have obstructed the resettlement process and complicated the relationship between the local government officials and international organisations, potentially causing significant damage to those concerned.

The bigger picture, however, should also be considered in such circumstances; and the price of continuing versus challenging such practices needs to be weighed up. In this refugee case, it could be a few people's well-being versus an improved and more efficient bureaucracy ultimately permitting to assist a more significant number of refugees as well as changes in the public's perceptions and tolerance of corrupt practices. This example illustrates that, in order to combat corruption it is imperative to consider the motives of all the stakeholders engaging in or condoning corruption. In this case it would not have been greed but rather a willingness to help others. Addressing corruption would therefore involve clearly setting out the bigger picture and long-term effects of eradicating corruption. The illustration by Pawel Kuczynski (2016) sums up this point (see Figure 3.1).

Figure 3.1 An illustration of short-term versus long-term approaches.
Source: author: Pawel Kuczynski (2016).

3.2 Measurement of corruption

Corruption is intrinsically difficult to quantify and significantly more difficult to measure progress on than other development undertakings, such as healthcare or economic growth. There is a large and growing number of methods that are being used to measure corruption, with a number of NGOs, aid agencies, multilateral organisations, think tanks and private sector actors generating indicators and indexes.

As with other crimes, it is challenging to accurately measure the pervasiveness of corruption due to its secretive nature and the reluctance of victims to report the crime. In the case of corruption, the notion of victims is vague as the victims of corruption may be unaware of the crime having been committed. This could be the case of, for example, enterprises that lose contracts due to their competitors paying a bribe. UNODC further points to three factors that make measuring corruption even further complicated (UNCAC, 2010, p. 3). First of all, the borders between licit and illicit activities within national legislation and the UNCAC can be blurred. Second, as the UNCAC names a wide range of offences that fall under the umbrella of the term 'corruption', as shown in Table 2.3, accurately quantifying the extent of corruption would require data to be collected for all of the offences. Third, victims of corruption may be less prone to report corruption to the authorities due to, among other reasons, fear of retaliation, reluctance to fight established institutions or participation in the crime.

Moreover, the currently predominant forms of measuring corruption – whether in terms of the incidence of scandals, estimates of secret funds or various corruption indexes, such as the Corruption Perception Index (CPI) or the Global Corruption Barometer compiled by Transparency International (TI, 2016a, 2016b) – are all proxies for the real situation. For example, the number of government corruption scandals will inevitably be lower in non-democratic countries where the state controls the press; however, bureaucrats in such countries may also be more prone to corruption as they are aware of the lower likelihood of public scrutiny for corruption and have relatively low checks of accountability to the population as a whole.

The subjective and politicised nature of corruption has also been noted in the literature. For example, Widmalm (2008, p. 113) writes:

> Corruption is a highly charged aspect of political life and has been so for a long time. Therefore, we have to be extremely careful when we apply it for scientific purposes because, like labels or terms such as ethnic, class or gender, corruption is not just a term liked by social scientists – it is a politicised term that can capture a reader's mind and lead it to domains where scientific dialogue has little point.

The fact that corruption can mean different things to different people (in particular in relation to connotations) makes data collection and comparison difficult.

The CPI, one of the most commonly cited measures of corruption, is largely based on 'expert' opinions, including from foreign business people who do business in the country they rate for corruption (and who contribute to the data for the CPI). These, however, are inevitably subjective, possibly biased, and, most importantly, incomparable among different countries where different businesspeople are being interviewed. Razafindrakoto and Roubaud (2010) compare a large sample of households' and 'experts' opinions on the extent and nature of corruption, and demonstrate a mismatch between two groups' estimates of the prevalence and the extent of corruption in a given country. The authors noted that experts may be influenced by their ideological inclinations and extrapolate from anecdotal experiences. Households, on the other hand, might be less aware of the levels of grand corruption within their country. Therefore, it becomes very difficult to assess how much corruption has influenced a given country's economic development, as it is impossible to accurately verify how pervasive the issue of corruption is in one country compared to others.

There is also the issue of measuring perceptions (CPI) versus actual experiences of corruption. Regional corruption barometers and other surveys such as the WB's World Business Environment Survey do in fact attempt to measure people's actual encounters with corrupt practices. This, however, also poses problems of comparison as there will inevitably be only a sample of people surveyed; and as offences of corruption on a grander scale (such as political corruption involving large sums of money) are only encountered by a small number of people (as opposed to, for example, corruption within the traffic police or administrative offices), it is unlikely that such corruption will be adequately captured by the surveys.

Nevertheless, it is important to note that public perception of corruption can also be an interesting factor in itself, even if it does not accurately correspond with actual levels of corruption. Perceptions of corruption can influence investors' decisions and general levels of trust within society and trust in institutions. These effects are discussed in more detail later on in this chapter. As such, cost–benefit analyses of the effects of corruption, which do not adequately take into account the effects of corruption on public confidence in institutions and developing countries' business environment, security and the environment (see, for example, the early works on corruption by Nye, 1967), are bound to be inaccurate.

Furthermore, Widmalm (2008) and Oldenburg (1987) note that as corruption and other variables, such as poorly functioning institutions and poverty, tend to correlate, they can get labelled under the same term. This, in turn, would make efficient reforms difficult to identify: 'If we throw cases of "inefficiency" which are not caused by corruption into the box, we will fail to understand why some bureaucrats manage to behave in a non-corrupt way although the structural constraints are severe' (Widmalm, 2008, p. 134). The same would apply if historical reasons for certain institutional structures are not identified. The causal relationships between corruption and a number of development indicators are explored in section 3.4.

The CPI and other global anti-corruption indexes, such as the World Bank's Control of Corruption Index, the PRS Group's International Country Risk Guide and Transparency International's Bribe Payers' Index, are also subject to aggregation problems, when data collected using different methodologies and incomparable samples are compiled to construct a single index.

3.3 Nature and causes of corruption

Academic analyses of corruption have largely focused on the factors that incentivise and enable corruption. These consider various economic variables, institutional arrangements and the form of government, culture and history. It is most useful to consider the determinants of corruption, as a good understanding of these can enable a more efficient programme design. Factors such as cultural and moral motivations for engaging in corrupt behaviour were discussed previously in this chapter. This section will present the dominant theories in the literature, from both economic and political science approaches. The section builds on the work done by Robinson (1998), Fitzsimons (2007, p. 46) and Johnson (2014) in categorising the theoretical approaches in the literature to the causes of corruption.

Economic approaches

Economic approaches have had the most significant influence on aid agencies' anti-corruption programme design. These theories focus on rent-seeking[4] and transaction costs, which makes them more pertinent to explain petty corruption rather than institutional or political corruption (Johnson, 2014). This section will review various economic approaches that have been put forward in the literature to explain the rationale behind engaging in corruption and consequently the methods that could be used to tackle corruption.

The limitations of these theories will also be presented. Overall, however, it is worth mentioning that, as put by Fitzsimons (2007, p. 46), the 'idea of unethical behaviour is difficult for economists to analyse given their assumption that all individuals and organisations simply pursue self-interest opportunistically'. This can lead to missing a range of social, institutional, psychological and cultural factors that might influence individuals' choices of whether to engage in corruption or not.

Public Choice Theory (PCT)

The Public Choice Theory considers individuals' decision-making processes and the incentives for individuals to obey or to disobey rules. The theory assumes that bureaucrats, politicians and ordinary citizens will act 'rationally' to maximise their own interests. Huther and Shah (2000, p. 3) suggest that '[c]orruption will only take place when officials expect to derive net positive benefit from the transaction. Successful anti-corruption programs will lower the expected gains and raise the expected penalties of corrupt behaviour.'

On a more granular level, bureaucrats are seen to calculate whether either fulfilling their duties and acting in the general public interest or bending the rules would be more favourable to them. This could involve, for example, public officials creating additional 'rents' such as licences for business to operate, in addition to the classic corrupt behaviours such as bribery and nepotism. Such licences could help create unfair competition or even monopolies. Businesses will, in turn, have increased incentives to engage in corrupt activities and bribe bureaucrats for such licences (see Krueger, 1974).

As such, PCT considers the institutional arrangements that determine the extent to which individuals can successfully intervene in markets and bend the rules in their favour, at the expense of the general public. The theory therefore propagates a minimal state, arguing that economic reforms and reducing a state's bureaucratic apparatus will result in fewer opportunities for bureaucrats' discretion regarding rent and resource allocation and thus limit the scope of rent-seeking and corruption.

Reforms to downsize the state on their own, however, will not eliminate corruption. Social policies and regulation of reforms is needed to ensure that benefits from economic liberalisation are not appropriated by the same corrupt elites that were in power previously. Similarly, benefits of such reforms will be limited if the public sector remains the primary source of income and formal employment while other economic opportunities remain scarce. The role of international actors in shaping the nature and prevalence of corruption is also often overlooked (see Robinson, 1998, pp. 1–14 for a more in-depth discussion of these factors).

PCT rationale can be seen in a large number of aid agencies' anti-corruption interventions, particularly those that consider the incentives or individuals to act with integrity, adopting a 'carrot and stick' philosophy (Johnson, 2014). An example of the 'carrot' approach would be ensuring an adequate remuneration for employees to be able to lead a dignified life. A competitive salary would both diminish the need for supplementary income and also increase the losses incurred if one gets caught for corruption and dismissed from his role. One of the factors that has been put forward for the pervasive nature of corruption in Indonesia has been the historically extremely low wages for public servants and bureaucrats, which, according to some calculations, only covered a third of one's household needs (see Robertson-Snape, 1999, p. 590). The 'stick' side of the approach would involve increasing the sanctions for breaking the rules as well as improving the monitoring systems (see Akerlof and Yellen, 1990).

PCT proponents consider that almost all key state stakeholders – the politicians who make the laws, the bureaucrats who implement the laws, as well as businesses and lobby groups are corruptible and 'solely motivated by self-interest' (Robinson, 1998, p. 4). This, in turn, disregards the possibility of active interventions by state actors to combat corruption and cannot explain the different levels of pervasiveness of corruption between different institutions (ibid.).

Moreover, the theory to a large extent ignores the international actors and their role in shaping the corruption landscape in developing countries. These

52 *Theoretical approach*

international actors include multinational corporations, UN agencies and other multilateral institutions, international NGOs and government departments' international development agencies.

New Institutional Economics (NIE)

NIE, drawing on the principal–agent approach, considers corruption through an institutional lens, focusing on transaction costs and 'rents'. As put by Khan (2010, p. 9), NIE's key contribution 'was to highlight that institutions mattered because rules were essential to make social interaction possible'. NIE has a focus on micro-economics, and considers people's behaviour using a rational choice framework.

Douglass North is considered as the key author who shaped the NIE approach. North (1990) examines the historical development of states and the extent to which different institutions succeed in minimising transaction costs, thus facilitating economic growth. North (1990) defines institutions as 'the framework within which human interaction takes places', which provide 'a structure to everyday life'. They are 'the codes of conduct, norms of behaviour, and conventions'. This includes both formal institutions – such as the police, regulators and courts – as well as informal institutions, such as a non-written rule 'that jobseekers who come with a recommendation from the local mafia boss should be given the job' or an 'internalized norm of respect for property that may restrain individuals from appropriating assets owned by others even if the property rights are not well enforced' (see Khan, 2010, p. 10). Khan further notes that the latter norm would significantly lower the costs of enforcing formalised property rights through official state institutions. As such, NIE proposes that different types of institutions will have different implications on the feasibility of various types of social activity as, in the absence of particular rules, the costs of these activities might be too high for successful cooperation (see Khan, 2010; North, 1990, 1995; Rodrik, 2002).

North builds on the seminal works of Coase (1988) who pioneered the transaction costs approach, with a consideration of information asymmetries and market failure. The transaction costs that are most relevant to the study of corruption are the costs of gathering information on the possible exchanges, the determining of satisfactory conditions for commitments ('bargaining') as well as policing and enforcement of contracts (ibid.).

North's approach and terminology influenced the work of international organisations in the sphere of anti-corruption (World Bank, 2012, pp. 15–21, 2002). The approach, however, has been criticised as lacking in political, cultural and social insights, as under NIE individuals are still understood to be making decisions unilaterally, based on rational self-interest (see Harriss *et al.*, 2003). Rose-Ackerman (1999, pp. 5–6) has noted that '[c]ultural differences and morality provide nuance and subtlety, but an economic approach is fundamental to understanding where corrupt incentives are the greatest and have the biggest impact'. Here Rose-Ackerman acknowledges the complexity of factors that influence the extent of corrupt practices, however she reverts to an economic approach when considering 'the biggest impact'. The NIE approach is therefore more useful to explain individuals' behaviour and petty/bureaucratic, rather than systemic/political corruption.

Furthermore, Khan (2010, p. 14) notes that NIE's focus on aggregate transaction costs is too simplistic. A reduction in some types of transaction costs while others persist might not in sum achieve efficiency improvements. A distinction also has to be made between overall transaction costs and transaction costs per unit of transaction. As put by Khan (ibid.),

> Advanced countries pay for a significant part of their aggregate transaction cost in the form of a collective enforcement of property rights and other economic rules as part of the 'rule of law'. Aggregate transaction costs (when we include the cost of enforcing the rules) may be very high, but collective provision ensures that the cost per unit of transaction facing individuals or organizations is relatively low.

The NIE approach suggests that changing 'the incentives public managers face in conducting public business' is a key factor that will determine the success of anti-corruption programmes (Shah, 2007, p. 6). As a remedy, Shah (ibid.) suggests extending the anti-corruption interventions to broader elements of a country's governance system:

> because corruption is itself a symptom of fundamental governance failure, the higher the incidence of corruption, the less an anticorruption strategy should include tactics that are narrowly targeted to corrupt behaviors and the more it should focus on the broad underlying features of the governance environment.

Political economy approach

The political economy approach emphasises power dynamics and focuses on agency rather than individuals' self-interest. Corruption is consequently seen as a multifaceted phenomenon, depending on the balance of power, influence and resources between the key stakeholders within a state. Historical structures and influences are therefore taken into account when explaining the prevalence of different types of corruption (Robinson, 1998, p. 5).

Robinson (1998, p. 6) further points out that there is a need to update and reconsider one's analysis of the position, power and preferences of the different actors within a state, arguing that the 'same actors that promote corruption in the first place can also be instrumental in its demise'. This would apply, for example, to businessmen tolerating high levels of corruption, payment and procurement irregularities while they are establishing their positions with the economy and are in the earlier stages of acquiring wealth, but once they have established themselves, would be more in favour of predictable contracts and a strong legal system to

54 *Theoretical approach*

ensure that the gains are protected and perhaps regularised. Regular contextual analysis and tailoring of anti-corruption programmes, targeting and incentivising different social groups and stakeholders in different ways, may therefore be necessary for anti-corruption programmes to achieve their intended goals.

Kang (2002) provides an interesting classification of four different types of corruption, based on the strength and concentration of state institutions and businesses, see Figure 3.2 below. Kang (2002, p. 15) suggests that the larger and more diversified businesses are (such as the Korean chaebol as opposed to individual artisans), the more likely they will be to attempt to influence government policies. Building on Shleifer and Vishny's (1993) work, Kang (2002, pp. 13–14) considers the state to be either 'fractured ... when leaders survive only tenuously, when they engage in constant conflict with political organizations over the form and content of the state, and bureaucrats can play off "multiple principals" to their own advantage' or 'coherent if it can formulate preferences independent of social influences and if political leaders have internal control over their bureaucrats'. In the case of a coherent state, leaders can be expected to use domestic politics to ensure they stay in power.

As shown by Figure 3.2, Kang (2002, pp. 13–17) suggests that the nature of the state and businesses will determine the type and the amount of corruption prevalent within society. Within the 'mutual hostages' scenario, there might be collusion between the state and businesses, but neither side is strong enough to take considerable advantage of the other without suffering significant repercussions themselves. A rent-seeking situation will occur when the businesses are more powerful than state institutions and can force concessions (such as low-income loans or import quotes) from it. This would, in turn, leave others within the society worse off. A predatory state will be characterised by political elites engaging in expropriation and soliciting 'donations' from businesses. In a laissez-faire situation, neither the state nor businesses are strong enough to demand significant benefits for themselves as there are numerous interest groups and power is dispersed among the state. Kang (2002) considers this to be the situation where the least corruption occurs.

		State	
		Coherent	Fractured
Business	Concentrated	**I: Mutual hostages** Type: prisoner's dilemma collusion Amount: medium	**II: Rent seeking** Type: bottom-up Amount: large
	Dispersed	**III: Predatory state** Type: top-down Amount: large	**IV: Laissez-faire** Type: residual Amount: small

Figure 3.2 Types of corruption based on the nature of the state and business.
Source: Kang (2002, p. 15).

Suggested means to combat corruption within the context of a political economy approach would therefore suggest conscious political interventions, to increase the checks and balances that the ruling elite is subject to and distribute power among numerous decision makers. This could involve democratisation or decentralisation reforms to increase the checks and demands on the politicians that the public would be able to make. Democratisation reforms, however, will not necessarily result in lower levels of corruption, as noted by Singh (1997), having analysed the cases of India and Nigeria where the levels of corruption rose despite democratisation. Furthermore, decentralisation programmes have the risk of not only enabling new elites to establish themselves and increase the public's engagement in political affairs and scrutiny of bureaucrats and public spending, but also of providing opportunities for established elites to increase their access to rents, if reforms are not carried out well or in a favourable context (see Zaum *et al.*, 2012, p. 19). Public engagement, political willingness and technical capacity is also needed to carry out the reforms effectively.

Pluralistic socio-conscious approach

The pluralistic socio-conscious approach builds upon the observations of the political economy approach, in addition to incorporating the notion that government and institutional reforms, in order to be effective, should be complemented by civil society organisations' and general citizens' involvement to create the social foundation necessary for long-term change (see, for example, Johnston, 1998).

This approach is also subject to the need for high levels of political commitment and administrative and legal capacity to implement institutional reforms. Moreover, while empowering some citizen groups to demand change may lead to the desired outcomes, other social groups may be resistant to change and stand in the way of reforms if they stand to lose out from the reforms. Furthermore, foreign support to CSOs may not be welcome by some more nationalist groups within society.

Summary

This section has discussed the shift in the predominant analytical focus over the years – from primarily considering rents and licences to bribery and related offences; gradually paying attention not only to the formal government structures and laws, but also their implementation as well as informal institutions and the engagement of citizens. The focus of programmes shifts accordingly, from large-scale structural government reform (such as decentralisation) and mainly focusing on economic issues, towards considering the political structures as well as the pervasiveness of corruption within society and the engagement of citizens in political debates.

Political science approaches

The principal–agent and the collective action theories are currently the most widely discussed theories in an attempt to explain what drives individuals to engage in corruption. The two theories suggest different incentives and drivers of corruption. Consequently, the types of programming that are suggested by proponents of these theories will differ significantly.

Principal–agent theory

The principal–agent theory is widely applied in a diverse range of research areas, such as governance, management of businesses and finance (see, for example, Shah, 2014). The principal–agent approach has until recently been predominantly used to account for the existence and persistence of corruption in many developing country societies. This has been influenced by the seminal works of Rose-Ackerman (1978) and Klitgaard (1988).

The theory attempts to set out the reasoning behind individuals' cost–benefit calculations when deciding whether to engage in corrupt activities (see, for example, Groenendijk, 1997; Laffont and Martimort, 2009). The costs and benefits considered do not necessarily have to be the risk of punishment and material gains, but can also include considerations of, for example, reputational concerns. Collier (2000, p. 198), for example, speaks of moral norms and 'feeling bad' as a key disincentive to engage in corrupt practices:

> If someone breaks their own moral norm they feel bad about doing so, and this feeling bad acts as a disincentive. In societies which are habitually honest, probably the main incentive to individual honesty is not the public penalties against corruption but these private penalties: people don't want to end up feeling guilty. By contrast, in a society in which corruption is normal, the psychic penalties to being corrupt are obviously much less. A person who behaves corruptly in such a society may worry at some level that they have done wrong, but their sense of guilt can be assuaged by the knowledge that most other people are equally guilty. Hence, the same corrupt action is likely to generate much more severe feelings of guilt in societies where such behavior is rare than in societies where it is common.

Corruption is understood in the context of dishonest or criminal behaviour, when one person (the agent) is entrusted to act on behalf of others (the principal(s)). The agent will be in a position of power; his abuse of that power to act in his own interests rather than in the interests of the principal will be a corrupt act. This could be the case of a politician acting as an agent for his constituents (the principals) or a civil servant acting as the agent for cabinet ministers (the principals). The principal is assumed to be benevolent/honest.

The principal–agent model has its appeals, not least of which would be the relative ease of combatting corruption by changing individuals' incentives to participate in corrupt activities (for example, by increasing the penalties and the probability of being caught by investing in policing). Klitgaard (1988, p. 75) even suggested a formula to define corruption:

corruption = monopoly + discretion − accountability

Klitgaard's approach was very influential in academia and policymaking organisations; and was subsequently taken up by a number of multilateral institutions including the World Bank (1997, p. 12) and UNDP (2004, p. 2). Programmes and approaches to combat corruption were accordingly designed while keeping in mind such a formulaic and universalistic explanation of the causes and enablers of corruption.

There are, however, several issues with the principal–agent theory. Rothstein (2011, p. 99) notes that in a thoroughly corrupt system, it may be difficult to determine who the benevolent principle would be. Rothstein further points out that due to a lack of evidence that democratic elections work against corruption, there is no basis to consider 'the people' to be the (benevolent/honest) principle and political leaders the (corrupt) agent. In fact, considering the case of Italy, Golden (2003) notes that politicians engage in widespread bureaucratic corruption to enhance their re-election prospects, using an extensive compensatory constituency service.

It is also important to consider the incentives of the political elites in power to change the corrupt system that they themselves would mostly be benefiting from. Klitgaard (1988, p. 5) suggests considering

> an analogous question, 'Why would national leaders, who are mindful of their self-interest, ever undertake free-market reforms, privatisation, and related policies, all of which sacrifice their personal control over the economy?' Yet such reforms have swept the world, as has the remarkable 'third wave' of democratic reforms.

While a detailed study of the potential benefits to elites that privatisation can offer is outside the scope of this book, it is apparent that in some countries liberalisation did not amount to more than window dressing in order to receive support from international organisations such as the International Monetary Fund (IMF) (see, for example, Babb and Kentikelenis, 2017). Furthermore, the process of privatisation may have benefited the political leadership individually as well as its entourage. Similarly, when discussing the benevolent decisions taken by elites to carry out anti-corruption reforms, one has to analyse the depth of reforms in the country in question, and establish whether the changes made were not just cosmetic, designed, for example, to obtain international funding.

Collective action theory

Recently academic accounts for corruption have started centring around a collective rather than individual behaviour analysis. Put simply, the theory suggests that an individual will be unlikely to stop acting in a corrupt way when everyone else within the society continues to do so, as there will be minimal to no overall impact resulting from refraining to engage in corrupt activities; and the individual in question is likely to himself be worse off as a result of not engaging in corruption. Consequently, as put by Rothstein (2011, p. 100), 'in a political system plagued by systemic corruption, we are not likely to find benevolent "principals" at the bottom or at the top'.

Changing the incentives to engage in corrupt activities, as the principal–agent theory would suggest, can be difficult. Bardhan (1997, p. 1331) notes that 'our expected gain from corruption depends crucially on the number of other people we expect to be corrupt'. In a society where corruption is prevalent, therefore, people will be less responsive to incentives to refrain from corruption. For example, if the penalties are increased for engaging in corrupt practices, these will need to be enforced uniformly and consistently to have the desired effect; and if corruption is closer to being the norm, rather than the exception, that may be difficult.

Rothstein (2011, p. 100) also evokes a *second order* collective action problem:

> All of the agents may well understand that they would gain from erasing corruption, but because they cannot trust that most other agents will refrain from corrupt practices, they have no reason to refrain from paying or demanding bribes. The only reason they would do so is if institutions could be established that would make them trust that most other agents would refrain from corrupt behavior (Rawls, 1971, p. 240). However, establishing such credible institutions is in itself a problem of collective action.
> (Lichbach, 1997)

The authors therefore suggest that corruption is self-reinforcing. Most importantly, corruption can be rooted within the wider context of national and international politics, government institutions, as well as business and other pressure groups' interests.

A differentiated approach

Both of the aforementioned theories have a sound theoretical background and will be applicable in different contexts. Johnston (1996) provides a useful breakdown of the scales on which that corruption occurs – from incidental (individual), to institutional (corruption occurs in individual institutions such as the police service but not necessarily others) and systematic (when corruption is pervasive in a society). Accordingly, the principal–agent theory may best account for incidental corruption which refers to individuals' decision-making processes;

and the collective action theory can best explain systematic corruption in the context of high prevalence of corruption within society.

It may be particularly useful to consider institutional corruption, which bridges the divide between the individual and society, in the context of a 'figuration', as explained by Norbert Elias (1978, p. 130):

> If four people sit around a table and play cards together, they form a figuration. Their actions are interdependent. In this case, it is still possible to bow to tradition, and to speak of the 'game' as if it had an existence of its own. It is possible to say, 'Isn't the game slow tonight?' But despite all the expressions which tend to objectify it, in this instance the course taken by the game will obviously be the outcome of the actions of a group of interdependent individuals. It has been shown that the course of the game is relatively autonomous for every single player, given that all the players are approximately equal in strength. But it does not have substance; it has no being, no existence independently of the players, as the word 'game' might suggest. Nor is the game an idea or an 'idea-type', constructed by a sociological observer through observing the separate behaviour of each individual player, abstracting the particular characteristics which several players might have in common, and deducing from them a regular pattern of individual behaviour. The 'game' is no more an abstraction than the 'players'. The same applies to the four players sitting around the table. If the term 'concrete' means anything at all, we can say that the figuration formed by the players is as concrete as the players themselves. By figuration we mean the changing pattern created by the players as a whole – not only by their intellects but by their whole selves, the totality of their dealings in their relationships with each other. It can be seen that this figuration forms a flexible lattice-work of tensions. The interdependence of the players, which is a prerequisite for their forming a figuration, may be an interdependence of allies or of opponents.

Therefore, if we are to consider institutions as 'figurations', these will be naturally influenced by both the decisions of the individuals that make up the institution and their calculations of what would constitute the best course of action, as well as the general norms, rules and traditions which prevail within the institution. Institutional corruption can be explained using a mixture of both the principal–agent and collective action theories. This could refer to individual state institutions such as the police service or customs; or a particular sector, such as extractives.

See Figure 3.3 for an illustration of when the different theories would be more analytically useful to explain individuals' corrupt behaviour.

The principal–agent and the collective action theories have received the most attention within the literature on corruption. A number of other approaches, however, also provide valuable insights into the study of corruption, its effects and the success of various methods to combat it.

60 *Theoretical approach*

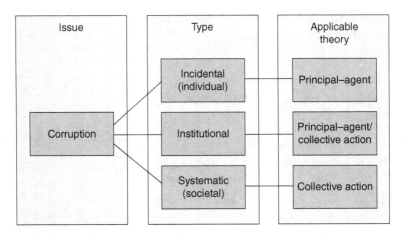

Figure 3.3 Theoretical approaches to corruption.

Migdal (1994, p. 8) suggests a 'state in society' approach, which 'break[s] down the undifferentiated concepts of the state – and also of society – to understand how different elements in each pull in different directions, leading to unanticipated patterns of domination and transformation'. Migdal argues that, in presenting a state as holistic, or as 'a unitary actor that assesses its situation strategically and then acts accordingly to maximise its interests ... scholars have obscured state formation and the dynamics of the struggle for domination in societies' (ibid.). Following Migdal's logic would lead to discrediting rational choice and some of the political economy perspectives presented earlier in this chapter, as these accept a largely coherent logic to how certain groups within a state come to dominate and make 'rational' decisions to achieve goals such as maximising state revenue or increasing the welfare of a state's citizens. In reality, the 'state' makes decisions to incorporate the interests of various groups within the state and society. Different groups (such as different levels of state bureaucracies, unions, businesses, etc.) can dominate in certain geographic or thematic areas. State decisions are also influenced by individual state officials' personalities and preferences.

Summary

The study of corruption and the considerations of its nature and causes has evolved significantly within the field of political science. Corruption, having been initially considered primarily within the principal–agent framework, weighing the incentives for an individual to participate in corrupt acts or not, has become considered within its wider social context. While this development has helped to further our understanding of the phenomenon and subsequently to design anti-corruption programmes that are more likely to achieve their intended results, authors such as Migdal (1994) have pointed out that more nuance within the study of corruption might be necessary. Migdal (1994, p. 9) discusses the often disjointed and conflicted nature of a state, which often does not itself have clear priorities and has to balance the interests of a number of different groups within the state, concluding that 'to glean the patterns of domination, one must focus on the cumulation of struggles and accommodations in society's multiple arenas'.

Policy implications

A host of various methods and combinations of approaches has been suggested to combat corruption, building on the aforementioned theoretical classifications of the causes and factors enabling corruption. Proponents of the principal–agent theory and incentive-based arguments suggest interventions to vary the incentives for engaging in corrupt practices – increasing the potential costs (by increasing the probability of getting caught and the penalties for when one is caught) and decreasing the benefits (for example, by ensuring more consistent and efficient asset freezing and recovery measures). More long-term approaches, such as education and media-based initiatives, are proposed by those suggesting a collective action issue, to gradually change people's attitudes and behaviours in relation to corruption.

Michael (2004, p. 1068) groups the anti-corruption project types undertaken into four main categories: universalistic, state-centric, society-centric and critical approaches to corruption. Michael argues that universalistic approaches regard corruption as 'a universal phenomenon occurring in organisations which run according to well-defined social laws' (ibid.). The state-centric approaches allow more scope for the influence of individual personalities and power struggles, and in so doing, to consider political and sociological causes of corruption. Society-centric approaches tend to consider corruption as socially constructed, thus emphasising the role and influence of social and cultural institutions. The critical approach views anti-corruption efforts as futile, as having unintended consequences, or even as counterproductive in combatting corruption. Michael summarises these approaches in Table 3.1.

A combination of these approaches can usually be seen in the current works of academics and international organisations. The universalistic approach lends itself to the development of international legal approaches to eradicating corruption as well as the ability to use 'toolkits', or pre-defined approaches to corruption that would be replicable in different contexts (see, for example, Klitgaard's (1988) proposed anti-corruption 'toolkits'). State-centric approaches to corruption can lead to projects tackling corruption indirectly, for example by means of institutional reforms to increase transparency and accountability in a government's operational processes. Society-centric approaches in practice suggest a programme focus on non-state actors, and civil society and advocacy in particular. Often, however, a mix of reforms is suggested. For example, Rider (1997, p. 3) states that the 'so-called "three-pronged attack" – firm enforcement,

Table 3.1 Summary of anti-corruption programme foundations

	Universalistic	State-centric	Society-centric	Critical
Who	'Society'	State	Civil society	Power institutions
What	Mechanic programmes	Government reform	Social reproduction	Epistemic contestation
Where	In all 'stakeholder groups'	State	Outside of the state	In discursive practices
Why	Social rules dictate change	State 'machine' is broken	People know what is best	Hegemony
How	Technocratic programmes	Public sector reform	Participation	Semiotic control
Main areas	Integrity systems	Civil service reform, budget reform, administrative reform	Media, schools, NGOs, cultural institutions	International organisations and governments
Author examples	Klitgaard et al. (2000)	Schick (1998)	Jenkins and Goetz (1999)	Polzer (2001)

Source: Michael (2004, p. 1068).

prevention and education' is the best strategy to develop control mechanisms for corrupt practices. The example of DFID's anti-corruption work, discussed in Chapter 4, illustrates the organisation's willingness to combine the aforementioned approaches to addressing corruption.

It is also worth noting that the differentiated and multifaceted approach to combatting corruption was not always featured as a key theme in the literature. Individual aspects of the types of governance, such as the democratic nature of a country's government or the level of centralisation and market liberalisation in the economy, had been proposed as the key factors affecting the prevalence of corruption within a state (see, for example, Little and Posada-Carbó, 1996). Current debates acknowledge the complexity in such relations, namely that decentralisation of power and control over the economy can simply have the effect of decentralising corruption; and democratic structures 'have proved markedly ineffective in developing countries' Robinson (1998, p. 2).

Migdal (1994, p. 9) states that '[s]cholars and journalists alike have paid far too much attention to who controls the top state leadership positions, as if those at the summit speak and act for the entire complex state organization'. In reality, the struggle for different policies, resources and power occurs at various levels of the state and society. This complexity has to be recognised when taking measures to curb corruption: the different actors and interest groups, their goals, approaches and power bases, need to be considered when designing anti-corruption strategies and programmes.

3.4 Consequences of corruption

The mainstream literature and the reports of international organisations and development agencies almost exclusively stress the negative and often quantifiable effects of corruption on various aspects of development,[5] including the economy, bureaucratic institutions, inequalities and social stability. A number of these are often presented in DFID business cases, justifying the need to intervene and wider benefits of addressing corruption (see, for example, DFID, 2015).

It is also important to keep in mind, however, that proving the exact effect of corruption on the economy, as well as broader development indicators, is difficult due to confounding factors that affect a variety of different institutions and indicators simultaneously: including the levels of corruption, economic output, levels of education, institutional efficiency, the profile and number of multinational companies entering in a developing country's market, historical legacies or the type of government ruling the country. Also, historically some authors have suggested positive or negligible effects of corruption on the economy, stability and other factors, as discussed in this section.

On the economy

Numerous studies have examined the effects of corruption on economic growth (see, for example, Dreher and Herzfeld, 2005; Mauro, 1995; Ugur and Dasgupta,

2011). Whereas, historically, researchers have advocated for both a positive ('greasing the wheels') and a negative effect of corruption on economic growth, the latter is currently the most widely accepted conclusion. Research has demonstrated that corruption results in reductions in levels of competition and investments in an economy; and diverts resources inefficiently and away from public provision of goods (see Bardhan, 1997; Gupta et al., 2002; Kaufmann, 1997; Mauro, 1995). Robinson (1998, p. 2) argues that corruption is of 'particular concern for developing countries because it undermines economic growth, discourages foreign investment and reduces the resources available for infrastructure, public services and anti-poverty programmes'.

Econometric studies have attempted to quantify the effects of changes in countries' corruption index measures on economic growth variables (see, for example, Dreher and Herzfeld, 2005; Rahman et al., 2000; Swaleheen, 2011). Due to the difficulties in measuring corruption and the problems with indexes analysed earlier in this chapter (section 3.2), these will not be considered in detail here.

Corruption has not always been seen as a hindrance to investments within a country or its economic growth. Scholars such as Leff (1964) and Lui (1985) have argued that corruption might actually 'introduce an element of competition into what is otherwise a comfortably monopolistic industry ... [where] payment of the highest bribes [becomes] one of the principal criteria for allocation ... Hence a tendency toward efficiency is introduced into the system'. The argument suggests that the most efficient firm should be able to afford the highest bribe, therefore competitively winning government procurement contracts. Kaufmann (1997, pp. 117–188), however, argues that the highest bidding capacity may be an indication of sub-standard quality rather than efficiency; and that the bribed money can easily be syphoned out of the country, as it has often happened, for example, in Nigeria. Furthermore, those with connections might be favoured over the most efficient companies, which can distort the market and discourage investors from investing in the more corrupt markets. Longer-term investments would also be discouraged by the uncertainty caused by frequent government policy changes due to corruption.

Kang (2002, p. 201) notes that 'bribes are transfers', therefore corruption affects the distribution, but not necessarily the quantity of funds within an economy. Kang further suggests that in the case of scarce resources in a country, concentrating them in the hands of a few people (corrupt companies, state officials and their entourage) who could then invest them productively could arguably be better for the economy than having many more people spending a little more on consumption. Leff (1964) argues that as the success of such corrupt investments would directly benefit the investors, these will have the incentives to be innovative and productive; corruption might therefore be beneficial for a poor country's economic growth. Murphy et al. (1993), however, warns that this might disadvantage entrepreneurs and innovators outside established companies, who will in such circumstances have limited access to credit or funds for bribery.

Furthermore, investments that are made to benefit businesses are not necessarily incompatible with public interests. For example, a factory owner might invest in infrastructure to transport his goods from the factory to the sales points and in electricity networks and power stations to ensure continuous power supply for the production of goods that will cause increased profits. This will also directly benefit the population living in the area. Kang (2002, pp. 178–179) argues that

> the Korean state intervened the way it did because doing so was in the interests of a small group of business and political elites. Producing public goods was often the fortunate by-product of actors competing to gain the private benefits of state resources.

Infrastructure built by businesses and employment opportunities created will not have equal social benefits across the board, as demonstrated by the colonial infrastructure which was not as useful as it could have been to the local populations and artisanal businesses in many African countries (Mentan, 2010, p. 194). In South Korea, however, large industrial conglomerates, which were favoured by the state, built significant amounts of infrastructure, created employment opportunities and significantly contributed to the Korean economy (Kim, 2006; Ungson *et al.*, 1997). A number of these conglomerates later developed into giants such as Samsung and Daewoo. Similarly, Allswang (1998) and McCaffery (2010) have argued that the United States' industries also developed at a time when corruption was rampant, propelling the United States into the World's largest economy.

There is, therefore, a need to carefully consider the factors that enabled these countries to thrive, or at least did not inhibit them in doing so, despite the high levels of corruption. This is necessary to be able to concentrate resources to tackle the types of corruption that are most harmful to countries' economic and other development indicators.

Corruption has also been cited as an effective way to 'cut through the red tape', or to reduce the amount of time it takes to navigate through bureaucratic procedures to establish a business or complete other procedures (see, for example, Egger and Winner, 2005; Lui, 1985). However, the possibility to obtain rents from reducing the normal bureaucratic procedures provides an incentive for bureaucrats to erect more obstacles, which then could be circumvented for a bribe. Such behaviour may result in a vicious cycle where corruption breeds more corruption (Kaufmann, 1997, pp. 116–117).

When discussing the effects of corruption, it is worth keeping in mind that it is impossible to establish how countries' economies would have performed in the absence of lower levels of corruption. For example, some industries might have been headed by more talented entrepreneurs and as a consequence developed faster; or, conversely, in the absence of political corruption or nepotism at the highest levels, resources might have been spread too thinly among entrepreneurs and might not have permitted the rapid development of large and

66 *Theoretical approach*

productive industrial conglomerates. Campos *et al.* (1999) argue that even in the countries where corruption has not inhibited growth, less corruption would have resulted in even higher levels of growth. Deconstructing the varying effects of corruption on different development indicators allows one to note which appears to be the most damaging to society and a country's development. Money taken out of a developing country, to go into corrupt officials' private bank accounts or invest in property in developed countries, appears to be particularly damaging to a country's economy, as discussed in section 4.2.

In addition to discussing the effect of corruption on the economy, the effect of the economy on corruption should also be noted. Corruption could in some cases be considered as a coping mechanism at times of poor economic conditions. A country with a badly performing economy might not be able to afford, or willing to invest in, adequate salaries for its employees. These employees might, in turn, be forced to resort to corruption to be able to adequately provide for their families. For example, Suharto (in Schwartz, 1994, p. 136) has been quoted as saying:

> Corruption in our country is not the result of corrupt minds but of economic pressures. Eventually, when economic development has gone so far as to produce a good overall standard of living, government employees will receive adequate salaries and have no reason to practise corruption.

Such a two-way influencing pattern complicates policymaking and introduces a need to address a vicious cycle of bad economies contributing to higher levels of corruption and higher levels of corruption contributing to bad economies.

On the efficiency of the state's bureaucratic institutions

Corruption and bribery can have the effect of undermining both government legitimacy and levels of political participation, if corruption is seen as rampant within government institutions (see Anderson and Tverdova, 2003; Rose-Ackerman, 2010; Seligson, 2002). It is worth mentioning that the causal arrows may as well go the other way, with limited citizens' engagement with public institutions creating the possibility for corruption to go unchallenged (see Figure 3.4).

Corruption has also been noted by numerous studies to have an adverse impact on both the amounts invested as well as the scope and the quality of services provided by the government, particularly in the spheres of education, healthcare, housing and other social goods (see Gupta *et al.*, 2002; Lambsdorff, 1999; Widoyoko, 2007). This can further contribute to the lack of confidence that people may have in government institutions.

Some authors, however, have suggested that corruption can have a positive effect on the efficiency of an economy by diminishing the amount of 'red tape' (see, for example, Widmalm (2008, p. 116) and Nye (1970)); and as a consequence measures to curb bureaucratic corruption may impede

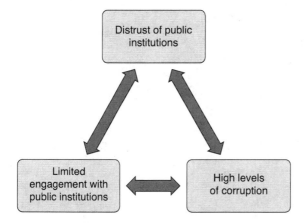

Figure 3.4 Corruption and state institutions.

the efficient operation of an administrative system, thus leading to bottlenecks and, often, widespread injustice. People who need quick action cannot but be harmed if the tedious routine procedures meant to assure against corruption actually make them avoid going through official channels or, conversely, actually punish them with crippling delays if they try to adhere to the law.

(Jordan, 2009, p. 218)

Such a view, however, is rather short-sighted, as many bureaucracies have effectively institutionalised higher payments for administrative tasks that are required to be performed urgently, such as issuing passports. In many countries a higher fee will have to be officially paid to the state authority if a passport is required urgently. Such a system allows for businesses' and individuals' needs to be met without recourse to corruption but rather via an official, yet adaptable, taxation system. Moreover, greasing some wheels within a bureaucracy might have the effect of stopping others.

On inequalities

Numerous studies have stressed that corruption has a disproportionate effect on the poor (see EP, 2015; Gupta *et al.*, 2002; ICAI, 2014). This can occur both on a larger scale and at the micro level: bribery in public procurement will normally lead to money being fraudulently awarded to larger programmes, for example in construction and infrastructure, at the expense of social programmes (USAID, 2005, p. 5). Companies can also resort to corruption in order to avoid paying the required taxes. This will also lead to the state having a smaller budget than it would have in the absence of corruption and most likely result in a smaller pot being available to fund social security and safety net programmes for the vulnerable.

Corruption in procurement as well as administrative corruption can mean that people will be required to pay bribes to access the basic services that they would otherwise be entitled to receive free of charge. This can include registration for documents or medical services. The poor will have less knowledge of the formal processes and less resources needed to access the available appeal mechanisms when faced with corrupt bureaucrats. Chetwynd *et al.* (2003) find that corruption works as a regressive tax, as lower-income households and businesses lose a higher percentage of their income to corruption than those with larger incomes. The authors further suggest that this disproportionate 'regressive taxation', in turn, contributes to lower levels of public engagement with, and trust in, public institutions.

As with the effects of corruption on the other development variables, the causal relationship between corruption and inequalities is hard to determine precisely. For example, Uslaner (2007) argues that high levels of inequality lead to lower levels of social trust and, in turn, foster corruption. The situation can therefore be one of a vicious circle, with corruption fostering inequalities and subsequently inequalities fostering corruption. The most significant type of inequality that corruption reinforces, however, is possibly inequality of opportunity. People with lower social capital miss out on education, employment, financing and other opportunities due to nepotism and patronage.

The importance of a thorough analysis of a given institutional, historical and cultural context before carrying out anti-corruption interventions has also been stressed in the literature. Dobson and Ramlogan-Dobson (2010) highlight the importance of the informal sector, which can have the effects of moderating the impact of corruption on levels of inequality. Formalisation under such circumstances could therefore adversely affect the levels of inequality within that context.

Studies have also suggested that corruption has a disproportionate effect on women (see, for example, TI, 2010). This is particularly acutely felt in the context of women accessing basic services such as healthcare and education, as well as the institutions that they would need to engage with to set up a small business and access credit. TI noted that women generally tend to be less aware of their entitlements and are often excluded from decision-making processes, and end up having to pay for the basic services and allowances that they are entitled to free of charge (see TI Bangladesh, 2005; UNIFEM, 2009).

On stability

The WB has suggested that corruption increases the risks of violence by 'fueling grievances and by undermining the effectiveness of national institutions and social norms' (World Bank, 2011). Research by Boucher *et al.* (2007) and O'Donnell (2006) has suggested similar causal links. Corruption has arguably had a particularly destabilising effect when the patronage networks are limited to a small number of people (Dix *et al.*, 2012).

Corruption might also indirectly influence a country's economic performance by contributing to political and social instability. Mo (2001) finds that a 1 per cent increase in the corruption level reduces a country's economic growth rate by about 0.72 per cent, suggesting that the manner in which corruption affects a state's economy is mostly via political instability (which accounts for 53 per cent of the effect); 20 per cent via reduction in private investment and 15 per cent by negatively influencing the formation of human capital. These figures, as mentioned in section 3.2, should be considered within the context of the limitations of measuring corruption and its effects on wider development indicators.

On the other hand, corruption has been suggested as having a stabilising effect under certain circumstances, particularly in fragile state contexts. For example, Huntington (1968) and Khan (2006) suggest that corrupt networks and patronage may be instrumental in ensuring peace and the support of competing groups that, without the corrupt payments and networks of patronage, would be prone to challenging the leadership often using violent means. The applicability of such reasoning will, of course, depend on the particular circumstances of the conflict and the institutional, social and other settings. For example, the abundance of natural resources could increase the likelihood of violence – a phenomenon that Arezki and Gylfason (2013) suggest will more strongly manifest in democratic rather than non-democratic states.

There is a need, however, to evaluate the short-term versus long-term benefits of such an approach, the unintended consequences and general signalling in terms of what can be acceptable in a post-conflict society if corruption is not to be accepted as having positive effects. As discussed in section 3.1, the wider implications and long-term consequences of different types of corruption should be considered when accepting a particular effect of corruption on development indicators in international development programming.

On the environment

Corruption can have a detrimental effect on the environment. In particular, failure to comply with regulations can result in pollution, deforestation, depletion of natural resources and destroy the livelihoods of, and endanger, various species as well as people's sources of income and livelihood (such as access to clean water). This can, in turn, have negative effects on the livelihoods of vulnerable members of the population (see Cole, 2007; Welsch, 2004).

Shaxson (2007) suggests looking at corruption through a 'tragedy of the commons' lens. Shaxson (2007, p. 1128) uses an oilfield example to illustrate this approach:

> In this 'common-pool' problem, participants compete to get oil out as fast as possible, before the others do, leading to overproduction and damage to the oilfield. This dynamic would be recognized by anyone familiar with corruption – or with the problem that politicians uncertain about their hold on power spend as much as possible, as fast as possible, leaving little on the table for future opponents.

70 *Theoretical approach*

Such behaviour can also be observed in other contexts where rents are to be made – when people try to extract as much as they can as quickly as they can, before others get into power and start doing the same. Excessive extraction of resources can lead to their depletion, in addition to being wasteful because of overproduction. This could be seen in the context of various resources, including oil (for example, in Nigeria – Human Rights Watch, 1999) and deforestation (for example, in Cambodia, Indonesia, Uganda – see Cavanagh (2012) and Hafner (1998)).

International instruments to combat the effects of corruption on the environment have been put in place, such as the Extractive Industries Transparency Initiative (EITI) and the EU's Forest Law Enforcement, Governance and Trade (FLEGT) initiatives. These initiatives create regimes to uphold principles of integrity and fairness within the sectors they focus on and their reach is expanding globally. Taken as a whole, their reach – in terms of the industries they address and the geographical coverage – is rather limited. For example, FLEGT is an EU initiative, however currently the majority of timber is being imported by large developing countries such as China. While a key part of the FLEGT initiative is in working with these other importers of timber to agree on standards to be required of timber importers, its practical effects have so far been limited (EU FLEGT, 2016). These international initiatives are discussed in more detail in section 5.3.

Policy implications

Policy suggestions to tackle the effects of corruption have been largely related to ideological perceptions of the nature of the state and the optimal extent of its involvement in market and other regulatory activities. For example, the neo-liberal school suggests that corruption is more likely to be rampant in countries where the market is severely regulated, as the state creates additional rents (such as licences and quotas), which provide the incentives for excessive competition for these rents, including bribery and corruption (see Klitgaard, 1988; Krueger, 1974). Minimising state intervention in the economy is therefore suggested to reduce corruption (Kaufmann, 1997; Mauro, 1995), and in the early 1980s, conditionalities of deregulation and economic liberalisation were attached to major World Bank loans to developing countries in the form of Structural Adjustment Programmes (SAPs).

It seems, however, that neo-liberal economists have at times selectively extrapolated conclusions from the examples that suit their own ideological conclusions. For example, Krueger (1990, p. 10), having analysed the inefficient investment programmes and predatory marketing boards in Ghana and Tanzania, argued that '[i]n many countries, there could be little question but that government failure significantly outweighed market failure'. However, she did not consider the evidence from other developed countries: the development path proposed by the SAPs is entirely ahistorical as no country has successfully developed following such open market and trade liberalisation policies (Chang,

2002, 2009; List, 1885). SAPs did not result in a reduction of corruption perception; nor did they facilitate economic growth in developing countries (Jerven, 2010, 2011; TI, 2013).

Decentralisation of administrative processes has also been suggested to reduce corruption (Banfield, 1985), due to increased competition between levels of government and between regions and other institutions in society that are engaged in the provision of goods and services (Breton, 1998). Evidence for such a relationship, however, is inconclusive (Fan et al., 2009). Decentralisation is a simple transfer of power and authority to the sub-national level, which is expected to bring about competition among regions. As pointed out by Bardhan and Mookherjee (2000), there may be a wide variety of context- and system-specific factors that can influence the level of state capture at different levels of governance. These include cohesiveness of interest groups, the extent of electoral competition, and the relative campaign sizes in local and national elections. Decentralisation of power may simply lead to decentralisation of corruption (Chabal and Daloz, 1999, p. 105).

There are dangers in assuming direct causal relations between complex phenomena such as corruption and economic performance, which are, themselves, influenced by a variety of factors. Sindzingre and Milelli (2010, p. 11) argue that 'the exact nature, extent and impact [of corruption] depend on the environment where the corrupt interactions occur: this environment influences and shapes the actions of corruption, while these actions, especially when repeated, modify the environment'. As such, the relationships between the various factors discussed in this section can be depicted as a two-way process, as illustrated by Figure 3.5.

Clearly, it is hard to assess what the span of a 'long-term' successful policy should encompass. The nuances and effects of different types of corruption should be kept in mind. These are analysed in the following section.

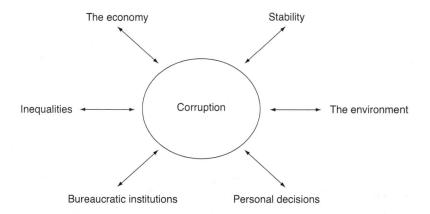

Figure 3.5 The influence on and of corruption.

3.5 The nuances

Over the years, scholars have presented a nuanced and opposing view of the effects of corruption on states' development, and states' economic growth in particular. Khan and Jomo (2000) point out that the net outcome, not only the costs of rent-seeking, should be considered: resources 'wasted' on rent-seeking may in fact be reintroduced in the economy; and if rent-seeking does not result in conflict, it may lead to institutional change and economic dynamism.

Very few states have been able to catch up with the 'Global North' in terms of development and economic growth. The 'miracle' growth of South Korea since the 1960s, when the state was situated among the poorest countries in the world, is often attributed to its meritocratic Weberian bureaucracy and sound economic policies. For example, Evans (1995, p. 51) argues that Korea's 'ability to facilitate industrial transformation … has been fundamentally rooted in coherent, competent bureaucratic organization'. South Korea is being portrayed as owing its impressive economic growth records to technocrats and austere military generals who emphasised export-oriented industrialisation; and corruption is not even evoked in many analyses of the Korean growth experience. Some accounts, however, suggest that corruption was nevertheless rampant during Korea's miracle growth era including, at the highest levels, two former presidents of Korea (Chun Doo-hwan and Roh Tae-woo), who were either imprisoned or exiled for corruption, and numerous other politicians, bureaucrats, bankers, businessmen and tax collectors who have been convicted (Kang, 2002, p. 177). It is interesting to consider the factors that enabled the rapid development of South Korea despite the prevailing levels of corruption, in order to establish which aspects are the most harmful to developing economies and to direct the focus of international efforts against corruption on those particular aspects, alongside general attempts to eradicate corruption.

Kang (2002, p. 177) notes that '[g]rowth was so spectacular that the reality of corruption was concealed or was dismissed out of hand'. The fact that corruption was compatible with regime stability and economic growth in South Korea suggests that corruption does not necessarily inhibit economic growth. The example of South Korea illustrates the nuances that have been presented in the anti-corruption debate, separating the different types of corruption and their effects on a country's development trajectory.

Authors such as Johnston (1996) and Hutchcroft (1997) pointed out a number of years ago that some forms of corruption will have the negative effects of slowing growth and/or threatening a country's political and social stability while others have fewer such effects. It is therefore important to pinpoint the factors that make corruption more corrosive to a country's wider development indicators.

Predictability and size

It is important to consider not only the presence but also the extent and predictability of corruption. Predictable levels of corruption might act as a form of tax (without, of course, the benefits of tax to the state and citizens in the form of increased state revenue which would be available to the state to reinvest for the benefit of the public in general – including in education, healthcare and infrastructure). Unpredictable and extortionate levels of corruption, however, will also have the additional effect of being destructive to businesses, by making financial planning extremely difficult and profits unpredictable; and ultimately driving businesses out of the country and discouraging investment. This can in sum have a significantly more devastating effect on the country's development in general.

South Korea offers an interesting example to consider in relation to the ultimate effects of corruption. Kang (2002) argues that the reason why corruption was not detrimental to economic growth in Korea was because the political strength of state agents and businesses was balanced, which meant that the business sector kept state corruption from spinning out of control and vice versa. Khan (1996) suggests that as the Korean state was resistant to societal and interest group demands, state officials and bureaucrats had incentives to maximise payments over the long term rather than the short term; which resulted in a non-detrimental 'efficient kleptocracy' over a long period of time rather than 'lump sum' corruption, which would have damaged the Korean economy even more.

Campos et al. (1999) suggest that while high institutionalisation in South Korea may have permitted corruption in the country to be predictable and therefore not inhibiting to the economy; in the long-term institutional change to meet the evolving political, social and economic circumstances and norms, may be successfully opposed by the bureaucrats in power and therefore have severe negative effects on the country's future economic growth.

Related to the issue of predictability of bribes and 'taxes' to be paid, which is an important factor affecting businesses' and investment decisions, is the distinction between extortive and transactive corruption. The former refers to situations where pressure is exerted on someone to give a bribe and the latter – to 'fee-for-service' bribes, which can be anticipated. Holmes (2015, p. 9) notes that in the latter, the two parties are practically equals negotiating a deal, whereas in the first situation there is a significant power imbalance. Pisani (2014) presents the example of Indonesia, which over the years has experienced both types of corruption:

> Indonesia's economy was, in the 1990s, chopped up into neat lines on a mirror to be sniffed up by the small handful of guests still standing at the Suharto party. Goodness knows there's plenty of corruption around now, but at least most of it is on a fee-for-service basis. Someone takes a percentage because they helped get a new mining contract, they pushed through the approval of another province or district, they delivered a jail term of just three or four years instead of fifteen. It's still corrosive, but it seems somehow less contemptuous of the majority than the brazen plunder of the Suharto years, when money was taken from farmers and companies and given to the President's children just because.

Pervasiveness

The pervasiveness of corruption is very much related to the arguments presented by collective action theorists (see section 3.3). Individuals' actions will often, to a large extent, be influenced by the behaviour of the general public.

Moreover, in the case of public office officials, their actions may be influenced by the conduct of their predecessors. Wrong (2009) presents the situation in the aftermath of the 2002 Kenyan election, when Kibaki became president on an anti-corruption platform. The author discusses the appointment of John Githongo, a known anti-corruption activist who had successfully led the Kenyan chapter of Transparency International, and Githongo's rapid disillusionment with the discrepancies between the Kenyan government's anti-corruption rhetoric and actions. The 'It's our turn to eat' approach, as described by Wrong (2009, p. 52) below, seemed to manifest again in Kenyan politics once again:

> Given how unfairly resources had been distributed under one ethnically-biased administration after another, starting with the white settlers, each succeeding regime felt justified in being just as partisan – it was only redressing the balance, after all. The new incumbent was *expected* to behave like some feudal overlord, stuffing the civil service with his tribesmen and sacking those from his predecessor's region.

Accordingly, Kanyinga (2006) presents figures that clearly show the ethnicisation of politics in Kenya, namely that each President in power staffs his cabinet with people of his own clan and that more resources are subsequently diverted to the regions mostly inhabited by the governing elite's tribes, at the expense of others.

Eradicating corruption in societies where corruption is pervasive will naturally require adequate efforts, tackling the entire system of corruption and prevalent behaviours. Pervasive and systemic corruption refers to the situations considered by the 'collective action' theory discussed in section 3.3. Sporadic corruption can more easily be explained by the rational choice and other economic theories presented in section 3.3, which more adequately explain individuals' behaviour and choice to engage in corruption, disregarding any social pressures to do so.

Level of society

The distinction between 'grand' and 'petty' corruption is perhaps most commonly discussed in the literature. A similar categorisation of corruption has been referred to as 'administrative' – 'political' corruption, or 'high-level' – 'low-level' corruption (see Hellman *et al.*, 2000). The distinction between 'high' and 'low' level corruption refers to the seniority of the official who is involved rather than the amount of money or resources involved in the act of corruption. As such, the distinction between these concepts refers to payments to, and influence on, the *formulation* versus the *implementation* of the 'rules of the game'.

Petty corruption can involve practices such as teacher absenteeism or charging people additional fees for access to basic services or other entitlements. The importance of combatting petty corruption was also stressed by the Independent Commission on Aid Impact (ICAI)[6] in its 2014 review of DFID's anti-corruption activities with a view to assessing their effectiveness on ultimately improving the lives of the poor (ICAI, 2014). The commission concluded that DFID should do more to eliminate petty corruption in developing countries, as it is the type of corruption that is most immediately experienced by the poor. The practicalities of doing so, however, are clearly ambiguous due to the relatively limited reach, or cultural and political influence, of donors on petty corruption practices in those countries. This is discussed in further detail in section 4.3.

Grand or political corruption involves top-level government and other officials. It takes the form of, for example, bribes to pass laws that would be beneficial for certain industries or businesses, or payments to award contracts for major projects. The sums of money involved in a given transaction, as well as the amount of money that a given individual can make overall within the context of grand corruption typically vastly exceeds that of petty corruption transactions. As certain individuals can gain substantial wealth from grand corruption, they will be likely to consider moving that money to a foreign jurisdiction, for various reasons including safety of the deposits/investments and more secretive arrangements in relation to ownership and details of bank accounts. Such drainage of funds can have a significant effect on a country, as discussed in the next section.

Nye (1970, p. 574) makes an interesting point in relation to the levels of society that would engage and condone corruption. The author notes that different groups and sub-cultures within society will have different levels of tolerance of corruption; the 'modern sectors', which Nye considers to be students, army and the civil service, being less tolerant of corruption than the traditional groups. Nye (ibid.) proposes the example of young army officers in Nigeria overthrowing the old corrupt regime to support his argument. While perhaps the Nigerian example, some 45 years later, has not proven to have resulted in a much less corruption-ridden environment, Nye's suggestion of evaluating the relative political power of the 'modern' groups that oppose corruption and working with them merits consideration.

Proceeds of corruption

Although corruption on its own does not necessarily inhibit economic growth, as demonstrated by the example of South Korea, discussed in section 3.5, it is very likely to reduce economic growth, most notably by depriving developing countries of scarce capital.

The proceeds of corruption is an important factor to consider in relation to determining the effects of corruption on a country's economic development trajectory, especially when money used for bribery is syphoned out of developing countries. Depriving a country of money that could otherwise be reinvested in its economy can have serious implications on its economic performance. Zinkernagel *et al.*

(2014, p. 7) note that '[i]dentifying, restraining, seizing, and repatriating ... assets to the countries from whence they were originally stolen is one of the greatest challenges for the global anti-corruption movement'.

Kar and LeBlanc (2013) estimate that Africa has lost in excess of a trillion US dollars to illicit financial flows over the last 50 years; and Baker (2010) suggested that 20 to 40 billion US dollars are stolen and hidden overseas as a result of high-level corruption. Despite the difficulties in accurately measuring the extent of damage that corruption does to a country's economic and social development, and the possible variances in the estimates of corruption, it is clear that corruption has a strong effect on facilitating the outflows of scarce capital from developing countries.

Corruption, however, does not necessarily imply capital flight. The government of South Korea had realised the dangers of losing the limited amount of foreign exchange available in the country during its industrialisation, and therefore had strict capital controls in place (just as Germany and Sweden during their rapid development in the twentieth century). These included restricting the possibilities of foreigners purchasing South Korean companies, as well as imposing severe penalties for taking money out of the country. South Korea introduced penalties of a minimum sentence of ten years in prison and a maximum sentence of death for violations of prohibitions on overseas capital transfers (Grabel, 1996, p. 1772).

Other factors also played a critical role in ensuring South Korea's rapid economic growth at the time. These include general acceptance of severely limited personal consumption levels and low labour remuneration, as well as the political will to enforce the aforementioned policies. Crotty and Epstein (1996, p. 144) argue that political commitment of the population was enforced by the stronger classes on the weaker ones, citing Korea's strict anti-strike laws. Furthermore, the unstable South Korean peace with North Korea has been argued to have instilled in South Korea a perception of the need to develop economically in order to be able to counter possible threats from the North (Harvie and Lee, 2003, p. 286). Favourable external circumstances such as access to the US market and financial assistance without conditionalities attached (see, for example, Painter, 1999), as well as the nature of the unsaturated international manufacturing market at the time of industrialisation, also played a role in the successful development of the country (see Cline, 1982, p. 89).

Rider (1997, p. 3) has argued that

> [i]n the majority of instances, the motive for corruption is simple greed. ... Hence, it makes a good deal of sense to focus on the illicit profit and at least make sure that the person who has received it is not allowed to retain it and its benefits.

The recovered funds could then be invested in developmental projects and contribute to society. As such, working on asset recovery in order to combat corruption, regardless of the existence of a transnational element to the crime, is an effective strategy to both deter and punish those engaging in corruption, and also to fuel development by returning illicitly obtained funds for use for other purposes.

3.6 Summary

This chapter has noted the need for a granular analysis of the effects of corruption on various aspects of a state's development processes, in order to be able to more efficiently direct the limited resources available for combatting corruption and for development. While corruption occurs in many forms in most, if not all, societies, not all forms of corruption are equally damaging to a country's economic, social and other aspects of development. There is a need to differentiate between the different types of corruption and the effects each one may have in a particular society, to identify how the efficiency of anti-corruption programmes could be maximised. This would entail discerning the varying effects that different types of corruption may have, thereby considering the scale of corruption, the levels of society that are affected, the flows of revenue from corrupt activities as well as the sectors affected.

International and governmental development organisations' resources available for combatting corruption and for development are inevitably limited, and the value for money of their use must be accounted for to the public. This adds to the necessity for international development organisations to focus on the areas where they can make the most impact. This is important not only to ensure that the limited resources available are not spread too thinly and help achieve tangible results, but also in order to demonstrate to society and government that tackling corruption is a feasible endeavour (i.e. that efforts to eliminate it can yield results).

This chapter has also noted that responsibility for addressing corruption falls not only upon individual governments and their civil society but also the private sector as well as the international community of other states and international organisations. The preamble of the UNCAC states that 'corruption is no longer a local matter but a transnational phenomenon that affects all societies and economies, making international cooperation to prevent and control it essential'. As such, states parties to this convention, currently amounting to 175, have acknowledged the international responsibility to tackle corrupt activities (UNODC, 2016). The extent to which the international community can contribute to fighting corruption in developing countries is discussed in the subsequent chapters.

Notes

1 Practically, however, both types of justice are interlinked and can affect one another. This is evident in the example of irregular migrants (such as refugees), who may not be given access to certain rights, such as the right to employment, due to a particular type of conception of distributive justice, which excludes non-citizens from the right to legally seek employment. Driven by the need to survive, these irregular migrants may seek illegal employment, which would render them accountable to the state's criminal justice system.
2 Where the principles of justice are agreed in an initial hypothetical situation of equitable social conditions, and none of the rational beings, deciding on what an equitable distribution of resources would look like, are aware of their own position in society or the talents with which they are endowed.

3 Rawls (1999, p. 89) suggests:

> [w]e do not deserve our place in the distribution of native endowments, any more than we deserve our initial starting place in society. That we deserve the superior character that enables us to make the effort to cultivate our abilities is also problematic; for such character depends in good part upon fortunate family and social circumstances in early life for which we can claim no credit.

4 Khan (2000, p. 21) defines rents as

> 'excess incomes' which, in simplistic models, should not exist in efficient markets. (…) Rents may take the form of higher rates of return in monopolies, the extra income from politically organized transfers such as subsidies, or the extra income which comes from owning scarce resources, whether natural resources or specialized knowledge.

5 The mainstream understanding of what 'development' entails has changed over time from mainly focusing on economic growth, to expanding the definition to include 'basic' necessities and comforts in life (such as food and shelter), to subsequently include civil and political rights, and personal freedoms and 'capabilities' (see the works of Amartya Sen, such as Sen (1999)) and inequalities.

6 ICAI is an independent body that scrutinises the UK government's overseas development assistance spending.

Bibliography

Akerlof, G.A., Yellen, J.L., 1990. The Fair Wage–Effort Hypothesis and Unemployment. *The Quarterly Journal of Economics* 105(2), 255–283.

Allswang, J.M., 1998. Franklin Delano Roosevelt and Tammany Hall of New York. *Journal of American History* 85(3), 1136.

Anderson, C.J., Tverdova, Y.V., 2003. Corruption, Political Allegiances, and Attitudes Toward Government in Contemporary Democracies. *American Journal of Political Science* 47(1), 91–109.

Arezki, R., Gylfason, T., 2013. Resource Rents, Democracy, Corruption and Conflict: Evidence from Sub-Saharan Africa. *Journal of African Economies* 22(4), 552–569.

Babb, S.L., Kentikelenis, A.E., 2017. *International Financial Institutions as Agents of Neoliberalism*. Sage Handbook of Neoliberalism. Sage, Thousand Oaks, CA.

Baker, B., 2010. The Future is Non-State, in: Sedra, M. (Ed.), *The Future of Security Sector Reform*. The Centre for International Governance Innovation, pp. 208–228.

Banfield, E.C., 1985. Corruption as a Feature of Governmental Organization, in: *Here the People Rule*. Plenum Press, New York, pp. 147–170.

Bardhan, P., 1997. Corruption and Development: A Review of Issues. *Journal of Economic Literature* 35(3), 1320–1346.

Bardhan, P., Mookherjee, D., 2000. Capture and Governance at Local and National Levels. *The American Economic Review* 90(2), 135–139.

Barry, B., 1989. *Theories of Justice*. University of California Press, Berkeley, Los Angeles, CA.

Bentham, J., 1948. *A Fragment on Government with an Introduction to the Principles of Morals and Legislation*. Blackwell, Oxford.

Boucher, A.J., Durch, W.J., Midyette, M., Rose, S., Terry, J., 2007. Mapping and Fighting Corruption in War-torn States. Henry Stimson Cent. Rep. No. 61, Washington, DC.

Bracking, S., 2013. A Qualitative Reframing of Private Sector Corruption: Considerations from the Natural Resource Sectors in South Africa. U4. Available at: www.u4.no/publications/a-qualitative-reframing-of-private-sector-corruption-considerations-from-the-natural-resource-sectors-in-south-africa/.

Breton, A., 1998. *Competitive Governments: An Economic Theory of Politics and Public Finance.* Cambridge University Press, Cambridge.

Buchanan, A., 1990. Justice as Reciprocity versus Subject-Centered Justice. *Philos. Public Affairs* 19(3), 227–252.

Campos, J.E., Lien, D., Pradhan, S., 1999. The Impact of Corruption on Investment: Predictability Matters. *World Development* 27(6), 1059–1067. doi:10.1016/S0305-750 X(99)00040-6.

Cavanagh, C., 2012. Unready for REDD+? Lessons from Corruption in Ugandan Conservation Areas. Policy Brief U4 Anti-Corruption Center. Chr Michelsen Institute. U4.

Chabal, P., Daloz, J.-P., 1999. *Africa Works: Disorder as Political Instrument.* International African Institute, London.

Chang, H.-J., 2009. *Economic History of the Developed World: Lessons for Africa.* University of Cambridge, Cambridge.

Chang, H.-J., 2002. *Kicking away the Ladder.* Edward Elgar, Northampton, MA.

Chetwynd, E., Chetwynd, F., Spector, B., 2003. Corruption and Poverty: A Review of Recent Literature. *Management Systems International* 600, 5–16.

Cline, W.R., 1982. Can the East Asian Model of Development be Generalized? *World Development* 10(2), 81–90.

Coase, R.H., 1988. *The Firm, the Market, and the Law.* University of Chicago Press, London.

Cole, M.A., 2007. Corruption, Income and the Environment: An Empirical Analysis. *Ecological Economics* 62(3–4), 637–647.

Collier, P., 2000. How to Reduce Corruption. *African Development Review* 12(2), 191–205.

Crotty, J., Epstein, G., 1996. In Defence of Capital Controls. *Social Register* 32, 118–149.

DFID, 2015. Anti Corruption Evidence 'ACE' Programme Business Case and Summary. DevTracker Project GB-1-203752 Doc. Available at: https://devtracker.dfid.gov.uk/projects/GB-1-203752/documents (accessed 3 September 2016).

Dix, S., Hussmann, K., Walton, G., 2012. *Risks of Corruption to State Legitimacy and Stability in Fragile States.* CMI, Bergen.

Dobson, S., Ramlogan-Dobson, C., 2010. Is there a Trade-off Between Income Inequality and Corruption? Evidence from Latin America. *Economics Letters* 107(2), 102–104.

Dreher, A., Herzfeld, T., 2005. *The Economic Costs of Corruption: A Survey and New Evidence.* Available SSRN 734184.

Dryzek, J.S., Honig, B., Phillips, A., 2006. *The Oxford Handbook of Political Theory.* Oxford University Press, Oxford.

Egger, P., Winner, H., 2005. Evidence on Corruption as an Incentive for Foreign Direct Investment. *European Journal of Political Economy* 21(4), 932–952. doi:10.1016/j.ejpoleco.2005.01.002.

Elias, N., 1978. *What is Sociology?* Columbia University Press, New York.

EP, 2015. Cost of Corruption in Developing Countries: How Effectively is Aid Being Spent? EP directorate-General for External Policies.

EU FLEGT, 2016. EU-China Cooperation: EU FLEGT Facility. EU-China Coop. EU FLEGT Facility. Available at: www.euflegt.efi.int/eu-china (accessed 17 September 2016).

Evans, P.B., 1995. *Embedded Autonomy: States and Industrial Transformation.* Cambridge University Press, Cambridge.

Fan, C.S., Lin, C., Treisman, D., 2009. Political Decentralization and Corruption: Evidence from Around the World. *Journal of Public Economics* 93(1-2), 14–34. doi:10.1016/j.jpubeco.2008.09.001.

Fitzsimons, V.G., 2007. Economic Models of Corruption, in: Bracking, S. (Ed.), *Corruption and Development: The Anti-Corruption Campaigns*. Palgrave Macmillan, New York, pp. 46–74.

Golden, M.A., 2003. Electoral Connections: The Effects of the Personal Vote on Political Patronage, Bureaucracy and Legislation in Postwar Italy. *British Journal of Political Science* 33(2), 189–212.

Grabel, I., 1996. Marketing the Third World: The Contradictions of Portfolio Investment in the Global Economy. *World Dev.* 24(11), 1761–1776.

Groenendijk, N., 1997. A Principal–Agent Model of Corruption. *Crime Law Social Change* 27(3–4), 207–229. doi:10.1023/A:1008267601329.

Gupta, S., Davoodi, H., Alonso-Terme, R., 2002. Does Corruption Affect Income Inequality and Poverty? *Economics of Governance* 3(1), 23–45.

Hafner, O., 1998. *The Role of Corruption in the Misappropriation of Tropical Forest Resources and in Tropical Forest Destruction*. FAO, Rome.

Harriss, J., Hunter, J., Lewis, C., 2003. *The New Institutional Economics and Third World Development*. Routledge, London.

Harvie, C., Lee, H.-H., 2003. Export-led Industrialisation and Growth: Korea's Economic Miracle, 1962–1989. *Australian Economic History Review* 43(3), 256–286.

Hehir, A., 2013. *Humanitarian Intervention: An Introduction*. Palgrave Macmillan, Basingstoke; New York.

Hellman, J.S., Jones, G., Kaufmann, D., 2000. Seize the State, Seize the Day: State Capture, Corruption, and Influence in Transition, Policy Research Working Papers. The World Bank, Washington, DC.

Holmes, L., 2015. *Corruption: A Very Short Introduction*. Oxford University Press, Oxford.

Human Rights Watch, 1999. *The Price of Oil: Corporate Responsibility and Human Rights Violations in Nigeria's Pol Producing Communities*. Human Rights Watch, New York.

Huntington, S., 1968. *Political Order in Changing Societies*. Yale University Press, New Haven, CT.

Hutchcroft, P.D., 1997. The Politics of Privilege: Assessing the Impact of Rents, Corruption, and Clientelism on Third World Development. Special Issue. *Political Studies* 45(3), 639–658.

Hutcheson, F., 1725. *An Inquiry Concerning Moral Good and Evil*. Online Library of Liberty.

Huther, J., Shah, A., 2000. Anti-corruption Policies and Programs: A Framework for Evaluation. World Bank Policy Res. Work. Pap.

ICAI, 2014. DFID's Approach to Anti-Corruption and its Impact on the Poor. Report.

Jenkins, R., Goetz, A.-M., 1999. Constraints on Civil Society's Capacity to Curb Corruption Lessons from the Indian Experience. *IDS Bull.* 30(4), 39–49.

Jerven, M., 2011. The Quest for the African Dummy: Explaining African Post-colonial Economic Performance Revisited. *Journal of International Development* 23(2), 288–307.

Jerven, M., 2010. A Level Playing Field? Revising Per Capita GDP Estimates in Sub Saharan Africa: From Structural Adjustment to SNA 2008. Available at: www.iariw.org/papers/2011/JervenPaper.pdf.

Johnson, J., 2014. *Corruption and Stabilisation: Aid Agencies' Anti-corruption Strategies in Fragile States*. University of Cambridge, Cambridge.

Johnston, M., 2006. From Thucydides to Mayor Daley: Bad Politics, and a Culture of Corruption? *PS Political Science and Politics* 39(4), 809–812.

Johnston, M., 1998. What Can Be Done About Entrenched Corruption? in: *Annual World Bank Conference on Development Economics 1997*. World Bank, Washington DC, pp. 69–90.

Johnston, M., 1996. The Search for Definitions: The Vitality of Politics and the Issue of Corruption. *International Social Science Journal* 48(149), 321–335.

Jones, P., 2001. *Rights*. Macmillan, London.

Jones, P., 1995. *Rights*. Macmillan, London.

Jordan, W.C., 2009. Anti-corruption Campaigns in Thirteenth-century Europe. *Journal of Medieval History* 35(2), 204–219. doi:10.1016/j.jmedhist.2009.03.004.

Kang, D.C., 2002. Bad Loans to Good Friends: Money Politics and the Developmental State in South Korea. *International Organization* 56(1), 177–207.

Kanyinga, K., 2006. *Governance Institutions and Inequality, in: Readings on Inequality in Kenya, Sectoral Dynamics and Perspectives*. Society for International Development, Nairobi.

Kar, D., LeBlanc, B., 2013. Illicit Financial Flows from Developing Countries: 2002-2011. Global Financial Integrity. Available at: http://gfintegrity.org/wp-content/uploads/2014/05/Illicit_Financial_Flows_from_Developing_Countries_2002-2011-HighRes.pdf.

Kaufmann, D., 1997. Corruption: The Facts. *Foreign Policy* 107(Summer), 114–131.

Khan, M., 2006. Governance, Economic Growth and Development Since the 1960s. DESA Working Paper. N54 New York: United Nations.

Khan, M.H., 2010. Political Settlements, Political Stabilization and Implications for Growth-Enhancing Governance. SOAS. Available at: http://eprints.soas.ac.uk/9968/1/Political_Settlements_internet.pdf.

Khan, M.H., 2000. Rents, Efficiency and Growth, in: Sundaram, J.K., Khan, M.H. (Eds), *Rents, Rent-Seeking and Economic Development: Theory and Evidence in Asia*. Cambridge University Press, Cambridge, p. 21.

Khan, M.H., 1996. A Typology of Corrupt Transactions in Developing Countries. *IDS Bull.* 27(2), 12–21. doi:10.1111/j.1759-5436.1996.mp27002003.x.

Khan, M.H., Jomo, K.S., 2000. *Rents, Rent-seeking and Economic Development: Theory and Evidence in Asia*. Cambridge University Press, Cambridge.

Kim, E., 2006. The Impact of Family Ownership and Capital Structures on Productivity Performance of Korean Manufacturing Firms: Corporate Governance and the 'Chaebol Problem'. *Journal of Japanese International Economics* 20(2), 209–233. doi:10.1016/j.jjie.2005.02.001.

Klitgaard, R.E., 1988. *Controlling Corruption*. University of California Press, Berkeley and Los Angeles, CA.

Klitgaard, R.E., Abaroa, R.M., Parris, H.L., 2000. *Corrupt Cities: A Practical Guide to Cure and Prevention*. World Bank Publications, Washington, DC.

Krueger, A.O., 1990. *Government Failures in Development*. National Bureau of Economic Research, Cambridge, MA.

Krueger, A.O., 1974. The Political Economy of the Rent-seeking Society. *American Economic Review* 64(3), 291–303.

Kuczynski, P., 2016. Canvas Collection. Available at: www.pictorem.com/collectioncat.html?author=Pawel+Kuczynski (accessed 16 September 2016).

82 Theoretical approach

Kymlicka, W., 1989. *Liberalism, Community, and Culture*. Clarendon Press, Oxford.

Laffont, J.-J., Martimort, D., 2009. *The Theory of Incentives: The Principal–Agent Model*. Princeton University Press, Princeton, NJ.

Lambsdorff, J.G., 1999. Corruption in Empirical Research: A Review. Transparency International Ninth International Anti-Corruption Conference Durban 10–15 Dec. 6.

Leff, N.H., 1964. Economic Development through Bureaucratic Corruption. *American Behavioral Science* 8(3), 8–14.

Lichbach, M., 1997. *The Co-operator's Dilemma*. University of Michigan Press, Ann Arbor, MI.

List, F., 1885. *The National System of Political Economy*, translated from the original German edition published in 1841 by Sampson Lloyd. Longmans, Green, and Company, London.

Little, W., Posada-Carbó, E., 1996. *Political Corruption in Europe and Latin America*. Macmillan Press, Basingstoke and London.

Lui, F.T., 1985. An Equilibrium Queuing Model of Bribery. *Journal of Political Economics* 93(4), 760–781. doi:10.2307/1832136.

Mauro, P., 1995. Corruption and Growth. *Quarterly Journal of Economics* 110(3), 681–712.

McCaffery, P., 2010. *When Bosses Ruled Philadelphia: The Emergence of the Republican Machine, 1867–1933*. Penn State University Press, Pennsylvania, PA.

Mentan, T., 2010. *The State in Africa: An Analysis of Impacts of Historical Trajectories of Global Capitalist Expansion and Domination in the Continent*. African Books Collective Bamenda, Cameroon.

Michael, B., 2004. Explaining Organizational Change in International Development: The Role of Complexity in Anti-corruption Work. *Journal of International Development* 16(8), 1067–1088.

Migdal, J.S., 1994. The State in Society: An Approach to Struggles for Domination, in: Migdal, J.S., Kohli, A., Shue, V. (Eds), *State Power and Social Forces: Domination and Transformation in the Third World*. Cambridge University Press, Cambridge, pp. 7–36.

Mo, P.H., 2001. Corruption and Economic Growth. *Journal of Comparative Economics* 29(1), 66–79.

Moran, M., Rein, M., Goodin, R.E., 2006. *The Oxford Handbook of Public Policy*. Oxford University Press, Oxford.

Murphy, K.M., Shleifer, A., Vishny, R.W., 1993. Why is Rent-seeking So Costly to Growth? *American Economic Review* 83(2), 409–414.

North, D.C., 1995. The New Institutional Economics and Third World Development, in: Harriss, J., Hunter, J., Lewis, C. (Eds), *The New Institutional Economics and Third World Development*. Routledge, London and New York.

North, D.C., 1990. *Institutions, Institutional Change and Economic Performance*. Cambridge University Press, Cambridge.

Nozick, R., 1974. *Anarchy, State, and Utopia*. Basil Blackwell, Oxford.

Nussbaum, M., 2007. *Frontiers of Justice Disability, Nationality, Species Membership*. The Belknap Press of Harvard University Press, Cambridge, MA.

Nye, J.S., 1970. Corruption and Political Development: A Cost–Benefit Analysis, in: Heidenheimer, A.J., Johnston, M., LeVine, V.T. (Eds), *Political Corruption: Readings in Comparative Analysis*. Transaction Books, New Brunswick, NJ, pp. 564–578.

Nye, J.S., 1967. Corruption and Political Development: A Cost–Benefit Analysis. *American Political Science Review* 61(2), 417–427.

O'Donnell, M., 2006. Corruption: A Rule of Law Agenda? in: Hurwitz, A., Huang, R. (Eds), *Civil War and the Rule of Law*. Lynne Rienner, Boulder, CO.

Oldenburg, P., 1987. Middlemen in Third-World Corruption: Implications of an Indian Case. *World Politics* 39(4), 508–535.

Painter, D.S., 1999. *The Cold War: An International History*. Taylor and Francis, New York.

Peters, J., Pierre, B.G., 2002. *Handbook of Public Administration*. Sage, Thousand Oaks, CA.

Pisani, E., 2014. *Indonesia Etc.* Granta Books, London.

Polzer, T., 2001. Corruption: Deconstructing the World Bank Discourse. Institute of Development Studies, DESTIN Work. Pap. 1, 18.

Rahman, A., Kisunko, G., Kapoor, K., 2000. *Estimating the Effects of Corruption: Implications for Bangladesh*. World Bank Publications, Washington, DC.

Rawls, J., 1999. *A Theory of Justice*. The Belknap Press of Harvard University Press, Cambridge, MA.

Rawls, J., 1971. *A Theory of Justice*. Oxford University Press, Oxford.

Razafindrakoto, M., Roubaud, F., 2010. Are International Databases on Corruption Reliable? A Comparison of Expert Opinion Surveys and Household Surveys in Sub-Saharan Africa. *World Development* 38(8), 1057–1069.

Rhodes, R.A., Binder, S.A., Rockman, B.A., 2006. *The Oxford Handbook of Political Institutions*. Oxford University Press, Oxford.

Rider, B.A.K. (Ed.), 1997. *Corruption: The Enemy Within*. Kluwer Law International, The Hague; Boston.

Robertson-Snape, F., 1999. Corruption, Collusion and Nepotism in Indonesia. *Third World Quarterly* 20, 589–602. doi:10.1080/01436599913703.

Robinson, M., 1998. *Corruption and Development*. Frank Cass and Co, London.

Rodrik, D., 2002. *Institutions, Integration, and Geography: In Search of the Deep Determinants of Economic Growth. In Search of Prosperity. Analytic Narratives on Economic Growth*. Princeton University Press, Princeton, NJ.

Rose-Ackerman, S., 2010. *The Law and Economics of Bribery and Extortion* (SSRN Scholarly Paper No. ID 1646975). Social Science Research Network, Rochester, NY.

Rose-Ackerman, S., 1999. *Corruption and Government: Causes, Consequences and Reform*. Cambridge University Press, Cambridge.

Rose-Ackerman, S., 1978. *Corruption: A Study in Political Economy*. Academic Press, New York.

Rothstein, B., 2011. *The Quality of Government: Corruption, Social Trust, and Inequality in International Perspective*. University of Chicago Press, Chicago, IL.

Schick, A., 1998. *A Contemporary Approach to Public Expenditure Management*. World Bank Institute, Washington, DC.

Schwartz, A., 1994. *A Nation in Waiting: Indonesia in the 1990s*. Allen and Unwin, Sydney.

Seligson, M.A., 2002. The Impact of Corruption on Regime Legitimacy: A Comparative Study of Four Latin American Countries. *Journal of Politics* 64(2), 408–433.

Sen, A., 1999. *Development as Freedom*. Oxford University Press, Oxford.

Shah, A., 2007. Overview, in: Shah, A. (Ed.), *Performance Accountability and Combating Corruption, Public Sector Governance and Accountability Series*. The World Bank, Washington, DC, pp. 1–14.

Shah, S.N., 2014. The Principal–Agent Problem in Finance. CFA Institute Foundation. Available at: www.cfapubs.org/doi/abs/10.2470/rflr.v9.n1.1.

84 Theoretical approach

Shaxson, N., 2007. Oil, Corruption and the Resource Curse. *International Affairs* 83(6), 1123–1140. doi:10.1111/j.1468-2346.2007.00677.x.

Shleifer, A., Vishny, R.W., 1993. Corruption. *Quarterly Journal of Economics* 108(3), 599–617.

Sindzingre, A.N., Milelli, C., 2010. *The Uncertain Relationship Between Corruption and Growth in Developing Countries: Threshold Effects and State Effectiveness*. University of Paris West-Nanterre la Défense, EconomiX.

Singh, G., 1997. Understanding Political Corruption in Contemporary Indian Politics. *Political Studies* 45(3), 626–638.

Smith, A., 1969. *The Theory of Moral Sentiments*. Liberty Classics, Indianapolis.

Swaleheen, M., 2011. Economic Growth with Endogenous Corruption: An Empirical Study. *Public Choice* 146(1–2), 23–41.

TI (Transparency International), 2016a. Transparency International – The Global Anti-corruption Coalition. Available at: www.transparency.org/cpi2015 (accessed 16 September 2016).

TI, 2016b. Transparency International – Global Corruption Barometer 2013. Available at: www.transparency.org/gcb2013 (accessed 16 September 2016).

TI, 2013. Research – CPI – Overview. Available at: www.transparency.org/research/cpi/overview (accessed 30 April 2013).

TI, 2010. *Corruption and Gender in Service Delivery: The Unequal Impacts*. Transparency International, London.

TI Bangladesh, 2005. *Corruption in Bangladesh: A Household Survey*. Transparency International Bangladesh, Dhaka, Bangladesh.

Tomuschat, C., 2014. *Human Rights: Between Idealism and Realism*. Oxford University Press, Oxford.

Ugur, M., Dasgupta, N., 2011. *Evidence on the Economic Growth Impacts of Corruption in Low-Income Countries and Beyond: A Systematic Review*. EPPI-Centre, Social Science Research Unit, Institute of Education, University of London, London.

UNCAC, 2010. Methodologies, Including Evidence-Based Approaches, for Assessing Areas of Special Vulnerability to Corruption in the Public and Private Sectors: Background Paper Prepared by the Secretariat. October 2010. Available at: www.unodc.org/documents/data-and-analysis/statistics/corruption/WG4_doc-4-FINAL.pdf.

UNDP, 2004. *Anti-Corruption Practice Note*. UNDP, New York.

Ungson, G.R., Steers, R.M., Park, S.-H., 1997. *Korean Enterprise: The Quest for Globalization*. Harvard Business Press, Boston, MA.

UNIFEM, 2009. *Who Answers to Women? Gender & Accountability. Progress of the World's Women 2008/2009*. UNIFEM, New York.

UNODC, 2016. Signatories to the United Nations Convention against Corruption. UNODC. Available at: www.unodc.org/unodc/en/treaties/CAC/signatories.html (accessed 17 September 2016).

USAID, 2005. *USAID Anticorruption Strategy (No. PD-ACA-557)*. USAID, Washington, DC.

Uslaner, E., 2007. Corruption and the Inequality Trap in Africa. Afrobarometer Working Paper No 69.

Welsch, H., 2004. Corruption, Growth, and the Environment: A Cross-country Analysis. *Environment and Development Economics* 9(5), 663–693.

Wheeler, N.J., 2000. *Saving Strangers: Humanitarian Intervention in International Society*. Oxford University Press, Oxford.

Widmalm, S., 2008. *Decentralisation, Corruption and Social Capital: From India to the West*. Sage Publications, India.

Widoyoko, D., 2007. *Tackling Corruption to Improve Housing Services in Indonesia, Partnering to Combat Corruption Series*. World Bank, Washington, DC.

World Bank, 2012. *Strengthening Governance: Tackling Corruption – The World Bank Group's Updated Strategy and Implementation Plan*. World Bank, Washington, DC.

World Bank, 2011. *World Development Report 2011: Conflict, Security, and Development*. World Bank, Washington, DC.

World Bank, 2002. *World Development Report 2002: Building Institutions for Markets*. World Bank, Washington, DC.

World Bank, 1997. *Helping Countries Combat Corruption: The Role of the World Bank*. The World Bank, Washington, DC.

Wrong, M., 2009. *It's Our Turn to Eat: The Story of a Kenyan Whistle Blower*. Fourth Estate, London.

Zaum, D., Taxell, N., Johnson, J., 2012. Mapping Evidence Gaps in Anti-Corruption: Assessing the State of the Operationally Relevant Evidence on Donors' Actions and Approaches to Reducing Corruption. U4 Anti-Corruption Resource Centre. Available at: https://assets.publishing.service.gov.uk/media/57a08a9ae5274a27b2000699/U4Issue-2012-07-mapping-evidence-web.pdf.

Zinkernagel, G.F., Pereira, P.G., De Simone, F., 2014. *The Role of Donors in the Recovery of Stolen Assets, U4 Issue*. Chr. Michelsen Institute, Bergen.

4 The UK's anti-corruption work in developing countries

> It is a common paradox: the world often becomes aware of corruption when someone is doing something about it. That leads to people to conclude that things are getting worse when they are, in fact, getting better. The incentives for countries can thus be perverse.
>
> (*The Economist*, 2016)

Corruption within the sphere of international development aid is addressed from two angles. First of all, corruption within, and as a result of, aid projects is considered. Direct budget support to developing states' governments is particularly susceptible to corruption. Accordingly, a number of scandals have emerged that cite aid money being diverted to corrupt leaders' personal bank accounts, such as those referred to in section 4.1. The second feature, which is increasingly gaining prominence in international development aid, is the general levels of corruption within developing states. This chapter will briefly touch upon corruption within development programmes, as far as it concerns DFID's approach to anti-corruption strategies, but will focus on DFID's efforts to eradicate corruption within other states.

It is important to note that international development organisations such as DFID do often take into account the fact that corruption is a symptom of wider issues within government institutions and generally part of prevailing social norms within a society. As such, the approaches to anti-corruption are diverse and varied in nature, some programmes being designed specifically to understand and address corruption in particular contexts, while in others corruption is only one of multiple aims attempting to induce government reforms on a larger scale. It can be difficult to separate out how large the anti-corruption element of a programme is, if tackling corruption is the secondary aim of the programme. This is discussed in more detail in this chapter. This chapter also fleshes out the paradox referred to by *The Economist* (2016), that actions against corruption (public information about these in the press or prosecutions) can create the impression that there is increasingly more corruption, when in reality the opposite may be true.

4.1 The UK's approach to anti-corruption programming

This section introduces the UK's approach to anti-corruption programming and also places it within the wider context of the UK's approach to international development.

Approach to development

The UK's ODA levels have been relatively consistently increasing since the 1970s, and reached £11,726 million in 2014 (DFID, 2015b, pp. 10–12). The trends in the UK's international development spending are illustrated in Figure 4.1.

The UK's dedicated agency for international development – DFID – spent £10.1 billion of ODA, or 86 per cent of UK ODA, in 2014.[1] DFID has a mandate to work towards reducing poverty globally, which is established by the International Development Act of 2002. The act, however, explicitly binds DFID, and not necessarily the other government departments that increasingly work on international development (including the FCO, MOD, DEFRA, etc.). These departments are nevertheless bound by OECD regulations as to what counts as ODA spending (details of these are set out in Chapter 1).

The International Development (Official Development Assistance Target) Act 2015 established in law the commitment of the UK to spend 0.7 per cent of its Gross National Income (GNI) on ODA annually. Such a legal requirement, however, can complicate efficient spending and programme forecasting. Efficient programming naturally requires planning in advance – for resources, and predictability of funding. A country's forecast of GDP and GNI, however, is likely to be slightly different from the actual figures. This can lead to last minute adjustments in the country's expected GNI levels and as a consequence a rush to spend the required remaining funds to reach the overall target of 0.7 per cent of the GNI before the end of the financial year. It is questionable, however, whether such last minute spending is wisely allocated to where it can help achieve the best results. Most international development organisations very much applaud

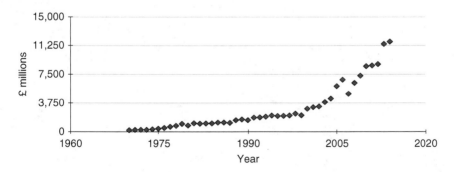

Figure 4.1 UK net ODA levels 1970–2014 (£ millions).
Source of data: DFID (2015b, p. 12).

the target. The OECD, for example, has praised the UK's meeting of the 0.7 per cent target as 'commendable' (OECD, 2014b, p. 17). The same page of the OECD report, however, was critical of the UK's spending targets, noting that 'they can make it more difficult for country offices to maintain context-based programming, and can undermine value for money by directing programmes into less performing areas in a given context' (ibid.).

DFID focuses on a set number of priority countries in Asia, Africa and the Middle East, many of which are its former colonies, although it also does work in other states to a smaller extent. This is particularly true in the case of humanitarian emergencies and Britain's aid dependent overseas territories – St Helena, the Pitcairn Islands and Montserrat. Priority countries are identified by taking into consideration the need for assistance within those countries, with the likelihood of assistance from the UK being effective as well as 'the strategic fit with UK government priorities' within the 2011 bilateral aid review (BAR) (DFID, 2011a; OECD, 2014b, p. 16). In 2016, DFID had 28 'priority countries'.[2] Focusing on those 28 priority countries following the publication of the 2010 BAR meant that UK aid was cut to middle-income countries such as China and Vietnam, as well as low-income countries where programmes were seen to be underperforming, such as Lesotho or Burundi (DFID, 2011; OECD, 2014b). Figure 4.2 depicts DFID's spending in 2014–2015 in its target countries; excluding the more global programmes that touch upon several different countries and regions. The split between bilateral and multilateral spending, including the share allocated to individual types of projects, is discussed in Chapter 6.

DFID's approach to development is constantly evolving. In November 2015, DFID published its new ODA strategy, entitled 'UK aid: tackling global challenges in the national interest' (HMT and DFID, 2015). The strategy was jointly

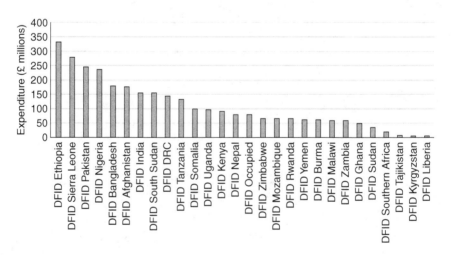

Figure 4.2 DFID spending in priority countries, 2014–2015 (£ millions).
Source of data: DFID (2015c, p. 12).

published by HM Treasury and DFID, which will have influenced the approach to the ODA strategy, citing the 'root causes of migration and disease, ... the threat of terrorism and global climate change' as the great global challenges that also directly threaten British interests (HMT and DFID, 2015, p. 3). The document continually stresses that the spending of money in developing countries by the UK government will be beneficial not only for the citizens of those countries but also to the UK and its citizens. The following statements from the strategy illustrate this particularly well:

> We recognise ... that spending has sometimes been controversial at home, because people want to know that it is squarely in the UK's national interest.
> (HMT and DFID, 2015, p. 3)

> We want to meet our promises to the world's poor and also put international development at the heart of our national security and foreign policy.
> (HMT and DFID, 2015, p. 3)

> We believe this fundamental shift in how we use 0.7 per cent of our national income will show there is no distinction between reducing poverty, tackling global challenges and serving our national interest – all are inextricably linked.
> (HMT and DFID, 2015, p. 4)

> This strategy sets out how the government will build on these successes and make UK aid even more effective in tackling the great global challenges of our age, in order to eliminate poverty and – *crucially* – also advance the UK's national interest.
> (HMT and DFID, 2015, p. 5, emphasis added)

The strategy sets out four strategic objectives, which much of the UK's ODA will be aimed at achieving (HMT and DFID, 2015, p. 9):

- Strengthening global peace, security and governance (this includes corruption);
- Strengthening resilience and response to crises;
- Promoting global prosperity; and
- Tackling extreme poverty and helping the world's most vulnerable.

It is also interesting to note that each of these objectives is presented with a note on how achieving it will also benefit the UK: it 'will also strengthen our own national security at home', 'strengthen UK trade and investment opportunities around the world' and 'build security and stability that will benefit us all' (ibid.). Clearly stating how overseas aid fits into the overall government strategy might be necessary for different parts of the government to work together effectively and to prevent government agencies inadvertently undermining other agencies' work. The OECD peer review of the UK's international development assistance in 2014 noted that at the time 'the overall rationale for international development in relation to other UK policies is [was at the time] not clearly stated – hampering cross-government work in support of development' (OECD, 2014b, p. 16). The review suggested that '[e]laborating a more comprehensive UK approach to international development would help drive support across policy areas, while communicating how the UK will contribute to achieving the goals of the post-2015 development agenda' (ibid.). While it might facilitate cross-departmental collaboration, clearly stating UK national interest as being a key focus of the UK's international development assistance, however, might have repercussions on the perception and acceptance of the UK's assistance, particularly technical assistance in politically sensitive areas such as anti-corruption. As noted by the (IDC, 2016a, p. 22), the

> strategy's status as a Treasury-led document with little explicit focus on poverty reduction risks creating an impression that the objectives regarding the UK's national interest, and therefore security and prosperity, were drawn up first, with DFID left to connect the dots with poverty reduction.

Figure 4.3 represents the sector mix within the UK's bilateral aid spending in 2014. Most of the categories used in this section can roughly be grouped into the

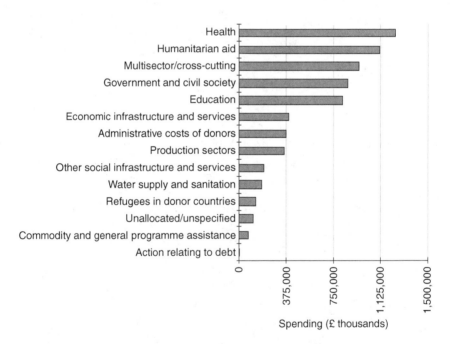

Figure 4.3 UK bilateral aid spending in 2014 by sector (£ thousands).
Source of data: DFID Statistics on International Development data (DFID, 2015b).

four mentioned in the strategy (for example, health and humanitarian aid would fit into goal number 2 'strengthening resilience and response to crises'; education, social infrastructure and services and water supply and sanitation would correspond to goal number 4, 'tackling extreme poverty and helping the world's most vulnerable'). Nevertheless, the focus on fragile states and prosperity-building around the world, with a view to developing and opening up markets for UK trade, can already be noticed. The UK has created two large interdepartmental funds – the Conflict, Security and Stability Fund worth £1.3 billion and the Prosperity Fund (£1.3 billion over 5 years). These interdepartmental funds are discussed in more detail in section 6.2.

Historically, much of international development aid has been given with conditions attached. These included requirements to spend the funds on services or goods from the donor countries and constituted the notion of 'tied aid' (Arvin and Baum, 1997; Kemp and Kojima, 1985). This can effectively reduce the concessionality of aid being provided as the goods or services might be cheaper to be procured from other countries; their purchase outside of the recipient country can reduce the amount of tax collected by that country and the demand for the local labour force (see Morrissey and White, 1996). The OECD notes that in both 2012 and 2013 all of the UK's ODA (excluding administrative costs and in-donor refugee costs) was untied, while the DAC average was 83.2 per cent (OECD, 2015a, p. 168). Gulrajani (2016, p. 11), however, notes that 'developing countries continue to suspect bilateral channels of neo-imperial aspirations, even when such aid was provided unconditionally'. The particularities of bilateral and multilateral approaches are discussed in detail in section 6.3.

Approaches to anti-corruption

Numerous aid agencies and academics have suggested that failing to address endemic corruption will undermine all other development efforts, which in part explains the recent proliferation of international development programmes on anti-corruption (DFID, 2015a; ICAI, 2014; USAID, 2005, p. 6). The approaches taken to combat corruption, however, vary significantly between agencies. A few key variables will be highlighted in this section as well as DFID's approaches to these.

First of all, the internal UK government's coherence in addressing corruption internationally will be discussed. The OECD DAC peer review of the UK's development assistance cites anti-corruption as one of the 'issues of common interest' within government organisations that has been able to bring different agencies together to work towards a common goal (OECD, 2014b, p. 15). The review notes that the 'Secretary of State's seat in Cabinet and membership of National Security Council ensure DFID is well placed to promote coherence between policies to support development' (ibid.).

It was, however, only in the last several years that clear avenues for leadership and the coordination of the UK government's anti-corruption activities on a high level were established. This includes two institutions that were set up, following the recommendations in the UK Anti-Corruption Plan of 2014: the inter-ministerial group on corruption, which provides a framework and director-level leadership; and the Joint Anti-Corruption Unit (JACU) in the Cabinet Office, which has a convening power to organise other agencies to work on corruption and to oversee progress towards achieving the 66 commitments that were made in the UK Anti-Corruption Plan (HMG, 2014).

The conservative government that took power in the UK in 2015 has indeed brought issues of corruption to the forefront of the UK government's agenda. Most notably, the former Prime Minister David Cameron organised an international summit on Corruption in May 2016, which brought together a large number of government, international organisations and some business and civil society leaders to discuss and commit to actions against corruption globally. This summit is discussed in further detail in section 6.4.

Overall, DFID has a structured approach to corruption and produces country strategy reports, where it considers corruption on two levels: (1) 'the risk of taxpayers' money in DFID programmes being fraudulently spent or stolen' and (2) the abuse of entrusted power for private gain within a country and its institutions, with the negative impact that it has on development prospects (see, for example, DFID's Anti-Corruption Strategies for Zambia (DFID, 2013a) and for Uganda (DFID, 2013b)). Accordingly, the DFID country strategies are split into two parts: protecting UK funds and supporting efforts to reduce corruption in countries. It is worth noting, however, that the strategies vary significantly in terms of detail of the proposed actions within countries, some outlining specific initiatives to be taken while others are more high level (Heywood, 2016). Transparency International noted that in preparing the 2013 anti-corruption strategies, its chapters were rarely consulted, and that the 2013 strategies in general were 'not well known or promoted' (TI, 2016c).

There is, furthermore, a mismatch between the timelines that are required for meaningful social and behavioural change to occur and DFID's (and more generally, the international development projects') timelines. The latter are typically two to five years, and DFID's anti-corruption strategies were for three years (2013–2016). It is, however, very difficult to achieve significant and visible changes on anti-corruption within that timeframe, particularly in states ridden with systemic corruption.

Risk of corruption within international development programming

Although the book focuses on donor approaches to corruption in developing countries rather than within its programmes, it is important to briefly discuss the latter and how it influences donor and international institutions' corruption work more generally.

Since corruption became a significant issue, considered by international development organisations, traditionally donors have emphasised the risk of corruption within international development programming (see, for example, European Parliament, 2015). This is not least due to international development assistance being under particular scrutiny from the public and media, compared to other government departments. It is important for governments' international development departments to ensure continuous public support for their activities. Some media outlets, however, are eager to report on incidents where inefficiencies or leakages occur with attention-grabbing headlines such as 'British aid money is funding corruption overseas' (Riley-Smith, 2014). Similarly, the European Parliament's Directorate-General for External Policies 2015 report states that EU project and financial management guidelines are 'oriented towards safeguarding own fiduciary risks as opposed to corruption risks from a societal perspective' (European Parliament, 2015, p. 7).

The case of Uganda is interesting to analyse in more detail in order to illustrate the potential leakages within international development programmes. TI has classified Uganda as 'highly corrupt' every year since 1996; TI's Global Corruption Barometer (GCB) 2013 notes that 79 per cent of their respondents believe that the country's judiciary was either corrupt or extremely corrupt (TI, 2016b; TI, 2013). There seems to be a significant number of laws and strategies adopted by the various institutional bodies in Uganda, such as the Anti-Corruption Act of 2009, the Whistleblowers Protection Act of 2010, The Public Finance and Accountability Act of 2003, the Public Procurement and Disposal of Public Acts of 2003 and five year National Anti-Corruption Strategies. Their implementation, however, appears to be more problematic, given the results from the aforementioned surveys. DFID had planned to spend a budget of £283 million over a 3-year period from 2012 to 2015 in Uganda, however, in 2012 several major international donors, including the UK, Sweden, Norway, Ireland and Denmark, had suspended financial aid to Uganda in 2012 due to corruption charges brought against the Office of the Prime Minister; and millions of dollars of donor funding were found to have been embezzled (DFID, 2012).

Direct budget support, as illustrated by the example of Uganda, is susceptible to corruption within aid programmes. Accordingly, development agencies such as DFID have been favouring technical assistance and capacity-building programmes or working with civil society organisations and other stakeholder groups, especially in countries where the fiduciary risk of misdirection of funds is deemed high.[3] Strictly focusing on technical assistance, however, can have limited results if other issues are not addressed. For example, training sessions to inform officials of the detrimental effects of corruption are unlikely to yield the desired results if government officials' salaries are insufficient to meet their needs without the additional income from engagement in corrupt activities. An appropriate balance needs to be struck between direct budget support and technical assistance, most importantly, focusing efforts where they are likely to have the most significant impact, given the limited resources that international development organisations have at their disposal.

Strict measures against corruption within the funding agency's own funding are key for the public's continuous support for international development funding. The International Development (Reporting and Transparency) Act of 2006 establishes a requirement for DFID to report annually to Parliament 'on total expenditure on international aid and breakdown of such aid; (…) the proportion of expenditure in low income countries and about the effectiveness of aid expenditure and the transparency of international aid'. DFID now publishes all non-sensitive project information on its DevTracker website, detailing the department's spending down to the individual project level, projects' business cases, annual reviews and publications resulting from projects. DFID is also currently asking its suppliers to publish details of how DFID project money is spent, in an attempt to track all DFID aid money's impact on the intended beneficiaries.

Overall, DFID has adopted a policy of blanket zero tolerance of corruption. This is in contrast to, for example, the World Bank which takes a more pragmatic approach to corruption and had noted that the

> ultimate goal of a Bank strategy to help countries address corruption is not to eliminate corruption completely, which is an unrealistic aim, but to help those countries move from systemic corruption to an environment of well-performing government that minimizes corruption's negative effect on development.
>
> (World Bank, 1997, p. 23)

Professor Heywood has noted that a zero tolerance of corruption approach is necessary to give a clear and consistent message that corruption is not to be tolerated, arguing that 'it would send a very unfortunate message to suggest in any official documentation or literature that some degree or element of corruption is somehow "acceptable"' (Heywood, 2016). Transparency International also noted the reputational risks that DFID would face 'if it was found not to operate with a zero tolerance approach to corruption' (TI, 2016c). The practicalities of operating on a policy of zero tolerance of corruption, however, are complex. Often, fragile states have high levels of corruption (see Figure 4.11), weak governance systems and are in particular need of development assistance. Operating a strict policy of zero tolerance of corruption, however, would imply not giving assistance to those countries where corruption is identified. A more nuanced approach to this, however, could in the long term be more beneficial towards eradicating corruption within such states, such as focusing on technical assistance support and reduced and carefully overseen budget support to minimise the potential for leakage, implementing robust monitoring systems and strengthening the country's governance systems. Professor Khan suggests that '[z]ero tolerance towards ... entrenched societal forms of corruption must be a longer term goal that is achieved using "nuanced" and targeted anti-corruption interventions' (Khan, 2016).

Programming to address corruption within developing countries

DFID addresses corruption within developing countries and their institutions by working with those developing countries directly as well as working through international organisations and treaties to contribute to multilateral efforts to combat corruption.

DFID programming has followed the predominant thinking and theories about the drivers of corruption, elaborated upon in section 3.3. DFID has incorporated the theoretical considerations within the literature into its programming, having refocused elements of its programming from traditional assistance in the form of capacity-building to interventions focusing on collective action. Concrete examples of this can also be seen in individual DFID programmes, such as the DFID's £11 million Strengthening Tanzania's Anti-Corruption Action (STACA) programme (Johnson et al., 2016). After the first year of the programme, DFID refocused elements of the programme from more traditional capacity-building on collective action, particularly regarding the police and judiciary.

DFID attempts to address corruption in developing countries in a variety of ways. This is evidenced by an increasing number of projects addressing corruption, the production of country corruption strategies and investing in anti-corruption research agencies such as U4, which is funded by eight states' governments, including the UK. DFID's expenditure on anti-corruption from 2007–2018 is shown in Figure 4.4.

It is worth noting that this data refers to DFID's expenditure on anti-corruption organisations and institutions as defined by the OECD, namely, as expenditure to support:

> [s]pecialised organisations, institutions and frameworks for the prevention of and combat against corruption, bribery, money-laundering and other aspects of organised crime, with or without law enforcement powers, e.g. anti-corruption commissions and monitoring bodies, special investigation

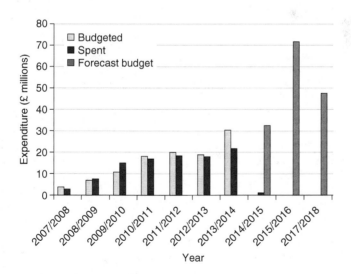

Figure 4.4 DFID's anti-corruption expenditure, 2007–2018 (£ millions).
Source: ICAI (2014, p. 5).

services, institutions and initiatives of integrity and ethics oversight, specialised NGOs, other civil society and citizens' organisations directly concerned with corruption.

(OECD, 2016c)

These are direct approaches to combatting corruption. Solely focusing on DFID's work with the aforementioned institutions and organisations, however, fails to capture the breadth of projects aiming to address corruption indirectly, as well as the organisation's support of anti-corruption projects carried out by multilateral organisations.

Two main reasons can be identified for including corruption interventions under broader programmes or labelling them as indirect interventions. First of all, as will be discussed in more detail in this chapter, successfully tackling corruption requires working with a number of institutions and institutional systems, to ensure that they all work well and corruption is disincentivised and tackled promptly and efficiently. Second, corruption can be a sensitive issue for foreign donors to discuss and intervene in, in some country settings. As noted by Jennett (2006, p. 3),

> In some countries it is downright impossible for donors to suggest a clear-cut anti-corruption project. The challenge is then to rewrite the project documentation so that it becomes less of a threat to the partner government. In some instances almost identical projects have been 'sold' as two quite different things.

Such 'relabelling' of anti-corruption interventions to 'transparency' or 'accountability' programmes can be necessary in some political settings. In other countries, however, where the leadership of the country is seen to be taking a strong stance against corruption and there is less resistance to foreign states' interventions in local governance systems, mentioning an anti-corruption component or focus of a programme does attract substantial interest from government officials. Examples of such countries in 2016 would be Kenya and Nigeria, which were two major participants in the Anti-Corruption Conference in London in May 2016.

A related issue also arises regarding the progress of interventions and the potential political issues associated with either criticising parts of the government for inefficiency or corruption, or the difficult decisions that have to be made in relation to continuing or pulling out in cases of multi-year programmes not achieving their objectives in the first years and not showing significant signs of improvement.

It is worth noting, however, that if corruption programmes have to be labelled as other types of interventions for them to be 'signed off' or allowed by some developing country governments, it becomes difficult to accurately assess how much is being spent on anti-corruption interventions and also how effective the different types of interventions are at achieving the aim of reducing corruption.

DFID's official spending on anti-corruption is illustrated in Figure 4.5,[4] based on the available data on programmes that touch on anti-corruption on the UK Government's devtracker website.

The graph in Figure 4.5 clearly illustrates only a small proportion of DFID's anti-corruption work; it is nevertheless interesting to analyse in more detail. Although the graph shows the amount of money invested in anti-corruption programming rather than the number of programmes active, one can see that Nigeria, Uganda, Zambia and Tanzania get the largest share of country-specific anti-corruption funds. This does not directly relate to the currently perceived good or bad performance of the countries in relation to corruption, as the aforementioned states receiving the largest shares of funding are distributed along the spectrum of corrupt states, as measured by TI's CPI, see Figure 4.6.

One of the main methods used by DFID to address corruption indirectly is increasing transparency and accountability. DFID attempts to do this by tackling the 'supply' and 'demand' aspects of corrupt practices. The former refers to projects designed to increase transparency and the accountability of the government in question via projects to, for example, strengthen the country's legal and financial systems and institutions so as to reduce the opportunities for, and increase the risks of, engaging in corrupt practices. The latter refers to efforts to mobilise civil society and the awareness of citizens of their rights and entitlements to ultimately be able to demand more transparency and accountability from their governments. This could be done by using the media, local political representatives or other forms of citizen mobilisation (ICAI, 2014, p. 1). DFID also attempts to

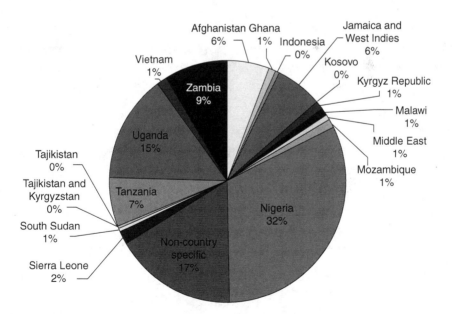

Figure 4.5 DFID spending on anti-corruption, aggregated from information published on DFID 2004–2020 programmes on devtracker, in 2016.

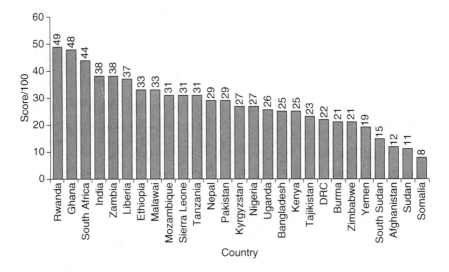

Figure 4.6 CPI ratings.
Source of data: CPI 2014 Index.

incorporate anti-corruption elements into sector-specific programmes, by tackling absenteeism in schools and hospitals, and conducting surveys and analyses to verify that the goods obtained as part of DFID's programmes have reached the intended beneficiaries (ICAI, 2014, p. 10).

An overview of the different approaches is presented in Figure 4.7, adapted from an initial mapping of anti-corruption interventions by Zaum *et al.* (2012, p. 2).

Figure 4.7 also illustrates where the multitude of different organisations, which DFID works with to address corruption, fit in. These include the following initiatives, which are discussed in more detail in section 4.2:

- International initiatives, such as:
  ○ Regional or international anti-corruption cooperation initiatives
  ○ Support to multilateral organisations tackling corruption, asset tracing and recovery
  ○ Assistance to governments to implement their obligations under international agreements, such as UNCAC
- National and sub-national initiatives, for example:
  ○ Supply side:
    △ Civil service reforms
    △ Parliamentary and PFM reforms
    △ Legislation drafting (on anti-corruption, procurement, right to information, etc.)

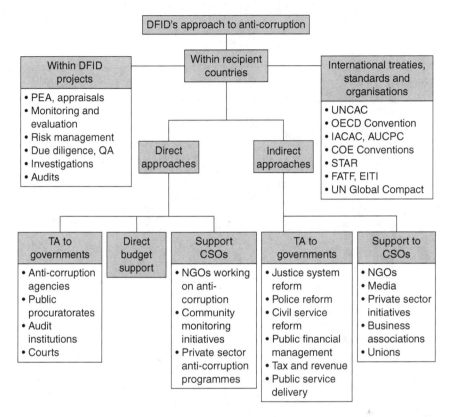

Figure 4.7 DFID's approach to anti-corruption.

- Demand side:
    - Work with NGOs
    - Work with the private sector
    - Education programmes in schools
- Monitoring:
    - Work with anti-corruption organisations
    - Work with law enforcement institutions
    - Work with the media

In 2014 the Independent Commission on Aid Impact (ICAI) reviewed DFID's efforts to 'reduce corruption as experienced by the poor', concluding that DFID has not

> developed an approach equal to the challenge [of corruption], nor has it focused its efforts on the poor. While some programmes show limited

> achievements, there is little evidence of impact on corruption levels or in meeting the needs of the poor.
>
> (ICAI, 2014, p. 1)

This report was picked up by the popular media, inspiring headlines such as 'Confirmed: Our foreign aid fuels corruption' (Martin, 2014). The response from academics and practitioners, however, was a lot more nuanced, criticising the report's methodology and its approach to corruption (Marquette et al., 2014). In particular, the potential of an external agency such as DFID, with finite resources and its own accountability systems, to influence a culture and habitual practices in a different environment is arguably rather limited. DFID does not, as pointed out by the report, primarily focus on corruption as experienced by the poor, but rather corruption in higher-level government institutions as well as technical assistance to increase the risks and reduce the potential rewards for individuals engaging in corrupt activities. This would then help ensure that the money in government institutions' budgets is spent where it is intended (such as education, healthcare and infrastructure). The debate illustrates the well-wishing ambition of some stakeholders in international development to address a multitude of issues at once and deliver results promptly, which, in turn, may lead to spreading too thinly the finite resources available and severely reducing their impact.

It is also worth noting the impact that political parties in place can have on the focus and types of programmes DFID engages in and funds. The conservative government has indeed brought issues of corruption to the forefront of the UK government's agenda, particularly with the organisation of the international summit on Corruption in May 2016. Political parties will also have influence on shaping development programmes. For example, the conservative party included the following commitment in its manifesto (Conservative Party, 2015, p. 80): 'We will boost partnerships between UK institutions and their counterparts in the developing world'. Subsequently support and funding for partnerships such as those between UK law enforcement agencies and their counterparts in developing countries were mentioned in DFID's economic development strategy published in 2017.

Significant knowledge and data gaps relating to DFID anti-corruption programming still exist. DFID is, however, also working to address these. The DFID business case for the Anti-Corruption Evidence programme has identified a number of these: (1) a general analysis of 'what works' in anti-corruption interventions; (2) the interdependencies[5] between different types of anti-corruption interventions, asking researchers to consider the bigger picture of 'surgical' interventions aiming to reduce corruption in developing countries; and (3) corruption that relates to the private sector (DFID, 2015a). Accordingly, further research into these themes is currently being undertaken.

The European Parliament (2015) raises the point that in fragile and post-conflict states prioritisation of security, development and anti-corruption policies is often lacking. This results in conflicting goals of development agencies, on the one hand attempting to facilitate rapid and stable reconstruction, working with existing government structures; and on the other hand attempting to ensure that posts are appointed solely based on merit and implementing other anti-corruption measures which may eventually target some of the existing society leaders. Some authors, such as North *et al.* (2009), Le Billon (2003) and Dix *et al.* (2012), argue that corruption may actually have a stabilising effect in the short to medium term in fragile countries, by allowing for redistribution through existing patronage networks. In the long term such an approach, however, can have significant negative consequences, as discussed in Chapter 3.

Scrutiny of UK aid

The UK's aid policies and expenditure is being heavily scrutinised by a number of institutions and bodies. The International Development Committee (IDC) is the parliamentary oversight body that has the mandate to monitor 'the policy, administration and spending of the Department for International Development (DFID) and its associated public bodies and takes an interest in the policies and procedures of the multilateral agencies and non-government organisations to which DFID contributes' (IDC, 2016b). The committee is an investigative body and chooses topics on which it conducts enquiries. The IDC was founded in 1997, at the same time as DFID was created from what had previously been the Overseas Development Administration. Prior to that, the UK's spending on international development had been subject to parliamentary oversight by the Select Committee on Overseas Aid (then renamed the Select Committee on Overseas Development).

The Independent Commission on Aid Impact (ICAI) is an organisation independent of the UK government, founded in 2011, responsible for scrutinising official UK overseas development assistance. ICAI's agenda and reports are led by four commissioners in four-year terms at the commission. ICAI reports to the IDC of the UK parliament; its budget is funded by DFID (see DFID, 2016b; IDC, 2016a). The government is required to publish a management response to each of ICAI's reports, detailing whether it accepts, partially accepts or rejects each of its recommendations and setting out the concrete actions (together with a timeline) that it will take in response to the recommendations. The International Development Committee's Subcommittee on ICAI then holds an evidence session on the report, where its members question the review team on their findings and DFID officials on their response to these.

A number of NGOs analyse and track the UK's spending in international development (including AidWatch and the UK Aid Network), and the transparency requirements under IATI and the OECD guidelines have been discussed in Chapter 1.

The harshest scrutiny, however, probably comes from the right-wing and tabloid media. Headlines such as 'Britain may have blown £2m in foreign aid helping Nigerians to export ROCKS: Corrupt officials are filling containers with boulders instead of leather so they can pocket the money' (Brown, 2015) and 'Nigeria aid farce (cont.): As UK gives £1bn to nation joining the space race, its corrupt officials allow £2bn of oil to be stolen every year' (Doughty, 2013) are increasingly common. Consultants working in the sphere of international development have suggested that some publications 'will not let the truth get in the way of a good story', particularly regarding the UK taxpayers' money being misspent in developing countries. Nevertheless, close scrutiny of the media does play a role in nudging the UK government and other organisations it works with to pay close attention to ensuring that aid money is not misspent and, to the extent possible, delivers the intended results.

Organisational learning and knowledge management within the sphere of development is also becoming a significant part of numerous DFID programmes. DFID engages in extensive consultation processes, which include early market engagement meetings, where potential bidders for programmes and other stakeholders are invited to give DFID feedback on the proposed design and focus of its forthcoming programmes. DFID also often engages private firms, consultants and academics in assisting it in designing and writing business cases for upcoming programmes.

In summary, UK aid is subject to intense scrutiny from a number of different organisations. This prompts DFID and other UK government departments that spend UK ODA to do their best to ensure that UK aid is well spent and is delivering 'value for money'. Issues, however, persist over the type of scrutiny that the UK's ODA spending receives. This has led the department to move to 'payment by results' (PBR, or paying for demonstrating particular results rather than inputting a certain level of effort into programmes) for its contracts. DFID noted that between April and October 2015, PBR contracts constituted 'nearly 80% by value of all new centrally procured contracts over this period' (quoted in IDC, 2016a, p. 22). Concurrently, DFID has committed to spending at least 50 per cent of its funds in fragile states (HMT and DFID, 2015).[6] The programme timelines (usually from three up to five years), and particularly those required to meet tight payment by results programme deadlines (up to six months for the contractors to receive payment), are incompatible with those that are needed for substantial change particularly in fragile states, and in those that have widespread corruption. As noted by the IDC (2016a, p. 18), '[t]ransformative impact in fragile states will take a generation to achieve and is dependent upon development of in-country state capacity'. This can create incentives for programmes to focus on easily achievable short-term goals and away from tackling the roots of issues in difficult environments, where assistance might be most needed, as well as reducing the flexibility of adapting a programme as it goes along (IDC, 2016a, p. 22).

4.2 Programme foci

Corruption is clearly a complex phenomenon which many have argued needs to be addressed holistically – looking at all levels of society – from grand to petty corruption; organisations – governments, public institutions, NGOs, religious institutions and others; as well as methods of enforcement – legal, educational, procedural. Put simply, the people (politicians, bureaucrats, law enforcement

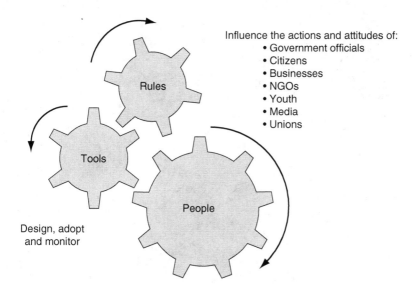

Figure 4.8 Key factors in anti-corruption programming.

officers, media, citizens, etc.), rules (laws, regulations and customs) as well as the tools to enforce these rules (including the judiciary and law enforcement) should all be functioning together, as illustrated by Figure 4.8.

Working with a large variety of organisations that address corruption at different levels and fora enables the UK to assist countries with the issue of corruption at all stages – from prevention, design and implementation of the necessary safeguards and laws, through to monitoring compliance with these systems, investigating and prosecuting breaches and ultimately redressing wrongdoings, as illustrated in Figure 4.9.

These approaches will be presented in more detail in the subsequent sections of this chapter. This section will also discuss the ability of a foreign government to deliver substantial change in all these respects in a different country with a very different culture, history, institutional architecture as well as political and economic climate, through bilateral or multilateral initiatives. This subsequently points towards the need to work with partner organisations and institutions, as well as to prioritise funding and to undertake the interventions that are most likely to achieve their intended impact.

Creating and strengthening anti-corruption agencies and strategies

The remit of anti-corruption organisations is to coordinate a country's anti-corruption efforts, and to liaise with international counterparts and institutions (such as, for example, the National Crime Agency of the UK) when transnational issues of corruption arise.

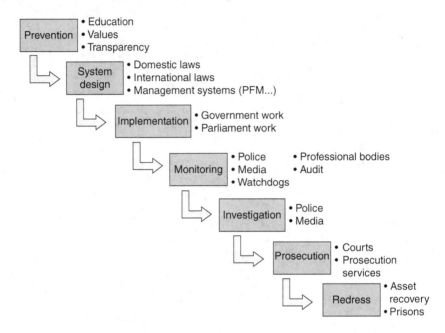

Figure 4.9 Stages of corruption interventions.

Corruption, especially grand corruption, is a sophisticated crime usually conducted in secrecy from both engaging sides. Specialised institutions will often therefore be better placed to pursue it than regular police forces. On the other hand, however, it might be easier to corrupt and influence a specialised agency than an organised police force. In particular, in most developed police forces it is customary within ordinary police to rotate posts frequently. This limits the opportunities for officers to create significant networks within a post and contributes to keeping corruption levels relatively low within the force. Of course, a number of other negative and positive incentives and regulations are important to control corruption within the police force; Punch (2000, p. 322) outlines these as:

> sending out clear and consistent messages reinforced by exemplary personal example; a well thought out, multi-faceted strategy of control and compliance; a robust, vigorous, and well-resourced internal investigatory unit; proactive techniques of uncovering and pursuing bent police; persistent efforts to build pride and to instil professional standards of conduct; and a contract with the public and stakeholders that promises an open, transparent organisation that publishes its mistakes and tries to learn from them (while recognising that some information will be restricted by security, investigative and privacy considerations).

Incentives for clean government institutions, however, can at times be taken too far and threaten human rights and justice for citizens. A particular example is the Philippines, where President Duterte has offered sizeable rewards for denouncing corrupt policemen and has himself released a list of more than 160 policemen, judges and officials who were allegedly taking corrupt payments from drug traffickers (*Reuters*, 2016). This has resulted in large numbers of extrajudicial killings – from June to August 2016, 889 people were reportedly killed by vigilantes, which has attracted criticism from the US and the UN (Murdoch, 2016; *Reuters*, 2016). Duterte was also reported to have dismissed thousands of government officials for corruption, without having produced evidence of their wrongdoing (Murdoch, 2016). This threatens people's human rights and the possibility to carry out trials and justice according to the law. This is particularly concerning as law enforcement leaders in the Philippines have endorsed such extrajudicial killings. For example, the National Police chief Ronald dela Rosa, in a speech in August 2016, encouraged people to kill drug lords:

> You want to kill them, then kill them, you can kill them because you are their victims here. You know who are the drug lords here, go to their houses, pour gasoline, set it on fire, show them you are angry at them.
> (Ronald dela Rosa quoted in *Reuters*, 2016)

Supporting anti-corruption agencies to combat corruption might be particularly difficult in practice if the country in question is suffering from an endemic corruption problem and there is corruption among the leadership. Multilateral organisations setting up anti-corruption agencies in developing countries can, if they are not politically astute and do not carefully vet their local partners and employees, further exacerbate institutionalised corruption. For example, the person appointed to set up and subsequently head the anti-corruption agency might be found selling posts within the agency for sizeable amounts of money.

Even if independent and 'clean' anti-corruption agencies are established, the question of entry points for anti-corruption efforts to other institutions, and the government and society persists. A 'big bang' approach to anti-corruption, which has been attempted in, for example, Georgia in 2003, consists of large-scale dismissals of public servants and/or policemen, their replacement with new recruits, and changes within the legal, administrative and institutional frameworks (Kupatadze, 2015). Politically, however, such a 'big bang' approach might be difficult to take within the majority of countries, due to the requirements of independence and commitment of the leadership, their ability to enforce such changes, a supply of experienced and skilled civil servants to take the place of those who are dismissed, as well as the public's support.

Hong Kong's Independent Commission Against Corruption (ICAC), established in 1974, is often argued to have successfully transformed Hong Kong from being perceived as endemically corrupt to one of the cleanest societies, undertaking the functions of investigation, prevention and education (see Lethbridge, 1985; Manion, 2004). In a society that was endemically corrupt, however, another policy decision played a key role – in 1977, amnesty was granted collectively to the Hong Kong Royal Police Force (David, 2010, p. 396). Simultaneously, severe repercussions for those who engage in corruption from that point in time onwards were introduced (ibid.). The amnesty was an important strategic decision, as it might provide the incentives on a larger scale to abandon corrupt practices, thus transitioning from an endemically corrupt society to a much cleaner one. Gong and Wang (2012) also stress the importance of civil engagement and informal institutions in Hong Kong's anti-corruption efforts. Furthermore, the legal powers and authorities that are granted to anti-corruption agencies are important to consider.

The ICAC model, however, might not be easily sustainable or replicable in other countries and environments. The application of the ICAC model has been attempted in other countries, including Botswana, South Africa and Namibia, but they have not been particularly successful at bringing high-level corrupt officials to justice, due to a combination of a lack of resources, the political will to prosecute high-level corruption, a lack of political power within the anti-corruption organisations and the model being based on a social setting in African states that is very different to Hong Kong (Sebudubudu, 2002). Furthermore, recently ICAC itself has experienced a number of corruption scandals within the leadership of the organisation. For example, ICAC's former commissioner left the organisation amidst accusations of, and investigations into, his lavish entertainment spending and 42 cases of breach of conduct (But and Chan, 2013; ICAC, 2016).

A way forward might be to begin with reforms that appear not to be threatening to the senior leadership of a country or institution in question, for example, introducing the requirements for junior members of staff to produce receipts for reimbursable expenses in government departments. It has been suggested that once such a practice is relatively widespread it would become difficult for the senior leadership to justify why it is only the junior members of their organisations who are subject to such requirements. Similarly, the reform could include asset declaration for new junior staff (to assist in identifying cases of illicit enrichment), which could then be naturally extended to all staff.

Overall, Zaum et al.'s (2012) research suggests that there is a fair amount of evidence to support the argument that anti-corruption agencies are ineffective in combatting corruption. Meagher (2005, p. 69) offers a more nuanced point of view, suggesting that anti-corruption agencies will not be effective where the preconditions of 'minimum political, legal, and socio-economic conditions for effective governance' are not yet present. DFID's (2015d, p. 64) literature review of a number of such studies suggests that this is due to three main reasons:

1 'Uneven or insufficient financial support';
2 'Limited independence from political influence'; and
3 'Weak institutional mandates'.

Nevertheless, DFID (ibid.) criticises these studies' methodologies and, in particular, the way that success of the agencies is measured, often using the CPI which makes attribution of results to the particular agency's work difficult, and has other flaws, as discussed in section 3.2.

As one-off individual reforms are unlikely to have the desired effect, it is important to consider the systems of corruption and the interdependencies between different institutions that are discussed below.

Adequate legislation and strengthening legal systems

A country's sound laws and strong legal and judiciary institutions can contribute to its development in a variety of ways. They can bring the corrupt to justice and strip them of their illicitly obtained gains, returning the funds to the victims of the crimes. As such, not only do they contribute to upholding the values of a society (including justice and fairness), but they also can make a monetary difference.

The strength of both the laws and the law enforcement and judiciary institutions, which determine the possibility of convicting offenders domestically, can make a significant difference to the amount a country's budget can receive. A key difference between UK and US legislation in prosecuting companies will help illustrate this point.

Both the UK and the US have legislation against corruption which has significant international reach – the UK Bribery Act 2010 and the US Foreign and Corrupt Practices Act (FCPA).[7] The UK Bribery Act came into force in 2011 and it in fact goes further than FCPA, the first legislation to criminalise acts of transnational corruption, in criminalising certain acts of bribery. For example, the UK Bribery Act prohibits private sector bribery in addition to bribery that involves public officials (Shulman, 2013, p. 729).

In the UK, however, a company can only be convicted under the Bribery Act 2010 in accordance with the identification principle, which provides that 'corporate liability arises only where the offence is committed by a natural person who is the directing mind or will of the organisation' (Ministry of Justice, 2011, p. 9). Therefore, a very senior director or manager, who can be said to embody the company as the 'directing mind and will', has to be identified and proven to be individually guilty of the crime for his company to be convicted. This principle provides several difficulties, including making going after smaller companies easier as the 'directing mind' can be identified more easily than in large multinational companies with more complex management systems. It also creates conflicting incentives for senior executives to distance themselves from operational knowledge while advocating for compliance in their company. By contrast, in the US if an employee commits a criminal offence while at least in part intending to benefit his or her company, the company will be vicariously liable (Weissmann and Newman, 2007). This has meant that some crimes are prosecuted and companies fined in the US rather than the UK, with the money going to the US Treasury rather than the UK (see, for example, LIBOR benchmark interest rate manipulation sentencing by US authorities) (US Department of Justice, 2013). An offence modelled under section 7 of the UK Bribery Act

2010, for companies failing to prevent economic and financial crimes of persons associated with the company, has been proposed to address this shortfall in legislation and encourage companies to develop sound management systems that could act as their defence against such an offence.

Similarly, convictions of bribery will more commonly be successful in jurisdictions where parent companies are liable for bribery by their subsidiaries. For example, the French power and transport company, Alstom, has been under investigation in a number of jurisdictions for bribery in Saudi Arabia, Egypt, Tunisia, Malaysia, Indonesia, Singapore, Egypt, Taiwan, Brazil, Italy, Zambia, Poland, Mexico, Latvia, the Bahamas, Hungary, Slovenia and Taiwan (CW, 2015, p. 11). It paid fines in Italy, Switzerland and the US. No investigations resulted in fines or convictions in France, however, where the company is headquartered (ibid.).

These examples help illustrate the importance of strong and adequate laws against offences of corruption. Another key point in legislation, which would facilitate prosecution in cases of corruption, would be reversing the burden of proof that some countries still have – from the law enforcement having to prove that officials' money was illicitly obtained, to the officials themselves having to prove that the sources of their funds were legitimate.

For a legal system and its institutions to be able to take on and successfully convict high-level cases of corruption, law enforcement institutions have to (a) be able to resist corruption (for example to resist bribes for burying evidence or making an unjust judgement), (b) have adequate laws and (c) have enough capacity to undertake their roles and implement legislation competently and swiftly. As such, tackling corruption in law enforcement requires ensuring that a significant number of institutions are well functioning:

- strong and independent legislatory bodies;
- the judiciary that would carry out just sentences to those who have engaged in corruption;
- the prosecution services to put forward a case in court; and
- the investigatory institutions (such as the Ethics and Anti-Corruption Commission (EACC) in Kenya or the Economics and Financial Crimes Commission (EFCC) in Nigeria and the police).

Some parts of the last three roles can be merged within one institution designed to tackle corruption: for example the EFCC in Nigeria undertakes investigatory and prosecutorial roles; and the SFO in the UK also investigates and prosecutes high-profile cases on economic crime, despite the UK having a separate prosecutorial office – the Crown Prosecution Services (CPS), and investigations for other crimes being carried out by the National Crime Agency (as well as the police units).

Even if these functions are carried out separately, all of the institutions responsible for the aforementioned functions are interlinked in the way their results get measured in relation to tackling corruption. The number and profile of prosecutions will be the measure of whether evidence was gathered well and thoroughly, whether it was well presented in court and whether an acceptable judgement was reached. Therefore, building the capacity of one of these institutions will not be likely to have the intended results if another function is not adequately performed. For example, even if investigations are carried out very thoroughly and sound evidence is gathered and presented to the court, a corrupt judge could undermine the other agencies' efforts to bring those engaging in corruption to account. If no admissible evidence is presented to a court, it will be difficult for an honest judge to convict people for corruption while following adequate procedures. This is illustrated in Figure 4.10.

Lawson (2009, p. 73) suggests that the EFCC having its own independent prosecutorial powers gives the organisation 'a measure of success'. Along the same lines, Quah (2009) argues that separating the powers between different institutions will be likely to increase the likelihood of mal-coordination and unhelpful competition between the different authorities. The institution does indeed acquire a greater degree of autonomy, however its success will be very much dependent on the individual institution's staff, circumstances as well as the wider environment they operate within. Awarding one institution a range of different investigatory and prosecutorial responsibilities could, in some cases, place an excessive burden on organisations that are already overstretched, if adequate resources to fulfil these functions are not provided.

The capacity of an organisation to fulfil its duties is also important to consider. The case of Kenyan institutions following devolution in 2013 provides an interesting example. The mandate of law enforcement and oversight of institutions was significantly expanded to provide adequate support for regional governments. For example, the Office of the Directorate of Public Prosecutions (ODPP) saw its staff numbers significantly expand to cater for all the newly established county offices (Makabila, 2013). There was, however, a limited supply of experienced prosecutors to employ, which meant that despite the new recruits being generally competent and from a variety of backgrounds, their sheer lack of experience would be a significant disadvantage in court. A very inexperienced prosecutor standing up against an established lawyer for a corruption case would be less likely to win the case to bring a perpetrator to justice. This is in addition to an ongoing shortage of staff in the agency (Makabila, 2013).

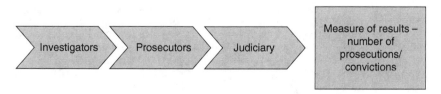

Figure 4.10 Interdependencies between different institutions in the legal sector in achieving results.

110 *The UK's anti-corruption work*

Similarly, the Auditor General's (AG) office in Kenya saw its mandate expanded from auditing the central government's institutions to also auditing the 47 regional government institutions, without comparable increases in resources. This comes at a time when audit institutions are attempting to move towards value for money auditing, that is, evaluating the results of investments, rather than following a check-box approach to confirm that the money did indeed go where it was meant to go. This can create a significant strain on the institution, despite it being considered as one of the leading AGs in the region. The particular issues pertaining to audit and oversight institutions are discussed in further detail in the subsequent section.

Strengthening parliaments, national bureaucracies and national audit offices

DFID has a long history of working with developing country parliaments and government departments. This is done directly, via contractor-delivered programmes overseen by DFID, and support is also provided by the House of Commons (usually facilitated by one of the two NGOs – The Westminster Foundation for Democracy or the Commonwealth Parliamentary Association), National Assemblies (such as the Northern Ireland Assembly), or government departments such as the UK's tax authority – Her Majesty's Revenue and Customs (HMRC). The UK's National Audit Office (NAO) also has a long history of providing assistance to developing country parliamentary and government institutions.

Just as law enforcement institutions are inherently interlinked in their capacity to achieve results in fighting and preventing corruption, so are many other government institutions. For example, a national audit system will only be fully operational and fulfil its purpose of holding to account those who divert public money to inefficient or illicit use if (a) the national audit office (or the auditor general's office, depending on the country) is able to conduct efficient investigations without political interference, and (b) if the reports produced by the audit office are then validated by the Public Accounts Committee (PAC) of the country in a timely, independent and efficient manner, and can be used to hold institutions and individuals to account, as demonstrated in Figure 4.11.

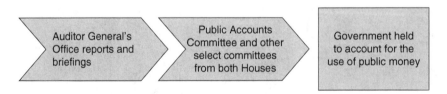

Figure 4.11 Interdependencies between different institutions in achieving results from national audits.

Most such work fits under the umbrella of public financial management (PFM) reforms work. DFID (2015d, p. 56) distinguishes between five different types of PFM reforms and summarises the existing evidence on each of these reforms' effectiveness in reducing corruption:

1 **Decentralisation**: a significant number of studies have considered the effectiveness of decentralisation on reducing corruption; the findings, however, produce mixed and inconsistent evidence. DFID (ibid.) concludes from such evidence that decentralisation will not on its own reduce levels of corruption. This is discussed in further detail in sections 3.1 and 3.4.
2 **Public expenditure tracking**: a number of studies have found public expenditure tracking to be 'generally consistent in showing budget tracking reduces leakage (a proxy indicator for corruption)' (ibid.). Studies have suggested that the 'very act of monitoring public finances has preventive effects on corruption, particularly if done repeatedly' (see DFID, 2015d, p. 58).
3 **Revenue and customs**: a few case studies that look into the effectiveness of tax, revenue and customs reforms produce inconsistent findings.
4 **Procurement**: several experimental, quasi-experimental and observational studies suggest that procurement reforms can effectively reduce corruption.
5 **Central budget planning and management**: often conducted via the ministry of finance, this has been identified by a small number of observational studies as having 'positive effects on reducing corruption' (DFID, 2015d, p. 56).

There are, however, many caveats to be considered when applying such conclusions to programming. Just because a certain type of reform can work, it does not mean that it always will. The systematic review of evidence points out that the most effective interventions appear to be those that combine two or more interventions, thus adopting a more holistic and integrated approach (DFID, 2015d, pp. 56–57). This is applicable to the five types of interventions mentioned above, as well as the other types of work discussed in this chapter, including supporting independent media, civil society organisations as well as asset recovery initiatives.

A few other observations on the types of PFM programmes mentioned above are worth mentioning. The health of a country's taxation system can rather accurately reflect a country's overall performance and level of political stability (Di John, 2010). Tax reform programmes will often not particularly target corruption, but rather incorporate it as one of the programme objectives (see ICAI, 2016).

There have, however, been less-than-successful attempts at reforming countries' tax systems. The IMF has been advocating for developing countries to introduce Value Added Tax (VAT) systems. VAT is a very complicated tax system (where tax is paid on gross sales but can be reclaimed on the inputs purchased, so as to pay tax only on the value they add to the purchased inputs). It is difficult to administer and adds an extra layer of bureaucracy and with it opportunities for corruption: for example, counterfeit receipts for inputs, such as transportation, equipment and communications, could be sold and bought by companies to reduce the taxes they owe the state (Tanzi and Davoodi, 2000; Toye and Moore, 1998). In developing countries with comparatively weak bureaucratic capacity and higher levels of corruption it might therefore be worth starting by introducing simpler tax reforms, gradually introducing VAT and other more complex tax systems.

Monitoring has in fact been noted to have a preventative effect in and of itself, even if done rather sporadically and at a high level (see Johnson and Soreide, 2013). This relates to the logic of spot checks, where a small number of recipients of state funds are audited and asked to account for their expenditure; however, everyone is at risk of being asked. In electoral democracies, audit findings that reveal corruption were shown to decrease the probability of incumbents being re-elected (see, for example, Ferraz and Finan (2008) who analyse the case of municipal audits leading to a reduction in the re-election of incumbents where cases of corruption were unveiled; and higher rates of re-election for those who are found to be less corrupt).

Rendering the audit process open and transparent, by publishing financial data and various audit reports online thus sharing information with the general public and civil society organisations (CSOs) can significantly increase the scrutiny levels of public spending. As demonstrated with the example of mayors' re-election in Brazil, making audits available to the public will be likely to provide disincentives for individuals to engage in corruption by affecting people's reputation and social standing, even if formal charges are not brought against them. Reinikka and Svensson (2004, p. 16) noted a significant drop in the leakage of funds (13.8 per cent) when people had more access to information about state institutions' funding; for example – when data on the amounts of funding that local schools received in Uganda was published in local newspapers.

Furthermore, there is a very limited number of public officials and law enforcement representatives and a lot of information to go through. The public's scrutiny can be of invaluable assistance in identifying wrongdoing or suspicious behaviour/spending, which can then be further investigated by the authorities and appropriate action taken. In some places such as Nigeria, however, the AG's annual reports have not been published since 2007 (OAG Nigeria, 2007). This can also be due to delays within the PACs and other parliamentary committees, when working with and approving the reports from the AG's office before these are released. Auditors' reports taking several years to be approved have resulted in a large backlog and reduced capacity of the audit institutions to hold the ruling government to account. As such, support can be needed to improve the capacity of the PACs to approve the AG's reports in a timely manner, as well as to ensure that the entire process is independent from political influences (as, for example, individuals within parliamentary committees could be offering to remove negative audit findings from audit reports in exchange for bribes).

CSO capacity-building

A strong civil society, able to challenge and keep the government in check, is seen by both academic researchers and international development agencies as a key pillar that could keep the levels of corruption in check (see Rose-Ackerman, 1999, pp. 162–174). Civil society's access to information on how public money is spent and the potential to organise to seek justice (by, for example, protesting) in case of perceived misconduct could indeed perform a key function in deterring people from corruption and bringing to account those who do engage in corrupt activities. A strong civil society, with shared values, trust and efficient networks, would also be key to solving collective action problems in relation to challenging corrupt behaviour (Paxton, 2002).

Nuances to the impact of differing types of civil society organisations on a country's political and economic development have been suggested in the literature. Putnam (2002, pp. 9–11) differentiates between horizontal and vertical social networks. Horizontal networks refer to citizens' networks that do not involve strict established hierarchical structures, such as various professional, student or cause-related associations. Vertical networks can refer to structures such as the church or the mafia. International development projects are typically designed to strengthen or form horizontal social networks, with democratic governance structures (see, for example, Holland et al., 2009).

There are, however, multiple complications that arise in relation to international development work aimed at strengthening civil society organisations. First of all, some governments, especially non-democratic ones, are reluctant to allow foreign entities to engage in such work in their countries, especially if it is seen as political (work on anti-corruption inevitably falls into this category). International aid organisations' continued access to work in a given region/country and support those who are worst off ultimately depends on receiving the local government's permission to do so. Dictators or abusive leaders may be unwilling to allow foreign organisations to strengthen civil society to challenge corruption and their methods of governance as ultimately that could evolve into a threat to their rule. This might require the organisations to assess their priorities (for example peace, stability, justice, economic growth, individuals' well-being and health, etc.) and consider which course of action and allies would be most conducive to achieving their goals (Magone et al., 2012).

An interesting way around this is being taken by some NGOs that choose to work on issues that are not political and that the dictatorial government will not be likely to object to in principle, such as environmental causes – cleaning up local parks, roadsides and engaging citizens to be environmentally conscious. This creates networks of activists, increases their reach to large numbers of citizens and allows for the indigenous development of strong civil society groups. The NGO then hopes that the groups, having established functioning networks to unite people to tackle issues relating to environment, would eventually move on to more governance and corruption-related issues.

An important distinction has also been noted about the composition, or levels of homogeneity, within civil societies (see Gibson and Gouws, 2000; Hardin, 1997). Authors have raised the question whether the strength of homogeneous civil societies (based on for example ethnicity or religion) and levels of trust within them influences the levels of trust within a society between different groups. Widmalm (2008, p. 167) cites the case of Hindus' social capital and trust within the group being used to mobilise against Muslims in Gujarat in 2002 as an example of social trust and the strength of a homogeneous civil society group being used against a weaker group. Widmalm's own field research, however, shows that a zero-sum game between intra-group and inter-group trust will not necessarily occur, that is, that increased trust within groups does not exclude the possibility of increased trust within the society between different groups (ibid.). Nevertheless, international development organisations supporting civil society organisations should carefully choose the types of organisations they support, taking into consideration the people who may lose out as a result of one social group being strengthened.

Gupta (1995) warns that the understanding of the distinction between what constitutes the 'state' and 'civil society' can be blurry in some circumstances. Gupta's fieldwork in Indian villages suggests that the conceptual separation of the two is a predominantly Western concept. Widmalm (2008, p. 123) notes that a number of researchers have relinquished the distinction between the 'state' and 'civil society', as the state was so intertwined in social relations that it was 'hard or impossible' for the researchers to separate them, and the villagers made no distinction between them. Widmalm, however, challenges this assumption, also noting that there is a distinction between people's understanding how the state and bureaucracies *do* and *should* operate. His field research in rural India reveals that people's ability to distinguish between the public and private spheres is related to the degree to which the individual is prepared to tolerate bribery within the public sector (Widmalm, 2008, p. 167). This, however, may be influenced by a person's education and knowledge of how the bureaucracies could operate and do operate elsewhere.

Whistleblower protection is a key element to consider in relation to civil society strengthening programming to address corruption. Citizens and civil society groups need to be given guarantees of protection and non-retaliation for people to feel safe to alert the relevant authorities when they come across information about incidents and networks of corruption. This, once again, requires adequate legislation, processes for whistleblowing (including hotlines and designated contact points) and institutions to follow up the claims and protect the whistleblowers. Furthermore, whistleblowing mechanisms and protection measures need to be widely understood by the public in order to have the desired effect of increasing numbers of people coming forward about questionable behaviour they witness. Successful programming in this area includes TI's work in Pakistan, where the TI chapter, in collaboration with USAID, established a hotline for reporting corruption within USAID programmes. This enabled 68 investigations, four arrests and the recovery of US$100 million (de Oliveira *et al.*, 2016).

DFID, together with government and civil society institutions, also engages in education and work on behaviour change programmes to address corruption (see, for example, Holland *et al.*, 2009). It is the hope of international development organisations, and a number of other organisations, that people would start behaving differently in relation to corruption – no longer engaging in it or tolerating it when they see others doing so. While changing behaviour on a large scale can be a difficult and lengthy process, government policies, policing and the support of civil society organisations can certainly, in some cases, help speed the process up significantly. One can compare such an attempt to large-scale campaigns to wear seatbelts in Western Europe, which largely succeeded in changing people's behaviour.

Directly attempting to change people's behaviour and engender certain types of values in societies very different from their own, however, is a risky undertaking, especially if those societies have a colonial history. DFID has openly stated that it is trying to engender behaviour change through some of its programmes (see Holland *et al.*, 2009). This can be a controversial undertaking, not always welcomed by host country governments and residents. While behaviour change can be influenced from the top down (as with the aforementioned example of wearing seatbelts), when it comes to cultural practices, such as gift-giving, such messages might be best received from local rather than international actors.

Religion, a significant aspect of many people's culture and everyday life, does not receive due consideration in relation to corruption. Research and surveys have long shown that religion generally tends to play a large role in lower-income societies (see WIN-Gallup International, 2012). Table 4.1 below suggests that people in bottom income groups are 17 per cent more religious than those in top income groups.

Most religions and traditions warn against corruption and bribery. Osborne (1997, pp. 12–14) highlights some key messages from a number of different traditions, as detailed in Table 4.2.

As religion is a fundamental pillar of many developing countries' social and community lives, it should not be ignored in favour of the more theoretical

Table 4.1 Percentage of people who identify themselves as religious in countries, by income levels

Income bracket	Proportion of people describing themselves as religious (%)
Bottom Quintile (Low Income)	66
Medium-Low Quintile	65
Medium Quintile	56
Medium-High Quintile	51
High Quintile (High Income)	49

Source: WIN-Gallup International (2012, p. 3).

Table 4.2 Attitudes to corruption and bribery in different traditions

Tradition	Key messages
The Hebrew scriptures	*Advice to Moses, 1,400 CE*: Look for able men … who fear God, are trustworthy, and hate dishonest gain; set … them as officers over thousands. Let them sit as judges. *The Law of Moses, 1,400 CE*: You must not distort justice; you must not show partiality; and you must not accept bribes for a bribe blinds the eyes of the wise and subverts the cause of those who are in the right.
Hindu writings	*Laws of Manu, about 600 CE*: Men who are appointed by the king to protect his subjects generally become hypocrites who take the property of others, and he must protect those subjects from them. The king should banish and confiscate all the property of those evil-minded men who take the money from parties to lawsuits.
Confucian	*Hsiao Ching, 145 CE (parts of an imperial edict)*: Anyone arresting or informing on a person guilty of bribery would be given the bribe received by the accused. Some officials … make a business of presents and bribes. *Wang an Shih, about 1050 CE*, attributed corruption to bad men and bad laws.
The teachings of Buddha	*About 585 CE*: If an important minister neglects his duties, works for his own profit or accepts bribes, it will cause a rapid decay of public morals. People will cheat one another … take advantage of the poor, and there will be no justice for anyone…. Unjust officials are the thieves of people's happiness … they defraud both rules and people and are the cause of the nation's troubles.
Christian	*Jesus said to tax collectors*: Collect no more than the amount prescribed for you. *And to soldiers*: Do not extort money from anyone … be satisfied with your wages. *Old Testament, Exodus 23:8*: 'Do not accept a bribe, for a bribe blinds those who see and twists the words of the innocent.'
Islamic	*The Qur'an, compiled about 600 CE*: And eat up not one another's property unjustly … nor give bribery to the rulers (judges before presenting your cases) that you may knowingly eat up a part of the property of others sinfully. *The sayings of the Prophet*: Allah curses the giver of bribes and the receiver of bribes and the person who paves the way for both parties. *The Fatwa Alamgiri*: (A present to influence a judge is unlawful, but) if a present be made to a judge from a sense of fear, it is lawful to give it, but unlawful to accept it.

Source: based on a compilation by Osborne (1997, pp. 12–14).

and academic considerations of corruption which tend to be more secular, when putting together anti-corruption policies and programmes.[8] Traditional religious and community leaders and international organisations are often advocating for the same values of integrity. They are well known by the communities and have a high standing within them, which means that they may be effective actors against corruption and significantly increase the effectiveness of anti-corruption interventions by foreign entities if they were to collaborate.

Supporting independent media

Support to the media can take a variety of forms – supporting media associations, journalists' associations or not-for-profit institutions such as BBC Media Action (BBCMA). The latter in 2016 published a policy working paper urging development actors to invest more in independent media, arguing that it is particularly needed given the economic pressures on independent media outlets (which are partially a result of the rising role of social media, but also given the increasing resources that are being invested to co-opt, control or intimidate media independence by those engaging in illicit and corrupt activities) (Deane, 2016). The paper also argues that apart from a few individual cases, 'the development system as a whole has weak capacity and a poor record' in supporting local and national media in developing countries, particularly in fragile states (Deane, 2016, p. 6). This is, however, a particularly important vehicle to promote accountability and anti-corruption, and one whose future sources of funding seem rather uncertain.

The media can perform two key functions to combat and challenge corruption: education and an investigatory function.

Traditionally, the radio has been the key media medium that performed an educational function in poor areas, informing citizens of their rights and entitlements. This has now been complemented by new types of media and technological advances. Accordingly, new initiatives have sprung up, such as informing citizens of the prices of public services and goods such as drugs via mobile phone requests, or providing information as to whether doctors are registered and qualified to be performing the services they are offering in remote parts of some countries. Deane (2016, p. 7) stresses that support to the media is most likely to achieve its intended results of engaging the public, exposing and ultimately tackling corruption, when not only a range of digital and analogue media platforms is used, but also when the programmes are 'grounded in strong contextual analysis and research'.

The investigatory function that the media performs has played a significant role in questioning and tracking public expenditure that might have been diverted for private gains. Deane (2016, p. 16) notes that even individual investigative journalists can significantly contribute to exposing and therefore disincentivising corruption, citing the example of the Ghanaian journalist Anas Aremeyaw Anas, who has exposed engagement in bribery of 12 high court judges, 22 lower court justices and 140 other court officials'. Media platforms such as the Organized

Crime and Corruption Reporting Project (OCCRP), which is partially funded by USAID, provides the platform for collaboration for a number of not-for-profit media organisations in Eastern Europe and Central Asia. The OCCRP generates more than 60 cross-border investigations a year, and since 2009, the organisation's work has contributed towards the following achievements, which represent a historical return of 'more than 47,000 percent to governments through seizures and fines' (OCCRP, 2016):

1 US$2.8 billion in assets frozen or seized with governments seeking to seize an additional US$1 billion.
2 55 criminal investigations launched as a result of its stories.
3 25 calls for action by civil or international bodies.
4 115 arrest warrants issued with 7 subjects on the run.
5 12 major sackings, including a President, a Prime Minister and CEOs of major international corporations.
6 Over 1,300 company closures and court decisions.

Media and the civil society can make a significant contribution to the law enforcement's work by providing and investigating leads, and subsequently handing over the cases to the authorities to take legal measures where wrongdoing has been identified.

A paradox has, however, been noted in relation to corruption scandals coming to the public's attention and people's perception of how corrupt a country is. *The Economist* (2016) noted that countries usually drop in corruption rankings following the exposure of major cases of corruption by the media (as happened in the UK following the 2009 expenses scandal, in Brazil following the 2014 Petrobras scandal and Guatemala in 2015). This can be misleading as the very fact that such cases are exposed and/or prosecuted is an indication of either the willingness of the authorities to do something about corruption, in allowing the publication of such cases (indicating a level of freedom of the press) and the willingness of the media or civil society to invest in investigating and exposing such behaviour. The scandals (such as the UK 2009 expenses scandal) do not necessarily indicate an increase in the incidence of abuse, rather just bringing them into the limelight (ibid.).

This has significant repercussions in relation to the compilation of indexes such as TI's CPI, which is largely based on public perceptions. If a country is seen as becoming more corrupt, as activists' efforts to bring those who have been engaging in corruption are successful, this can create the wrong policy incentives.

Whisleblower protection, as discussed in the previous section on civil society, is also key to a strong and independent media, able to bring corruption by government and business leaders to the public's attention. The OECD Foreign Bribery Report, however, notes that only 2 per cent of the 390 foreign bribery investigations, which were conducted in states parties to the OECD Anti-Bribery Convention between 1999 and 2014, were instigated by whistleblowers (OECD, 2014c).

Around the world there are vastly different attitudes towards financial incentives for whistleblowers, who are likely to be putting their jobs and future careers at risk. The regulations around whistleblower protection do not necessarily reflect a Global North–South divide. For example, in the US the Dodd-Frank Wall Street Reform and Consumer Protection Act (section 922) provides for compensating whistleblowers with 10–30 per cent of monetary sanctions exceeding $1 million, recovered as a result of the information provided by the whistleblower. The US Securities and Exchange Commission (SEC, 2015, p. 1) stated that in '2015 alone, more than $37 million was paid to reward whistleblowers for their provision of original information that led to a successful Commission enforcement action'. It has been noted that, while such compensation would provide strong incentives for people to report wrongdoing to the authorities, it would have little chance of being culturally accepted in the UK, due to UK citizens' reluctance to allow people who have personally benefited from, or have been accomplices to, crimes benefit substantially from reporting the crime.

The need for enhanced whistleblowers' and investigators' protection is also highlighted by the increasingly prominent role that journalists have been playing worldwide in uncovering corrupt practices. The 2016 leak of the Panama Papers, discussed in more detail in section 6.1, shows that it was journalists rather than multilateral or governmental institutions who were initially trusted with the evidence, as the papers were being analysed within the International Consortium of Investigative Journalists (ICIJ) for a year before being announced to the public. The information contained within the papers has resulted in numerous criminal investigations being pursued by law enforcement authorities, as discussed in section 6.1. Resources devoted towards, as well as collaboration between, different entities, such as foundations and development agencies, to support independent media in developing and fragile states, however, have been noted to be sparse (Deane, 2016, p. 11). The ICIJ, which is funded by philanthropic donations, was founded to enable cross-border collaboration of the media, and to support media outlets that have been finding it increasingly difficult to survive independently (Deane, 2016, p. 15).

The ability of the media to report on officials and others engaging in corruption can be compromised due to lack of media independence, with the government or businesses having significant influence over media outlets, particularly by owning them. As donor agencies strive to ensure that their programming is more demand-led and corresponds with recipient governments' objectives and priorities (in order to achieve senior level buy-in in recipient countries and, by extension, programme and policy synergies and with this – greater aid efficiency), programmes to support the independence of media are unlikely to be at the top of donors' intervention priority list in countries where there are high levels of grand corruption within the government (see Deane, 2016, p. 11). This might mean that independent media is not adequately supported where it might be most needed. The balance between independent and biased media might be further tilted in favour of the latter as Deane (2016, p. 13) notes that 'those who do not wish to be held to account have invested heavily in ensuring that traditional and online media is not independent and instead reflects and protects their interests', according to BBCMA's research in fragile states such as Afghanistan, Somalia, Kenya and Pakistan. This might take the form of direct action against media outlets, particularly in less democratic states, or subtler economic action by limiting the advertisement potential of particularly outspoken outlets or exercising influence through networks of patronage, such as board membership of media outlets (ibid.).

Asset recovery

Asset recovery has been defined as

> the effort by law enforcement and prosecutors to (i) identify and trace the proceeds of crime; (ii) restrain them to avoid their dissipation; (iii) link them to a criminal activity and its perpetrators; (iv) confiscate them from the perpetrators; and (v), where applicable, return them to their rightful owners.
> (Gray *et al.*, 2014, p. 15; Zinkernagel *et al.*, 2014, p. 8)

Asset recovery requires the involvement of specialists with a diverse range of skills, including accountancy, investigations, prosecution, financial analysis and cross-jurisdiction communication, in addition to adequate knowledge of the relevant legal and procedural frameworks (ibid.). As such, asset recovery is a lengthy process. As noted by Zinkernagel *et al.* (2014, p. 9), the fastest recovery of assets is considered to be that of Abacha funds from Switzerland, which took five years, whereas other cases, such as the recovery of Marcos's assets from Switzerland back to the Philippines took 28 years.

There are multiple reasons why recovering illicitly gained assets and capital is an important factor for legal and development organisations to focus on. Not only would more effective asset recovery play a role in discouraging people from engaging in criminal activities, but it would also ensure that the illicitly gained money is not used to finance further criminal or terrorist activities. It would also make it significantly more difficult for corrupt businesses to penetrate (and possibly subvert or corrupt) non-criminal businesses with proceeds of crime. Recovery of corrupt assets would also facilitate compensation for victims. The UN Secretary General Ban Ki-Moon has stressed that corruption deprives developing countries of more than a trillion US dollars every year through money laundering, illegal tax evasion and embezzlement (UN, 2014). A report on stolen assets produced by ONE estimates that $3.2 trillion of assets held offshore originate in developing countries; and if these assets were declared, they could yield yearly revenues of $19.5 billion in taxation (ONE, 2014). In section 3.5, the case of South Korea's stringent capital controls was discussed, along with the importance of keeping scarce capital within the developing economy in question.

International efforts to facilitate the recovery of stolen assets are therefore crucial in the fight against corruption. Initiatives such as the Stolen Asset

Recovery Initiative (StAR), established by the World Bank (WB) and the United Nations Office on Drugs and Crime (UNODC) have contributed to a joint international effort to 'end safe havens for corrupt funds (...) and to facilitate more systematic and timely return of stolen assets' (StAR, 2016b). As such, the StAR initiative influences policy in the sphere of the global fight against corruption, in addition to providing capacity-building, case assistance and facilitating the collaboration of experts from different jurisdictions (Fofack, 2009; Greenberg, 2009).

Zinkernagel et al. (2014, p. 7) note that there are five major ways in which international development organisations can and do support asset recovery:

> (i) supporting international standards and initiatives; (ii) providing technical assistance and capacity building (most often through third parties); (iii) encouraging policy coherence at home; (iv) helping build political will; and (v) providing assistance during the asset repatriation phase.

Acknowledging the importance of asset recovery efforts, DFID has supported such programmes, including: the International Centre for Asset Recovery at the Basel Institute for Governance, which provides strategic case advice, technical assistance, capacity-building and informs global policy discussions on setting standards in asset recovery, in addition to funding posts from other UK law enforcement agencies, such as the CPS, the Serious Fraud Office (SFO) and the National Crime Agency (NCA) (Basel Institute on Governance, 2014; Olson et al., 2016).

Furthermore, in addition to preventative measures, DFID has been incorporating activities to strengthen developing countries' abilities to tackle corruption by taking a broader criminal justice approach. This includes providing assistance to developing country governments when conducting investigations, prosecutions and facilitating international collaboration for asset tracking and recovery, with the aim to reduce the possible gains and increase the risks associated with engaging in corrupt activities. Programmes announced under this umbrella include the GREAT for Partnerships programme (DFID, 2016b) and Implementation of the Regional Facility for Strengthening Transnational Responses to Countering Illicit Financial Flows, Corruption and Organised Crime in Africa programme (DFID, 2016c). Since 2006, DFID has been funding the Proceeds of Corruption Unit (POCU) in the Metropolitan Police, which specialised in cases involving allegations of laundering of illicitly gained assets in the UK; funding the City of London Police Overseas Anti-Corruption Unit (OACU), which investigates allegations of corruption involving UK citizens, companies and financial institutions in developing countries; and, in addition, financially supporting posts within the Crown Prosecution Services, dedicated to executing confiscation orders in relation to developing country cases (Gray et al., 2014, p. 56). Many of these activities have now been subsumed by the International Corruption Unit (ICU) within the National Crime Agency (NCA), which was created in 2015 in line with the UK Anti-Corruption Plan.

DFID's track record to date in relation to the aforementioned initiatives has been regarded as positive – with £5 million invested in six years, more than £100 million in frozen assets were, in 2013, 'subject to judicial procedures with a view to confiscation' (ibid.). Other DFID programmes include support for asset recovery and related assistance, however these are not on a very large scale, particularly compared to the scale of DFID's investments in other sectors, as discussed at the beginning of this chapter.

Western countries' governments and their various departments have a comparative advantage globally in possessing the specialist legal, forensics and investigatory skills as well as strong legal institutions necessary for successful asset recovery. If the UK's international development funding is to be directed to, and concentrated where, it can make a real difference both in the long and short term, there is a rationale for asset recovery to feature more prominently in the UK's anti-corruption programming for developing countries.

It is worth noting, however, that, despite some frozen assets mentioned previously, the traditional criminal justice system has only very rarely succeeded in effectively depriving criminals of their illegally obtained assets. Lord Elwyn-Jones has noted that

> The public no longer believes that the legal system in England and Wales is capable of bringing the perpetrators of serious frauds expeditiously and effectively to book. The overwhelming weight of the evidence ... suggests that the public is right ... the present legal system is archaic, cumbersome and unreliable.
>
> (HL, 1986, p. 198)

The reasons for this are abundant, including the clandestine nature of economic crime, the often high profile of the people involved in such crimes, their complexity and international dimension, as well as often a lack of resources on the prosecuting side. Reflecting this, the courts have made amusing analogies in relation to the practical issues of tracing illicitly obtained property:

> In the course of this appeal some reference was made to the fact that assets, like the Cheshire Cat, may disappear unexpectedly. It is also to be remembered that modern technology and the ingenuity of its beneficiaries may enable assets to depart at a speed which can make any feline powers of evanescence appear to be sluggish by comparison.
>
> (*Derby & Co v. Wheldon* (Nos 3 and 4) (1989) 2 WLR 412 at 436)

Nevertheless, freezing assets will often have the effect of disrupting criminal networks, making it more difficult for criminals to take advantage of illicit activities. Furthermore, some cases do, or are likely to, lead to funds being returned to the developing countries from which they were stolen. The Ibori case is an important one to consider in this respect. In 2008, the UK issued a Restraint Order against assets owned and controlled by James Ibori, a former governor of

Nigeria's Delta State, and his companies; and froze $35 million of his assets (StAR, 2016a). In 2012, the UK sentenced Ibori to 13 years in prison for money laundering and conspiracy to defraud, with a confiscation hearing regarding some of his assets taking place in June 2016 (ibid.). The United States also restrained more than $3 million in corruption proceeds related to this case (DOJ, 2012). This can serve an important signalling purpose – alerting both the public and leaders around the world to the fact that cases of grand and transnational corruption can be successfully prosecuted in a number of jurisdictions.

Summary

The question remains as to what types of institutions should address which aspect of corruption: for example, local, foreign or international; governmental, private sector, grassroots or religious; legislatory, law enforcement, civil society or media. DFID has, to some extent, been attempting to address all of the aforementioned aspects of corruption, often working through programme delivery partners. It is therefore suggested that the UK government, in its overseas anti-corruption work, should perhaps concentrate on what appears to be the most effective interventions in order to achieve the maximum benefit from its investment (which would have both an impact on the vulnerable populations in developing countries and demonstrate the usefulness of such investments to the taxpayers who are funding the work), but also work with entire systems of corruption. This will inevitably require a more coordinated approach to working with other institutions and organisations to ensure that corruption is addressed holistically.

4.3 Issues with anti-corruption programming

A number of issues with anti-corruption programming have been discussed in the previous chapters. This includes definitional issues as to precisely what actions or behaviour is to be considered as 'corruption' under the programmes, cultural issues and concerns about sovereignty, as well as issues of measurement of progress and effectiveness of interventions. Several additional matters should be considered in the context of bilateral anti-corruption programming – politics, the existing evidence of what works, as well as the associated costs. These are discussed in detail in this section.

Politics

Political issues can arise from foreign actors intervening in issues of governance in other states. Organisations such as DFID, as well as the World Bank and organisations of the United Nations, attempt to maintain an apolitical stance when addressing the needs of vulnerable people rather than supporting particular sides within political debates. This can also be a requirement for gaining access to work in more politically volatile environments, where such organisations' assistance can make a significant difference to people's lives.

World Bank

An interesting case to consider in relation to politics is the World Bank's engagement with the issue of corruption. To illustrate the apolitical nature of the World Bank's engagement with the issue of corruption, we can refer back to the speech delivered at the annual meeting of the World Bank (WB) and the International Monetary Fund (IMF) in 1996, by James Wolfensohn, the then President of the World Bank. After having presented the damaging effects that corruption may have on issues of development, Wolfensohn noted:

> Corruption is a problem that all countries have to confront. Solutions, however, can only be homegrown. National leaders need to take a stand. Civil society plays a key role as well. Working with our partners, the Bank Group will help any of our member countries to implement national programs that discourage corrupt practices. And we will support international efforts to fight corruption and to establish voluntary standards of behavior for corporations and investors in the industrialized world.
>
> The Bank Group cannot intervene in the political affairs of our member countries. But we can give advice, encouragement and support to governments that wish to fight corruption and it is these governments that will, over time, attract the larger volume of investment. Let me emphasize that the Bank Group will not tolerate corruption in the programs that we support; and we are taking steps to ensure that our own activities continue to meet the highest standards of probity.
>
> (World Bank, 1996)

Navigating the sensitivities around being seen to intervene in a country's political affairs while engaging in anti-corruption work, however, is no easy task. The Bank's mandate and the Articles of Agreement clearly prevent it from engaging in political activity, under section 10 of art. IV, which states:

> The Bank and its officers shall not interfere in the political affairs of any member; nor shall they be influenced in their decisions by the political character of the member or members concerned. Only economic considerations shall be relevant to their decisions, and these considerations shall be weighed impartially in order to achieve the purposes stated in Article I.

There were doubts about whether such a change in policy would persist beyond Wolfensohn's presidency. Nevertheless, as the issue of corruption has been increasingly seen as a fundamental threat to countries' development, the World Bank has been more extensively engaging in anti-corruption activities, albeit still limited by its mandate. Cremer (2008, p. 4) notes that the timing of the Bank's change of policy in relation to corruption is also to be credited, in addition to Wolfensohn's personal devotion to the subject: the end of the Cold War meant that aid recipient countries lost their political allegiance as a bargaining tool and were in a worse position to oppose the Bank's anti-corruption undertakings. The General Counsel noted the following in relation to separating anti-corruption activities from political affairs:

> The Bank can, in my view, take many actions to help the fight against corruption. It can conduct research on the causes and effects of this worldwide phenomenon. It can provide assistance, by mutual agreement, to enable its borrowing countries to curb corruption. It may take up the level of corruption as a subject of discussion in the dialogue with its borrowing members. And, if the level of corruption is high so as to have an adverse impact on the effectiveness of Bank assistance, according to factual and objective analysis, and the government is not taking serious measures to combat it, the Bank can take this as a factor in its lending strategy towards the country. The only legal barrier in this respect is that in doing so the Bank and its staff must be concerned only with the economic causes and effects and should refrain from intervening in the country's political affairs.
>
> (World Bank, 1997, p. 24)

In practice, however the distinction between intervening in fights against corruption for economic versus political causes could be very difficult. A very different example to consider is China.

China

China's development assistance has been clearly focused on technical assistance and cooperation, 'not interfering in the internal affairs of the recipient countries' (Xinhua, 2014). China's involvement in African States' development as well as increased trade between the regions has been evaluated in differing ways. At one end of the spectrum one finds arguments such as those put forward by Pehnelt and Abel (2007), that 'China is guilty of backing corrupt political elites in "rogue states" in exchange for exploitation rights or other forms of access to raw materials'. Commercial deals with corrupt governments and businesses could have the effect of fuelling corruption and be damaging to a country's economy and wider development. Nevertheless, a differing point of view has also been put forward. Namely, that China's involvement in trade and industries in African States contributes to improved infrastructure, offers opportunities for increased trade relations and investment, which can, in turn, generally strengthen the country.

China has attempted to dispel the views that it mostly invests in Africa in order to obtain resources. In 2011 it published a white paper on its development assistance, suggesting that their investment has been driven by friendship and pointing out that the majority of its investments are in infrastructure (Xinhua, 2011). The report, however, does not provide a detailed breakdown of assistance by countries, rather suggesting that 80 per cent of its international development assistance goes to least developed and low-income countries in Asia and Africa. Its second white paper released in 2014 details China's increased focus on social issues, such as education and healthcare, carefully stressing in the introduction:

> When providing foreign assistance, China adheres to the principles of not imposing any political conditions, not interfering in the internal affairs of the recipient countries and fully respecting their right to independently choosing their own paths and models of development. The basic principles China upholds in providing foreign assistance are mutual respect, equality, keeping promise, mutual benefits and win-win.
>
> (Xinhua, 2014)

Condon (2012, p. 5) notes that the 'West, which typically conditions its loans on initiatives like democracy promotion and corruption reduction, has labelled China a "rogue donor", whose actions will be damaging to Africa in the long run'. It may be worth considering, however, that the Global West is not the only or the definitive moral authority that has the ability to define what can constitute 'corrupt' behaviour. As pointed out by Le Billon (2008, p. 355) and referred to by the OECD (2009, p. 2), many people in Afghanistan consider the high salaries and profits that foreign consultants, contractors and NGOs receive to be a form of corruption. It is therefore important to assess to what extent particular interventions to address corruption will have local uptake and therefore the intended effect; and likewise whether not stressing governance reforms in international development assistance and trade will result in a deteriorated corruption situation.

An interesting example to consider is Angola in 2004, when it was offered an IMF loan for reconstruction purposes after the civil war. The loan, however, came with governance and transparency conditions attached (see Taylor, 2006, p. 946). Angola had large petroleum reserves and had been named as a rogue and extremely corrupt state (Condon, 2012, p. 8). Angola, however, rejected the IMF loan in favour of a $2 billion low-interest loan offered by China's Exim bank, which had no transparency and its governance conditions deemed as 'humiliating' by Angolan state officials (Taylor, 2006, pp. 947–948). Despite the lack of conditionality and transparency requirements, the Angolan government has made a significant number of steps towards increasing the transparency of its revenue and expenditure, including publishing monthly petroleum receipts on the website of its Ministry of Finance. The National Governance Resource Institute (2015) notes that

> The country's last bid rounds for exploitation acreage, in 2006, earned the praise of many international observers for opening the contract process to scrutiny. The government publicized the selection criteria and the bidding rules clearly, opened bids in public, and announced the size and specifications of the winning bids, including the signature bonuses.

Other issues, especially regarding the government's interaction with the civil society, clearly persist; nevertheless, progress has been made under the government's own initiative.

China's anti-corruption work, however, has been concentrated and received most attention domestically, where the Chinese government has shown a ruthless approach to corruption. Since Xi Jinping took office as the General Secretary of the Chinese Communist Party, he launched an anti-corruption campaign against both the 'lions and the flies' – the rank and file and the common officers in China – to eradicate corruption in all levels of administration and society. China's new government has charged hundreds of thousands of public officials with corruption, including those of very high rankings within the government and the military (see, for example, Kwong, 2015; Zhu, 2015). The country has imposed sizeable fines on multinational companies such as GlaxoSmithKline; and has increased the scope of its anti-corruption campaign internationally by bringing charges to corrupt officials living abroad (Lafraniere and Grobler, 2009). China's anti-corruption actions could be criticised as a political move against dissidents (see, for example, (Zhu, 2015, p. 612); an in-depth analysis of this is outside the scope of this chapter, however the numbers and seniority of those convicted are larger than had initially been expected and speak for the Chinese government's serious approach to anti-corruption and the message it is sending about those who engage in it.

Internal politics

Working on governance issues such as corruption can also stir the social order within a country. Prominent politicians, businessmen and other social figures are likely to be placed under increased scrutiny and subsequently sanctioned. Furthermore, anti-corruption campaigns may be used, or seen to be used, by the government as a tool against dissidents or opposition members, rather than to engender real change and accountability (Bayart, 1993; Chabal and Daloz, 1999). This is particularly due to the fact that often those who are in a position to implement large-scale anti-corruption reforms are those who stand to substantially benefit from the status quo (Lawson, 2009, p. 74).

Evidence on what works and unintended consequences

Zaum *et al.* (2012) have evaluated the strength of evidence of the impacts of different types of interventions, noting that in the majority of cases the evidence that would support the efficiency of the various interventions is contested and at times even points towards the ineffectiveness of interventions. The authors grouped the various anti-corruption interventions into the following categories: Direct Interventions (D), Indirect Interventions (I), Oversight Institutions (O), Civil Society Organisations (C), Budget Support (B), Donors' own systems (S) and Multilateral agreements on anti-corruption standards (M). Their findings are presented in Table 4.3.

Table 4.3 The evidence on the effectiveness of various anti-corruption interventions

Impact of the interventions	Weak strength of evidence	Fair strength of evidence	Strong strength of evidence
Effective	• Judician Reform (I) • Judicial Independence (O) • Media (C)	• Procurement (I) • Tax Reform (I)	• Public Financial Management (PFM)
Contested	• National Anti-Corruption Strategies (D) • Financial Intelligence Units (D) • Police reform (I) • Parliament (O) • Private sector • Direct Budget Support (B) • Donor Systems (S) • Multilateral Agreements (M)	• Anti-Corruption Laws (D) • Decentralisation (I) • NGOs/community Monitoring	• Supreme Audit Institutions (O)
Ineffective	• Ombudsperson (O)	• Anti-Corruption Authorities (D) • Civil Service Reform (I) • Corruption Conditionality (S)	

Source: Zaum *et al.* (2012).

The table shows that some interventions appear to be more effective than others, and also that there is a significant lack of evidence regarding the effectiveness of a large number of different types of interventions. A classification of the effectiveness of different approaches could be used to focus work on the interventions that are more likely to achieve their intended results; it also demonstrates that more work needs to be done to establish the effectiveness of a large number of interventions regularly funded by donors.

Furthermore, it is worth noting that it is difficult to measure the effectiveness of anti-corruption interventions, just as it is difficult to measure the extent of corruption present, and to compare the evolution of that data across different countries and over time (see section 3.2 on this). Nevertheless, an interesting approach to measuring the effectiveness of anti-corruption interventions is presented by Deane (2016, p. 9) – to look at 'how much concern is expressed by those who are or who wish to be corrupt'. Deane argues that if these groups are not concerned about particular anti-corruption interventions or institutions, these are not likely to have a significant effect on the levels of corruption. Identifying such people and their concern about particular interventions is clearly not an easy undertaking, however Deane presents an example of when it has been done – the case of Peru in the 1990s.

McMillan and Zoido (2004) discuss in detail the nature of bribes paid during President Fujimori's rule in Peru, which the authors argue was de facto run by Peru's secret-police chief, Vladimiro Montesinos Torres. The authors use the 'meticulous records' that Montesinos kept of his 'methodical' bribery of judges, politicians and the news media. These records included contracts setting out the terms of the transactions, written receipts for the bribes, as well as videotapes of his negotiations (McMillan and Zoido, 2004, p. 69). Comparing the amounts Montesinos was paying different groups of people who could present a threat to the political status quo indicates which of these groups were perceived to be a greater threat. The authors conclude that it was the media that represented the greatest threat to the Fujimori-Montesinos rule:

> The typical bribe paid to a television-channel owner was about a hundred times larger than that paid to a politician, which was somewhat larger than that paid to a judge. One single television channel's bribe was five times larger than the total of the opposition politicians' bribes. The strongest of the checks and balances, by Montesinos's revealed preference, was television.
> (McMillan and Zoido, 2004, p. 69)

DFID acknowledges the gaps in the evidence of what works in anti-corruption interventions and committed to 'expand its existing anti-corruption policy team to gather evidence, disseminate lessons and cultivate expertise' (DFID, 2014, p. 5). Accordingly, DFID has also been investing in programmes such as the £9.6m anti-corruption research programme on Anti-Corruption Evidence (ACE) to generate reliable data and evidence on what works in anti-corruption interventions and the interdependencies between different types of development and anti-corruption interventions (DFID, 2015a).

Costs of interventions

This section highlights two types of unintended consequences and costs of international development interventions that should be kept in mind when designing anti-corruption programming. The first one relates to the salaries that local staff are paid on international development programmes and the second one to the perceived effectiveness of development programmes by those funding the interventions. In the UK government's case these are the UK's taxpayers.

International organisations such as the WB, the EU and states' international development departments have been criticised for their unintended effects on staffing within the governments of developing states. In 1993, Bayart (1993, p. xiii) noted the WB's practice of 'recruiting the best African intellectuals – and paying them salaries based on international pay scales whilst simultaneously enjoining African governments to pay their own civil servants less'. International development specialists have observed this tendency and note that competent and qualified civil servants in countries that receive substantial amounts of international development assistance funds are soon recruited by international development organisations that pay significantly higher salaries. International foundations that offer even more generous remuneration packages, such as the Bill and Melinda Gates Foundation, can then recruit competent staff from these organisations. The World Bank (2014, p. 207) suggested nuances in the approaches of different donors to government capacity and staffing:

> donors with a small share of the aid in a country may focus more on delivering successful projects, even at the expense of government capacity – for example, by hiring the most qualified government administrators to run their projects. This collective action problem may be less severe where there is a dominant donor, who has a greater incentive to take a broader and longer-term view of the country's development.

Of course, the author is not suggesting that well paid positions within international development organisations should not be offered to competent individuals, from developing countries, who work for their governments. A mechanism to reduce the corrosive effects on the ability of governments to staff their ministries with competent, ambitious, moral and entrepreneurial staff is, however, needed. This might involve secondments, rotation schemes and scholarships for further study with requirements to work in the civil service.

The level of public support for not only anti-corruption activities but also international development in general is important for state-level funding of such activities to continue, in the long term therefore attention should also be paid to the public's perceptions within donor countries of international development organisations' effectiveness in addressing corruption. It is therefore imperative, in undertaking international development programmes, to balance delivering both long- and short-term results – to keep the funding and public faith in the work, as well as to ensure that the harder-to-tackle and endemic problems are addressed where possible. Striving for positive public opinion of international development, however, inevitably impacts on the said organisations' willingness to be transparent and disclose various aspects of its operations, in particular the failures, as will be discussed in the following chapters.

4.4 Summary

This chapter has set out the UK's approach to international development and its approach to combatting corruption. The UK works with a large number of different organisations and attempts to combat corruption within different contexts and institutions. This chapter has stressed that it is important to work to improve the entire systems within which each of these institutions operates (for example, to work with the investigatory, prosecutory and judiciary institutions to improve the legal sanctions system; or with the media as well as with the state institutions that can guarantee protection for whistleblowers).

Given the increased focus and demand for international development projects and public undertakings to demonstrate value for money, resources should be directed to where they can have the largest impact and efforts not spread too thinly. The OECD's peer review of DFID's development assistance in 2014 noted that the UK has room to improve in this regard:

> while the rationale for individual programmes is well developed, country portfolios are spread over many topics/priorities and it is not always clear how an understanding of the development context (and the potential role of the UK) translates into strategic country programmes. Spreading its activities too thinly can undermine DFID's impact and efficiency.
> (OECD, 2014b, p. 19)

There is a scarcity of data on what works in anti-corruption interventions; an issue that DFID is also taking steps to address. Issues of resources, ambition and politics within anti-corruption interventions were also highlighted. The nature of politics and political processes can influence what is generally regarded as corruption or, alternatively, lobbying or even strong representation of one's constituents. Furthermore, anti-corruption activities may themselves form or be seen as a political tool.

This chapter considered the different types of interventions and the UK's comparative advantage to make the most of its resources and capabilities. An example of DFID-funded projects that appear to play to the UK's comparative advantage would be its international efforts to facilitate the recovery of stolen assets. Recovery of stolen assets is not only a powerful deterrent for corrupt activities, it also provides developing countries with more capital while reducing their dependencies on foreign states.

The bigger picture should feature more prominently in international development considerations, as the wide variety of projects that international development organisations engage in may end up being counterproductive in the long run. Ultimately, it is worth asking what makes more of a difference to developing states and what kind of change would the states themselves like to see happen. In this context, international cooperation and the combining of resources from other donor states and local government institutions, as well as private sector, civil society and media organisations, and directing them to where they can make the most difference is important, and will be discussed in the next chapter.

Notes

1 The remainder of ODA was spent by other UK government developments such as the Foreign and Commonwealth Office and the Department of Health (DFID, 2015b).
2 The priority countries in 2016 were: Afghanistan, Bangladesh, Burma, the Democratic Republic of Congo, Ethiopia, Ghana, India, Kenya, Kyrgyzstan, Liberia, Malawi, Mozambique, Nepal, Nigeria, Occupied Palestinian Territories, Pakistan, Rwanda, Sierra Leone, Somalia, South Africa, Sudan, South Sudan, Tajikistan, Tanzania, Uganda, Yemen, Zambia and Zimbabwe (DFID, 2016b).
3 Another example of a country approached in such a manner is Nigeria, as discussed in the 2014 ICAI report on DFID's Approach to Anti-Corruption and its Impact on the Poor (ICAI, 2014).
4 This graph was compiled by collating the information available on DFID's devtracker website on all the projects relating to corruption (62 in total found by searching for the key word 'corruption') in 2016.
5 Examples of interdependencies that are relevant for states' development would include considering the optimal levels of regulations (as well as the enforcement of those regulations) that would discourage corruption and the incentives and ability for businesses to invest and innovate. Significant regulation of the banking sector, as is prevalent in India, for example, can stifle the development of the MPesa-type innovations that took place in Kenya.
6 It is worth noting that currently 22 out of 28 of DFID's priority countries are classified as fragile states or regions (IDC, 2016a, p. 25).
7 The FCPA is discussed in detail in section 5.3.
8 While a thorough analysis of the reasons why religion and work with religious institutions do not feature particularly prominently in the work of multilateral and government institutions is outside the scope of this book, the reasons that could account for this are a fear of excluding from assistance, religious minorities or people of religions with whom the programme does not work, as well as the generally smaller roles that religion plays in the everyday lives of people in Western societies where development assistance policies tend to originate.

Bibliography

Arvin, B.M., Baum, C.F., 1997. Tied and Untied Foreign Aid: A Theoretical and Empirical Analysis. *Keio Economic Studies* 34(2), 71–79.
Basel Institute on Governance, 2014. Asset Recovery/ICAR. Available at: www.basel governance.org/icar (accessed 12 December 2014).
Bayart, J.-F., 1993. *The State in Africa – The Politics of the Belly*. Addison Wesley Publishing, New York.
Brown, L., 2015. Britain May Have Blown £2m Helping Nigerians to Export Rocks. *Mail Online*.

But, J., Chan, S., 2013. Former ICAC Chief Timothy Tong Criticised For Breaching Spending Rules. *South China Morning Post.* 12 September.

Chabal, P., Daloz, J.-P., 1999. *Africa Works: Disorder as Political Instrument.* International African Institute, London.

Condon, M., 2012. China in Africa: What the Policy of Nonintervention Adds to the Western Development Dilemma. Praxis. *The Fletcher Journal of Human Security,* 27.

Conservative Party, 2015. *The Conservative Party Manifesto 2015.*

Cremer, G., 2008. *Corruption and Development Aid Confronting the Challenges,* translated by Elisabeth Schuth. Lynne Rienner Publishers, Boulder, CO.

CW, 2015. Corruption Watch: Off the Hook: Corporate Impunity and Law Reform in the UK: Corporate Liability Reform: Overview and Options. Corruption Watch UK. Available at: www.cw-uk.org/wp-content/uploads/2015/09/Corruption-Watch-Off-the-Hook-Report-September-2015.pdf.

David, R., 2010. Transitions to Clean Government: Amnesty as an Anticorruption Measure. *Australian Journal of Political Science* 45(3), 391–406. doi:10.1080/10361146.2010.509309.

Deane, J., 2016. Curbing Corruption and Fostering Accountability in Fragile Settings: Why an Imperilled Media Needs Better Support. BBC Media Action Working Paper, London.

de Oliveira, I.S., Lain, S., Winterbotham, E., Kerusauskaite, I., Glanville, M., 2016. *Fighting Corruption: The Case for Inclusive and Risk-Based Approaches (Workshop Report).* Royal United Services Institute for Defence and Security Studies.

DFID, 2016a. *Department for International Development: Annual Report and Accounts 2015–16.* Williams Lea Group on behalf of the Controller of Her Majesty's Stationery Office: DFID, London.

DFID, 2016b. *GREAT for Partnership.* DFID devtracker, London.

DFID, 2016c. *Implementation of the Regional Facility for Strengthening Transnational Responses to Countering Illicit Financial Flows, Corruption and Organised Crime in Africa (CIFFs).* DFID, London. Available at: https://devtracker.dfid.gov.uk/projects/GB-1-204227/documents.

DFID, 2015a. Statistics on International Development 2015 – Publications. DFID, London.

DFID, 2015b. DFID Annual Report and Accounts 2014–2015. Williams Lea Group on behalf of the Controller of Her Majesty's Stationery Office, London.

DFID, 2015c. Anti Corruption Evidence 'ACE' Programme Business Case and Summary. DevTracker Project GB-1-203752 Doc. Available at: https://devtracker.dfid.gov.uk/projects/GB-1-203752/documents (accessed 3 September 2016).

DFID, 2015d. Why Corruption Matters: Understanding Causes, Effects and How To Address Them: Evidence Paper on Corruption, February. DFID, London.

DFID, 2014. DFID Management Response to the Independent Commission for Aid Impact Recommendations on DFID's Approach to Anti-Corruption and its Impact on the Poor. DFID, London.

DFID, 2013a. DFID's Anti-Corruption Strategy for Zambia, January. DFID, London.

DFID, 2013b. DFID's Anti-Corruption Strategy for Uganda, January. DFID, London.

DFID, 2012. Uganda: UK Suspends Aid to Government – News stories, November. DFID, London.

DFID, 2011. Bilateral Aid Review (BAR): Technical Report March 2011. DFID, London.

Di John, J., 2010. Taxation, Resource Mobilisation, and State Performance. Crisis States Res. Centre, Working Papers.

Dix, S., Hussmann, K., Walton, G., 2012. *Risks of Corruption to State Legitimacy and Stability in Fragile States*. CMI, Bergen.

DOJ, 2012. US Restrains More Than $3 Million in Corruption Proceeds Related to Former Governor of Nigeria. US Department of Justice.

Doughty, S., 2013. Nigeria Aid Farce (Cont.): As UK Gives £1bn to Nation Joining the Space Race, its Corrupt Officials Allow £2bn of Oil to be Stolen Every Year. *Mail Online*. Available at: www.dailymail.co.uk/news/article-2426122/Nigeria-accepts-1bn-UK-aid-corrupt-officials-allow-2bn-oil-stolen-year.html (accessed 20 September 2016).

European Parliament, 2015. Cost of Corruption in Developing Countries: How Effectively is Aid Being Spent? European Parliament, Directorate-General for External Policies, Policy Department, Belgium.

Ferraz, C., Finan, F., 2008. Exposing Corrupt Politicians: The Effects of Brazil's Publicly Released Audits on Electoral Outcomes. *Quarterly Journal of Economics* 123(2), 703–745. doi:10.1162/qjec.2008.123.2.703.

Fofack, H., 2009. Stolen Asset Recovery: The Need for a Global Effort, in: Minter, W. Scarnecchia, T., Ndikumana, L., Boyce, J. (Eds), *Special Bulletin*, 29.

Gibson, J.L., Gouws, A., 2000. Social Identities and Political Intolerance: Linkages within the South African Mass Public. *American Journal of Political Science* 44(2), 278–292.

Gong, T., Wang, S., 2012. Indicators and Implications of Zero Tolerance of Corruption: The Case of Hong Kong. *Social Indicators Research* 112(3), 569–586. doi:10.1007/s11205-012-0071-3.

Gray, L., Hansen, K., Recica-Kirkbride, P., Mills, L., 2014. *Few and Far: The Hard Facts on Stolen Asset Recovery*. World Bank Publications, Washington, DC.

Greenberg, T.S., 2009. *Stolen Asset Recovery: A Good Practices Guide for Non-Conviction-Based Asset Forfeiture*. World Bank Publications, Washington DC.

Gulrajani, N., 2016. Bilateral versus Multilateral Aid Channels. ODI Report. Available at: www.odi.org/sites/odi.org.uk/files/resource-documents/10393.pdf.

Gupta, A., 1995. Blurred Boundaries: The Discourse of Corruption, the Culture of Politics, and the Imagined State. *American Ethnologist* 22(2), 375–402.

Hardin, R., 1997. *One For All: The Logic of Group Conflict*. Princeton University Press, Princeton, NJ.

Heywood, P., 2016. Written Evidence – Professor Paul Heywood. Available at: http://data.parliament.uk/writtenevidence/committeeevidence.svc/evidencedocument/international-development-committee/tackling-corruption-overseas/written/29840.html

HL, 1986. Fraud Trials Committee Report (*Hansard*, 10 February 1986). *Hansard*. Available at: http://hansard.millbanksystems.com/lords/1986/feb/10/fraud-trials-committee-report.

HMG, 2014. UK Anti-Corruption Plan. December. Available at: www.gov.uk/government/uploads/system/uploads/attachment_data/file/388894/UKantiCorruptionPlan.pdf.

HMT, DFID, 2015. UK Aid: Tackling Global Challenges in the National Interest. Available at: www.gov.uk/government/uploads/system/uploads/attachment_data/file/478834/ODA_strategy_final_web_0905.pdf.

Holland, J., Thirkell, A., Trepanier, E., Earle, L., 2009. Measuring Change and Results in Voice and Accountability Work. DFID Department of International Development Working Paper.

ICAC, 2016. ICAC Statement. ICAC.

ICAI, 2016. UK Aid's Contribution to Tackling Tax Avoidance and Evasion. ICAI. Available at: http://icai.independent.gov.uk/report/tax/.

ICAI, 2014. DFID's Approach to Anti-Corruption and its Impact on the Poor. Report.

IDC, 2016a. UK Aid: Allocation of Resources: Interim Report, Third Report of Session 2015–2016.
IDC, 2016b. Role – International Development Committee. UK Parliament. Available at: www.parliament.uk/business/committees/committees-a-z/commons-select/international-development-committee/role/ (accessed 20 September 2016).
Jennett, V., 2006. *Categorization of Anti-corruption Interventions*. Anti-Corruption Resource Centre, U4 Helpdesk.
Johnson, J., Soreide, T., 2013. Methods for Learning What Works and Why in Anti-corruption: An Introduction to Evaluation Methods for Practitioners. *U4 Issue* 8, 40. Chr. Michelsen Institute, Bergen.
Johnson, J., Aiko, R., Messick, R., Mwombela, S., Schütte, S., Sengu, H., 2016. Strengthening Tanzania's Anti-Corruption Action (STACA) Programme. A Case Study Evaluation March 2016. Chr. Michelsen Institute in collaboration with REPOA. Available at: www.gov.uk/government/uploads/system/uploads/attachment_data/file/533695/Strengthening-Tanzania-Anti-Corruption-Action-Programme.pdf.
Kemp, M.C., Kojima, S., 1985. Tied Aid and the Paradoxes of Donor-Enrichment and Recipient-Impoverishment. *International Economic Review* 26(3), 721–729. doi:10.2307/2526716.
Khan, M., 2016. *Evidence to the International Development Committee on Tackling Corruption Overseas*. IDC.
Kupatadze, A., 2015. Georgia: Breaking Out Of A Vicious Cycle? Available at: www.againstcorruptioneuwp-Contentuploads201505D3-GeorgiaKupatadzepdf.
Kwong, J., 2015. *The Political Economy of Corruption in China*. Routledge, Abingdon, Oxon.
Lafraniere, S., Grobler, J., 2009. China Spreads Aid in Africa, With a Catch. *New York Times*.
Lawson, L., 2009. The Politics of Anti-corruption Reform in Africa. *Journal of Modern African Studies* 47(1), 73–100.
Le Billon, P., 2008. Corrupting Peace? Peacebuilding and Post-conflict Corruption. *International Peacekeeping* 15(3), 344–361.
Le Billon, P., 2003. Buying Peace or Fuelling War: The Role of Corruption in Armed Conflicts. *Journal of International Development* 15(4), 413–426.
Lethbridge, H.J., 1985. *Hard Graft in Hong Kong: Scandal, Corruption, the ICAC*. Oxford University Press, Oxford.
Magone, C., Neuman, M., Weissman, F., 2012. *Humanitarian Negotiations Revealed: The MSF Experience*. Oxford University Press, Oxford.
Makabila, S., 2013. Kenya : Director of Public Prosecutions' Office to Recruit 300 Staff in Bid to Devolve Services. August. *The Standard*. Standard Digital.
Manion, M., 2004. *Corruption by Design: Building Clean Government in Mainland China and Hong Kong*. Harvard University Press, Cambridge, MA.
Marquette, H., Mallett, R., Moore, M., 2014. Was UK Aid Watchdog Right to Accuse DfID of Failing to Tackle Corruption? *Guardian*.
Martin, D., 2014. Confirmed: Our Foreign Aid Fuels Corruption – Official Watchdog's Verdict on Aid Spending That Cameron Has Defiantly Ring-Fenced. *Mail Online*.
McMillan, J., Zoido, P., 2004. How to Subvert Democracy: Montesinos in Peru. *Journal of Economic Perspective* 18(4), 69–92.
Meagher, P., 2005. Anti-corruption Agencies: Rhetoric versus Reality. *Journal Policy Reform* 8(1), 69–103.

Ministry of Justice, 2011. The Bribery Act 2010 – THE BRIBERY ACT 2010 Guidance about procedures which relevant commercial organisations can put into place to prevent persons associated with them from bribing (section 9 of the Bribery Act 2010). Ministry of Justice, bribery-act-2010-guidance.pdf.

Morrissey, O., White, H., 1996. Evaluating the Concessionality of Tied Aid. *Manchester School* 64(2), 208–226. doi:10.1111/j.1467-9957.1996.tb00481.x.

Murdoch, L., 2016. 'I Still Hear Corruption': Philippines President Lays Off Thousands. *Sydney Morning Herald.*

National Governance Resource Institute, 2015. Angola. Available at: www.resource governance.org/our-work/country/angola.

North, D.C., Wallis, J.J., Weingast, B.R., 2009. *Violence and Social Orders: A Conceptual Framework for Interpreting Recorded Human History, 1st edition.* Cambridge University Press, Cambridge; New York.

OAG Nigeria, 2007. Report of the Auditor-General for the Federation to the National Assembly on the Accounts of the Government of the Federation for the year ended 31 December, 2007. Office of the Auditor General for the Federal Republic of Nigeria. Available at: www.oaugf.gov.ng/AuditReport.html.

OCCRP, 2016. Organised Crime and Corruption Reporting Project: About us. Available at: www.occrp.org/en/about-us (accessed 21 September 2016).

OECD, 2016. List of CRS Purpose Codes. Available at: www.oecd.org/dac/stats/documentupload/2012%20CRS%20purpose%20codes%20EN.pdf.

OECD, 2015. Development Co-operation Report 2015: Making Partnerships Effective Coalitions for Action. Organisation for Economic Co-operation and Development, Paris.

OECD, 2014a. *OECD Development Co-operation Peer Reviews: United Kingdom 2014, OECD Development Co-operation Peer Reviews.* OECD Publishing.

OECD, 2014b. OECD Foreign Bribery Report – An Analysis of the Crime of Bribery of Foreign Public Officials. OECD. Available at: www.oecd.org/daf/oecd-foreign-bribery-report-9789264226616-en.htm.

OECD, 2009. *Working Towards Common Donor Responses to Corruption: Joint Donor Responses Vis-À-Vis Corruption in Afghanistan: Myth or Reality?* OECD, Paris.

Olson, J., Kerusauskaite, I., Clarke, J., Francino, M., 2016. Financial Accountability and Anti-Corruption Partnerships Programme Scoping Report.

ONE, 2014. The Trillion Dollar Scandal. ONE. Available at: https://s3.amazonaws.com/one.org/pdfs/Trillion_Dollar_Scandal_report_EN.pdf.

Osborne, D., 1997. Corruption as Counter-culture: Attitudes to Bribery in Local and Global Society, in: Rider, B.A.K. (Ed.), *Corruption: The Enemy Within.* Kluwer Law International, The Hague; Boston, pp. 9–34.

Paxton, P., 2002. Social Capital and Democracy: An Interdependent Relationship. *American Sociological Review* 67(2), 254–277.

Pehnelt, G., Abel, M., 2007. *China's Development Policy in Africa (No. 1).* The South African Institute of International Affairs, SAIIA National Office Bearers.

Punch, M., 2000. Police Corruption and its Prevention. *European Journal of Criminal Policy Res* 8(3), 301–324. doi:10.1023/A:1008777013115.

Putnam, R.D., 2002. *Democracies in Flux: The Evolution of Social Capital in Contemporary Society.* Oxford University Press, Oxford.

Quah, J.S., 2009. Combating Corruption in the Asia-Pacific Countries: What Do We Know and What Needs to Be Done? *International Public Management Review* 10(1), 5–33.

Reinikka, R., Svensson, J., 2004. *The Power of Information: Evidence from a Newspaper Campaign to Reduce Capture.* World Bank Publications.

Reuters, 2016. Philippines' Duterte Offers Reward for Corrupt Police Linked to Drugs. *Reuters*.

Riley-Smith, B., 2014. British Aid Money is Funding Corruption Overseas, Damning New Report Finds. *Telegraph*.

Rose-Ackerman, S., 1999. *Corruption and Government: Causes, Consequences and Reform*. Cambridge University Press, Cambridge.

Sebudubudu, D., 2002. Combatting Corruption in Southern Africa: An Examination of Anti-corruption Agencies in Botswana, South Africa and Namibia (PhD). University of Leeds.

SEC, 2015. 2015 Annual Report to Congress on the Dodd-Frank Whistleblower Program. The US Securities and Exchange Commission. Available at: www.sec.gov/about/offices/owb/annual-report-2015.pdf.

Shulman, S., 2013. Criminalization of Bribery: Can the Foreign Corrupt Practices Act Be Applicable to the Anti-Bribery Provisions of the United Nations Convention Against Corruption? *The. Am U Intl Rev* 29, 717.

StAR, 2016a. Stolen Asset Recovery Initiative (StAR). Available at: http://star.worldbank.org/star/ (accessed 24 September 2016).

StAR, 2016b. StAR – Stolen Asset Recovery Initiative – Corruption Cases – James Ibori (United States).

Tanzi, V., Davoodi, H.R., 2000. Corruption, Growth, and Public Finances. IMF Working Paper, pp. 1–27. Available at: https://ssrn.com/abstract=880260.

Taylor, I., 2006. China's Oil Diplomacy in Africa. *International Affairs* 82(5) 937–959. doi:10.1111/j.1468-2346.2006.00579.x.

The Economist, 2016. Fighting Corruption: Cleaning Up. *The Economist* June, p. 16.

TI (Transparency International), 2016a. Written Evidence – Transparency International & Transparency International UK. IDC. Available at: http://data.parliament.uk/writtenevidence/committeeevidence.svc/evidencedocument/international-development-committee/tackling-corruption-overseas/written/29947.html.

TI, 2016b. Transparency International – Global Corruption Barometer 2013. Available at: www.transparency.org/gcb2013 (accessed 16 September 2016).

TI, 2016c. Written Evidence – Transparency International & Transparency International UK. Available at: http://data.parliament.uk/writtenevidence/committeeevidence.svc/evidencedocument/international-development-committee/tackling-corruption-overseas/written/29947.html.

TI, 2013. Research – CPI, Overview. Available at: www.transparency.org/research/cpi/overview (accessed 30 April 2013).

Toye, J., Moore, M., 1998. Taxation, Corruption and Reform. *European Journal of Dev. Res.* 10(1), 60–84.

UN, 2014. International Anti-Corruption Day, 9 December. UN.

US Department of Justice, 2013. *UBS Securities Japan Co Ltd Sentenced for Long-running Manipulation of Libor*. US Department of Justice.

USAID, 2005. *USAID Anti-corruption Strategy (No. PD-ACA-557)*. Washington, DC.

Weissmann, A., Newman, D., 2007. Rethinking Criminal Corporate Liability. *Indiana Law Journal* 82, 441–451.

Widmalm, S., 2008. *Decentralisation, Corruption and Social Capital: From India to the West*. Sage Publications, India.

WIN-Gallup International, 2012. Global Index of Religion and Atheism (Press Release). WIN-Gallup International. Available at: http://sidmennt.is/wp-content/uploads/Gallup-International-um-tr%C3%BA-og-tr%C3%BAleysi-2012.pdf.

World Bank, 2014. Helping Countries Combat Corruption: The Role of the World Bank. Available at: www1.worldbank.org/publicsector/anticorrupt/corruptn/cor02.htm.
World Bank, 1997. *Helping Countries Combat Corruption: The Role of the World Bank.* The World Bank, Washington, DC.
World Bank, 1996. Annual Meetings Address by James D. Wolfensohn President The World Bank, 1 October. Available at: http://web.worldbank.org/WBSITE/EXTERNAL/EXTABOUTUS/ORGANIZATION/EXTPRESIDENT/EXTPASTPRESIDENTS/PRESIDENTEXTERNAL/0,,contentMDK:20025269~menuPK:232083~pagePK:159837~piPK:159808~theSitePK:227585,00.html (accessed 3 September 2016).
Xinhua, 2014. *China's Foreign Aid (2014)*. Information Office of the State Council, The People's Republic of China, Beijing.
Xinhua, 2011. *China's Foreign Aid*. Information Office of the State Council, The People's Republic of China, Beijing.
Zaum, D., Taxell, N., Johnson, J., 2012. *Mapping Evidence Gaps in Anti-Corruption: Assessing the State of the Operationally Relevant Evidence on Donors' Actions and Approaches to Reducing Corruption.* U4 Anti-Corruption Resource Centre.
Zhu, L., 2015. Punishing Corrupt Officials in China. *The China Quarterly* 223, 595–617.
Zinkernagel, G.F., Pereira, P.G., De Simone, F., 2014. *The Role of Donors in the Recovery of Stolen Assets, U4 Issue.* Chr. Michelsen Institute, Bergen.

5 International law and development
Where anti-corruption interventions fit in

We have entered an era of international law in which international law serves not only the interests of individual States, but looks beyond them and their parochial concerns to the greater interests of humanity and planetary welfare.

(Judge Weeramantry, 1997)[1]

5.1 Law and development

Broadly, law and development, as initiatives, both aim to achieve the goal of improving society and the lives of individuals within it. Both have considered issues of access to rights and justice in the literature and in practical undertakings. Corruption in particular has become a key theme tackled by both legal institutions and approaches, as well as within the international development industry. Corruption is already being conceptualised 'as a violation of human rights' by various institutions, such as the African Commission and the Committee on the Rights of the Child (Olaniyan, 2014, p. 313). This is due to the corrosive effects that corruption has on the rule of law, governance and the application of human rights law. The South African Constitutional Court, in *S v Shaik and Others*, noted that '[c]ourts must send out an unequivocal message that corruption will not be tolerated and that punishment will be appropriately severe' (*S v Shaik and Others* [2007] (1) SA 240 (SCA) [223]).

This section will give a brief overview of how law and development have historically related to and influenced one another, and consider how law and development initiatives have historically been linked to address issues such as corruption.

A key theme running through this chapter relates to qualifying issues as those 'of concern to humanity' versus domestic issues of sovereign states (see, for example, Hey, 2010, p. 51). The latter would limit the extent to which foreign states and international organisations could intervene to address issues on those matters. The former, however, can provide reasons for interventions, particularly to empower people to demand, from their state – and failing that, using international fora – what they are rightfully entitled to.[2] As noted by Judge Weeramantry (1997), international law now pays a lot more attention to general interests of 'humanity and planetary welfare' rather than just the interests of individual states.

Corruption is now almost universally being understood as a key factor preventing people from accessing services, goods and opportunities that they are entitled to, as discussed in Chapters 2 and 3. The extent to which anti-corruption provisions empower individuals to challenge their governments and institutions, however, is less clear. This section will consider this question in relation to the provisions of international law and institutions on anti-corruption.

Historical evolution of the 'law and development' theory and practice

Traditionally, development studies literature has largely been focused on economic growth and economics as a discipline. Law has featured in the literature, though mostly as an instrument to enable and further economic growth and development. The relationship between law and economic development has been considered centuries ago by authors such as Marx (see, for example, Marx, 1995) and Weber (see, for example, Weber, 1978), however it was not until after the Second World War that legal issues and reforms became an important part of development agendas and literature. Trubek and Santos (2006) suggest the existence of three 'moments' in law and development theory, when the role of law in development had crystallised into a widely accepted and relatively comprehensive orthodoxy. These moments largely follow the predominant economic and development theories that guided the focus and works of international organisations and Western governments at the time.

Accordingly, Trubek and Santos (2006, p. 5) argue that the first moment, which emerged in the 1950s–1960s, can be characterised as the 'law and developmental state' period. Law was seen as an instrument for state policy to manage the economy and to modernise traditional societies. The moment was characterised by the following assumptions: 'that import substitution in the internal market is the engine of growth; scarce savings must be directed to key investment areas; the private sector is too weak to provide "take-off" to self-sustaining growth; and "traditional sectors" will resist change' (ibid.). The state was regarded as the best actor, capable of ensuring economic growth, by allocating surpluses to where it saw fit, directing the economy and regulating foreign capital. Development was seen as a linear process, as evidenced by Rostow (1990) evoking the 'five stages of development' that countries sequentially follow, from a traditional agricultural, to more specialised manufacturing and ultimately to a mass-consumption society, in their 'take off to sustained growth'. Law was considered to be a tool at the state's disposal to change economic behaviour, and create modern formal structures to enable efficient state macro-economic control. The first law and development moment was therefore primarily concerned with public law, and sought to transplant regulatory laws from more advanced states.

The second moment, starting in the 1980s and largely based on neo-liberal ideas in economics, expanded the role of law in development to it being regarded 'more as a framework for market activity than as an instrument of state power' (Trubek and Santos, 2006, p. 1). As the neo-liberal theory[3] in economics regarded well-functioning markets as necessary and largely sufficient for economic growth (which was at the time largely equated to development in general), due to its perceived role as a corrective mechanism for market failures, law became seen as a key part and an objective of development, rather than merely being its tool. Law was therefore considered the foundation for market relations, and a limit on state power; and subsequently received a lot more attention and funding. Emphasis shifted to private law (with the main aims of protecting private property, ensuring contract enforceability and facilitating market transactions) as opposed to the previous concern with public and administrative law. As markets and their rules were considered universal, the need for context-specific laws to foster markets and facilitate private transactions was not seen as necessary. The essence of the second moment in law and development is well explained by Trubek and Santos (2006, p. 2):

> Attention shifted from the establishment of an administrative state to the core institutions of private law, the role of the judiciary in protecting businesses against the intrusions of government, and the need to change local laws to facilitate integration into the world economy. Not much attention was paid to regulatory law. When it was, regulation was often presented as an unnecessary intrusion on the market. Neoliberal law and development thought focused primarily on the law of the market: relatively little concern was shown for law as a guarantor of political and civil rights or as protector of the weak and disadvantaged.

Scholars, governments and international organisations alike started to reassess the second moment theories and assumptions as the law and development projects, as well as the economies of many developing countries which, to some extent, implemented neo-liberal reforms, failed to perform as expected. As such, the third, and current, moment started emerging in the 1990s. The moment was characterised by the realisation that unregulated markets do not necessarily function efficiently (due to issues such as transaction costs and information asymmetries) or create desirable social outcomes; that social issues such as poverty, deprivation and inequalities would not automatically disappear with economic growth, but, in most cases, would have to be addressed separately; and ultimately that laws transplanted from different contexts, social norms and institutional environments are not likely to have the desired impact on other societies, therefore local legal and political institutions have a role to play in the development of their countries and communities (see Trubek and Santos, 2006, pp. 6–7). Thus, as the notion of development itself was expanded to include the social, human, political and legal aspects[4] in addition to economic considerations, state intervention once again became justifiable and addressable by law. This was notably accompanied by the development of international, human rights law and the legal frameworks to protect individuals' social, political and economic rights. It is within the context of this third moment of law and development that we examine the extent to which arguably the most vulnerable people in developing countries have been granted rights and access to systems of justice.

Legal pluralism

A significant undertaking relating to 'law and development' was an attempt to tackle legal pluralism. The multitude of sources of international law, which coexist with national and regional laws, as well as cultural and religious norms, or legal pluralism, poses the question of priorities and hierarchies, namely, in the case of conflicting laws, which sources are to be considered superior. Legal pluralism is also perceived to increase uncertainty and the unpredictability of others' actions, or the future validity of one law or another in decentralised justice systems, with local courts applying local laws and customs that would not necessarily be known or accepted by all the parties concerned in a dispute (see Janse, 2013). This is particularly relevant if a developing state or region is attempting to boost its economy by attracting foreign investment. Therefore, legal pluralism (including indigenous laws and dispute settlement mechanisms) was, until recently, largely considered as an obstacle to economic development, and 'law and development' projects have largely attempted to 'solve' the issue of a plurality of legal sources, especially in developing countries.

Legal pluralism on a national level

It is widely quoted that 80–90 per cent of disputes in developing countries are being resolved using non-state or informal justice mechanisms – this may include religious or customary justice systems (policing, adjudication mechanisms, etc.), vigilance groups, work-based security groups, restorative justice community-based organisations or peace committees (see Baker, 2010, pp. 208–209; Chirayath et al., 2005, p. 3; OECD DAC, 2007, p. 17; Wojkowska, 2006). This was, however, seen by Western states and international organisations as a negative issue to be addressed. The development industry and scholarship suggested that Western-style contract and property laws and judiciaries were necessary to attract significant levels of investment and therefore to bring about economic growth (Janse, 2013, p. 183). These views were largely influenced by the arguments of Hernando De Soto (2002, 2003), who argued that an official legal system, especially formal property rights, could help the poor in developing countries bring to life their previously 'dead capital' in order to obtain credit and expand or start businesses, and to access more impartial systems of justice in case of conflict (when the ownership of a business or a land could be proved). De Soto (ibid.) suggested that formalisation and enforcement of property rights would help the state and region to collect taxes and therefore improve the general welfare of the people. However, it would be very difficult to prove the existence of direct causal relationships between institutionalising formal legal systems and improving the welfare and access to justice of vulnerable people.

In fact, the importance and the potential benefits of informal or non-state mechanisms have recently been recognised by international organisations, Western states and their agencies, which had previously been largely focused on the formal state justice systems (Faundez, 2011). The law and development scholarship is now calling for more participatory and inclusive approaches to law in the context of development. Accordingly, Carfield (2011, p. 743) argues that:

> [s]cholars and practitioners must abandon the question, how can 'we' change 'them' and instead begin by asking a different question: in what ways, if any, does a community want to change the rules it operates by and how can external actors assist in that process?

It is indeed doubtful whether transposing systems of justice and laws, which people did not make or consent to, onto different states while ignoring their cultural, political and security situations can be effective. Authors such as Janse (2013, p. 183) argue that the majority of people in developing countries have either no access to, or little respect for, state systems of justice. Traditional justice systems are faster at dealing with cases, less costly, less bureaucratic and the general public is more familiar with, and accustomed to, their proceedings. The people who do have access to formal justice systems tend to be from the more advantaged social backgrounds, the more educated, middle and upper class and mostly men (see Otto, 2009; Otto and Hoekema, 2012; Tamanaha, 2009). Accordingly, the poor not only less frequently participate in these newly established formal legal state structures transposed from other societies and therefore do not benefit from them, but there are also examples of those who are more familiar with the system taking advantage of those who are not, further deepening social inequalities and disadvantaging the most vulnerable segments of society. In some societies women are likely to be severely disadvantaged by formal titling of land and the institutional processes that accompany it, as men are preferred in cases of ownership titling and transfer (Lund, 2008; Manji, 2006). It can also result in multiple and potentially clashing systems of justice (in the sense of enforcement and attribution of rights) which, in turn, would result in greater uncertainty (Tamanaha, 2008), thus not only not achieving the positive outcomes suggested by de Soto, but also generating new problems for developing societies.

On the other hand, Wojkowska (2006, p. 5) notes that one has to be wary of uncritically strengthening informal justice systems as they may be discriminatory in regards to minority groups, 'inferior' castes, women, etc. and can be susceptible to elite capture.

Legal pluralism on an international level

Theoretical approaches to the relationship between national and international laws in the legal literature have been largely revolving around the monism-dualism debate. The debate addresses the question whether international and domestic legal systems constitute one single, or two disparate legal orders, and which set of laws has primacy (either within the same order, or which order is to be considered superior). The debate is relevant to have an accurate understanding of the functioning of the international legal system and its hierarchies, which, in turn, is necessary for any alterations to the system to be made.

The dualist position views the international and national legal systems as distinct and rather independent, noting the different levels of social relations (individuals or states) addressed by each of the legal systems, and sources of the laws (a common will of states versus a state's own legislative mechanisms) (see, for example, Ago, 1957; Triepel, 1899). State laws are seen as superior in their jurisdictions to international law. Monism portrays national and international law as part of one legal order, assuming relative coherence between the two levels of law. Starke (1936, p. 70) argues:

> the state as a legal concept is merely a schema serving to embrace the totality of legal norms which apply over certain persons within a defined territorial area; the state and the law may indeed be described as synonymous terms ... [therefore the] responsibility of a state is nothing more than a normative expression denoting that the collectivity of individuals constrained by a defined totality of legal norms [is] bound to make a breach of a wrong which has been inputted to the state.

International law is therefore understood to bind individuals indirectly, through the state, and by extension is seen as superior to domestic laws. Kelsen (1945), who regarded jurisprudence as a science, argued that only monism was consistent with the legal character of international law.

Fitzmaurice (1957, p. 71) offers an alternative and practical view, rejecting the superiority of either national or domestic laws over one another, and suggesting that 'international and domestic law both exist independently, as the dualist view predicates, but ... they are both subordinate to a third, superior judicial order which governs them, delimits their respective spheres, and resolves conflict between them'. The two legal systems are regarded as addressing different spheres, and are therefore not in competition or conflict with one another. Shaw (2013, p. 132) calls such a view a 'recognised theoretical framework tied to reality'; and Fitzmaurice notes it would be more acceptable to proponents of the natural rather than the positive law school.

It is worth acknowledging, as noted by Rothwell and Kaye (2011, p. 160), the 'growing encroachment of international law upon areas of legal regulation traditionally considered within the confines of municipal law'. International law, as noted previously, is no longer simply concerned with inter-state affairs, but also directly addresses the rights and well-being of citizens within other sovereign states (human rights and humanitarian law). There is also a growing tendency for domestic courts to be used to address violations of international law.[5]

As international law has traditionally focused on the relations among states, transnational law was proposed by Philip Jessup in 1956 'instead of "international law" ... to include all law which regulates actions or events that transcend national frontiers. Both public and private international law are included, as are other rules which do not wholly fit into such standard categories' (Jessup, 1956, p. 136). Transnational law is therefore concerned with transborder issues involving states, corporations, NGOs, individuals, as well as interest and other groups. It would concern cases such as disputes arising from multiple companies from different countries implementing a World Bank financed project in a developing state; or, as suggested by Menkel-Meadow (2011, p. 98), '[a] woman, fearing domestic violence from her military officer husband in another country, seek[ing] political asylum in the United States'.

Scholars have also questioned whether the conflict of laws based on territorial boundaries (between different national laws or between international and national laws) is the most efficient one to study and characterise legal systems. Teubner (1988, p. 32) suggests that perhaps it would be more pertinent for legal scholarship to shift its emphasis towards the conflict between different subsystems (the economic sphere, the political sphere, culture, religion, family issues etc.) of the world. De Sousa Santos (1987, pp. 297–298) qualifies it as 'interlegality', which is the 'inter-section of different legal orders':

> [n]ot the legal pluralism of traditional legal anthropology in which the different legal orders are conceived as separate entities coexisting in the same political space, but rather the conception of different legal spaces superposed, interpenetrated and mixed in our minds as much as in our actions, in occasions of qualitative leaps of sweeping crises in our life trajectories as well as in the dull routine of eventless everyday life.

Whereas the nature of the relationship between international and domestic laws is a matter still contested among scholars, it is worth noting that there is an increasing dialogue between practitioners and academics working on law and development, and legal pluralism in particular. This is evidenced by projects such as the World Bank's efforts to bring together its staff with scholars critical of a number of the organisations' initiatives and approaches. This takes the form of conferences and round-table discussions, and results in insightful publications and the furthering of debates on the issues (see, for example, Harper, 2011; Tamanaha et al., 2012; Ubink and McInerney, 2011).

In any case, increasing cooperation and mutual influence of legal agreements can be noted not only in a vertical sense (between international and domestic legal institutions), but also horizontally (among states). For example, in the context of refugee law, Goodwin-Gill notes the importance and the increase of cases of states considering each other's case law when applying the Refugee Convention (see Lambert and Goodwin-Gill, 2010, chapter 11). The appropriateness of some international legal systems in non-Western contexts, however, is questionable, and it is worth keeping in mind power disparities, in addition to inherent differences among states, when addressing the relationship between states and international law. This is further elaborated upon in section 5.2.

5.2 International law

Theoretical accounts for international law

The foundations of modern international law are deeply rooted in Western (Judeo-Christian) philosophical, political and legal thought. The relations between states, sovereigns and their envoys were already debated in Roman times, in the form of the concept of 'ius gentum', or 'the law of nations'. 'International law' was a term was coined by Jeremy Bentham in 1789, and in the following century was established in preference to the terms 'ius gentum' and Vattel's 'droit des gens' (see Crawford, 2012, p. 3). Given the complexity surrounding its scope, conception, interpretation, policing and enforcement, it is not surprising that the nature of international law has been the subject of ongoing theoretical and philosophical debate – historically primarily within legal and international relations scholarship,[6] but has also been addressed by philosophers, sociologists, anthropologists and development scholars.

The question of whether international law can be considered as 'law', was notably discussed among legal philosophers in the eighteenth and nineteenth centuries, and is still relevant today. Austin defined law as commands backed by threats of sanctions (see, for example, Austin, 1832). Therefore, according to Austin, international law cannot be regarded as 'law' in its proper sense as there is no sovereign power to enforce it. Austin considered international law as a form of positive morality, which compares to the rules that govern clubs or societies. Authors such as Bentham (1789), however, considered that moral sanctions (fear of acts of hostility or denial of reciprocal benefits) formed a sufficient basis for international law to qualify as 'law'. Hart (1961) rejected the oversimplified perception of the centrality of sanctions in law, referring to the multitude of other functions performed by international law – such as facilitating cooperation, coordination and other administrative functions that do not require the threat of punitive action in order to be effective. As put by Rosenne (1984, p. 2), international law is 'a law of coordination' rather than of 'subordination'. More recently, Byers (1997) and Koskenniemi (2009) have been reiterating the normative and obligation-creating aspects of international law.

Some empirical studies, however, dispute the effectiveness of the normative aspects of international law. Although empirical studies on the effect of international human rights treaties on states' practices have been suggesting varying and often incompatible results (see, for example, Hill, 2010), some interesting theoretical analyses have been put forward. Vreeland (2008) observes that the effect that the ratification of the United Nations Convention against Torture (UNCAT) has very much depends on the domestic politics of the state in question. Namely, Vreeland (2008), citing cases from Nigeria, Gabon and Ivory Coast, observed that multi-party dictatorships (i.e. dictatorial regimes where political power is shared or to some extent contested) are more likely to sign and ratify the Convention than one-party dictatorships. At the same time, however, they are also more prone to violating their obligations under the Convention. The author explained his observations by suggesting that multi-party dictatorships are under more pressure from domestic actors to engage in international human rights treaties, and the government sees it as a low-cost mechanism to improve its image and legitimacy domestically and abroad. One-party dictatorships, on the other hand, are rather unwilling to cave-in to similar demands from their citizens and national groups, fearing to set a precedent or send the message that political dissent will be tolerated. Therefore, ratification of the UNCAT, according to Vreeland (2008), has little or no intended effect on state practices. Hill (2010) suggests interesting variations in the effects that different human rights treaties and regimes have on state practices. In particular, that the UNCAT and the International Covenant on Civil and Political Rights (ICCPR) lead to reduced respect for physical integrity rights, while ratification of the Convention on the Elimination of All Forms of Discrimination against Women (CEDAW) has a positive impact on women's rights situations. Hill (2010, p. 1172) argues that the reason for the differences in the effects may lie in the fact that women, as a subset of the population, do not generally pose a threat to the government's position in power, whereas political dissidents, for whom the UNCAT and the ICCPR are more relevant, may pose a threat to the stability of a non-democratic government.

Shaw (2013, p. 6), however, suggests:

> just as incidents of murder, robbery and rape do occur within national legal orders without destroying the system as such, so analogously assaults upon international legal rules point to the weaknesses of the system without denigrating their validity or their necessity.

In accordance with Louis Henkin's (1979, p. 47) famous quote that '[i]t is probably the case that almost all nations observe almost all principles of international law and almost all of their obligations almost all of the time', Shaw (2013, p. 6) suggests that the rare exceptions of states violating international law are the ones that receive the most publicity, hence the general public perception of international law being violated more often than it actually is.

Other scholars present a more critical view of the nature of the law itself. Teubner (1988, p. 16) calls law self-reproducing and self-referencing – 'not only in the sense of law made by human hands, but in the sense of law made by law'. Teubner (1988, p. 15) recalls a Talmudic story:

> once during a heated halachic discussion, when no agreement could be reached, Rabbi Eliezer, whose detailed, elegantly justified legal opinion was not shared by the majority, said that if he were right, a carob tree outside would move to prove it. When it did move, the other rabbis remained unimpressed. Eliezer claimed that if he were right, a nearby stream would flow backward – and it did; he claimed that the schoolhouse walls would bend – and they did. But the rabbis were not impressed by these wonders either. Finally, he said heaven itself would prove him right. Thereupon a Heavenly

Voice confirmed Eliezer's position. Yet the rabbis disagreed even with this voice, saying: 'We pay no attention to a Heavenly Voice, because Thou hast long since written in the Torah at Mount Sinai, after the majority must one incline.'

Therefore, while being dependent on the past, law can be essentially unpredictable (dictated by the majority opinion or previous, though not entirely relevant, laws). Furthermore, the self-referencing nature of law can be practically problematic. For example, the fact that the highest laws of a state, the constitution and its norms, can only be amended in accordance with the constitution (and the procedures laid out therein) and its norms, creates a self-referencing regime with no real checks and balances on 'the watchmen' (see Cappelletti, 1985, p. 550). This is particularly true in the case of international law, where there is no separation of powers – it is the same actors (states, often acting through international organisations), that are the principal authorities in the legislative process, as well as in interpreting and policing the laws.

Furthermore, Teubner (1988, p. 17) invokes the phenomenon of 'tangled hierarchies', coined by Douglas (1979), where, once the highest level of authority is reached in an argumentative process, the only method of validating the highest law (in the Rabbi's case – the divine law) is by recourse to the lowest law – the trivial procedural norms ('after the majority must one incline'). In the case of international courts and tribunals, this can be equated to jurisdictional and admissibility clauses, such as the crime in question being committed at a time that is outside the scope of a particular court, determining the fact that the cases will not be considered by the court, before even evaluating the committed acts or theoretical arguments for attempting to render justice for which the court was established in the first place. Social and economic interests also influence law by penetrating the formal rationality and calculability of law, adding political and utilitarian considerations (see, for example, Weber, 1978, p. 822). Legal conflict arbitration, therefore, can become swayed into, from a legal norms' point of view (i.e. considering what is right and what is wrong), rather inconsistent decision-making (Teubner 1988, pp. 30–31).

Sources of international law

International law has evolved particularly rapidly in the past 50 years, expanding its scope from just addressing relations between states to include individuals and other non-state actors. Such developments, it has been argued, reflect the changing values and morals globally, as well as the changing circumstances (particularly those of rapid technological advances and increased global interconnectedness). These require the cooperation of multiple states to be addressed. As put by Shaw (2013, p. 43), 'international law is a product of its environment'. However, the question as to whose environment and customs are being referred arises. The law has developed differently in various jurisdictions, based on differing challenges that legal institutions had to address, distinct philosophical influences, political and economic circumstances, as well as cultural norms and traditions.

In order to establish potential mechanisms for influencing the content and mechanisms of international law, it is important to consider its sources. International law is not a single body of law made by a central body, but rather a patchwork of treaties, accords, agreements, charters, compromises, conventions, memorandums, protocols, tribunals and understandings, as well as international custom. According to art. 38 (1) of the Statute of the International Court of Justice (ICJ),

> whose function it is to decide in accordance with international law such disputes as are submitted to it, shall apply:
>
> a international conventions, whether general or particular, establishing rules expressly recognized by the contesting states;
> b international custom, as evidence of a general practice accepted as law;
> c the general principles of law recognized by civilized nations;
> d …judicial decisions and the teachings of the most highly qualified publicists of the various nations, as subsidiary means for the determination of rules of law.

It is particularly interesting to consider the source (b), 'international custom, as evidence of a general practice accepted as law'. De Visscher (1957, p. 149) equates the formation of customary rules to the emergence of a road, where after the initial footpath taken by one or a few members becomes one adopted by others as well, in order to increase certainty. Eventually, the footpath develops into a larger road and becomes accepted as the path to be taken, even though the precise moment of its establishment as the route to be taken is difficult to pin point. De Visscher (ibid.) further suggests that the paths will inevitably be most significantly shaped by the travellers who are heaviest and therefore leave more visible footprints (which in the case of international law would be the politically and economically more powerful states); or those who take the path most frequently. In the case of customs in international law, however, it is usually rather difficult to identify those major paths that then evolve into roads. Even within one state with a single legal tradition, it is unclear whose statements in relation to international law should be considered as the most authoritative – heads of states', their legal advisors', judges, parliamentary members' statements, as well as the context or the expressly legal nature of these (interviews, parliamentary discussions, UN debates, written communiques, etc.)?

Furthermore, whereas customary law and various international organisations and legal mechanisms refer to global international community values, or what could be understood as 'universal' agreement of what rights each person should have, in practice the existence of global values is debatable. A good example is the 'universal' human rights discourse. The Universal Declaration of Human Rights has been repeatedly criticised by states such as Iran and Saudi Arabia, who believe that the declaration is largely based on secular principles that originated in Western, Judeo-Christian philosophy, ignoring possibly distinct local and regional contexts and moral, ethical and legal codes. Menski (2006, p. 41) went as far as to say that human rights jurisprudence has become a 'human rights industry', relying on the imposition of globally uniform standards and norm systems rather than the reconstruction of indigenous norms. Similarly, Cotterrell (1989, p. 44) argued that 'the universalization of human rights is a matter of the export, reception or transplanting of fundamental values or beliefs ... in legal form', rather than an expression of globally prevalent values and beliefs.

The signing of the Universal Islamic Declaration of Human Rights (UIDHR) in 1981, and the Cairo Declaration of Human Rights in Islam (CDHRI) in 1990, indicates a rather widespread discontent with the mainstream, the 'universal', approach of the international human rights regime. The reaction to these declarations from Western human rights activists and lawyers to the declarations has, unsurprisingly, been negative. For example, the Geneva-based International Commission of Jurists (2014) warned (and still warns today) that the CDHRI 'gravely threatens the inter-cultural consensus on which the international human rights instruments are based'. However, the message that the signatory states of the aforementioned declarations were trying to send was, arguably, that such a consensus does not in fact exist in the way that Western states may think it does.

A detailed analysis of the deliberations in international law-setting discussions also reveals mechanisms of how larger political, economic and military powers are able to steer international law to address the issues and to address them in a way that is convenient for the aforementioned powers (instead of just leaving a heavier footprint, as suggested by De Visscher (1957), discussed previously). For example, the London Charter laid out the principles, rules and procedures by which the Nuremberg trials were conducted, and was proclaimed by the International Military Tribunal (IMT) as not being

> an arbitrary exercise of power on the part of the victorious nations, but (...) the expression of international law existing at the time of its creation; and to that extent is itself a contribution to international law.
> (IMT Judgement, 2014)

Sir Maxwell-Fyfe, the convenor of the London International Conference on Military Trials (ICMT), which was called for the purpose of formulating the London Charter, however, proclaimed that the victors of the Second World War should 'declare' what international law is:

> What we want to abolish at the trial is a discussion as to whether the acts are violations of international law or not. We declare what the international law is, so that there won't be any discussion on whether it is international law or not.
> (ICMT, 1945)

Such a statement, combined with the fact that only judges from the victor countries participated in the Nuremberg trials and that only those from the vanquished states were tried, can hardly be labelled as an affirmation of 'universal' principles of rights and justice. Davies argued that a treaty concluded at the end of a war will not be based on justice, but will simply represent the policy of the victors imposed upon the vanquished (Davies, 1932).

It is also worth noting that values and morals inevitably change over time, with the development of economies and new opportunities. Accordingly, certain human rights, that are now by many considered as non-negotiable, may not have been considered as non-negotiable rights not very long previously by the same communities, and may currently be accorded different levels of consideration and importance by different communities. Basu (2003) refers to global labour standards, which prohibit phenomena such as child labour and bounded labour. The author notes that it is rather hypocritical of Western states to apply regulations that limit the types of employment people can engage in in other states, especially when, during their own development stages, child labour and other practices that would now be considered as exploitative in the Global West were common in the same Western states during their equivalent stages of development. In a similar vein, the present concept of children working in, for example, shops or the market (in non-exploitative conditions) is not necessarily foreign or considered negative in some states; the lack of financial contribution to their families on the part of the children would, at times, have a more negative effect on their well-being.

Similarly, Chang (2007) notes that the Trade Related Intellectual Property Rights (TRIPS) agreement of the World Trade Organization (WTO) not only disadvantages developing states as the vast majority of the world's patents are held by citizens and corporations of developed countries, it also encourages the diversion of scarce developing countries' resources to policing compliance with TRIPS instead of investing in more strategic and productive sectors. Chang (ibid.) concludes that it prohibits the currently developing countries from using some of the techniques that the now developed countries used during their initial stages of development (such as reverse engineering).

State sovereignty

Sovereignty has for a long time been considered in the sense of states' right to freedom from interference of other countries in their domestic affairs, and was in fact the foundational doctrine of the international system. For example, Louis XIV stressed the perception of absolute sovereignty as a God-given right, claiming 'L'État, c'est moi' (or 'I am the State', see, for example, Summerton, 1996). The UN Charter, art. 2(7), states that 'Nothing contained in the present Charter shall authorize the United Nations to intervene in matters which are essentially within the domestic jurisdiction of any state'.

The traditional concept of sovereignty, however, has been challenged by the development of international humanitarian and human rights law, the establishment of super-sovereign organisations such as the UN and the EU, and the rising influence of non-traditional and non-state actors in the international arena (such as large international Non-Governmental Organisations (iNGOs) and Multinational Corporations (MNCs)). Sovereignty has, more often than not, become referred to in relation to states' obligation to provide their citizens with basic rights and freedoms, upon which the right to freedom from interference from other states and international organisations is contingent. The principle of Responsibility to Protect (R2P) accordingly gained currency over the previously dominant principle of non-intervention and respect of territorial independence, articulated in art. 2 of the UN Charter, thus legitimising phenomena such as military intervention on humanitarian grounds (see ICISS, 2001).

The extent to which the sovereignty of smaller and politically or economically less powerful states is respected by larger world powers, however, is questionable, especially when it does not fit with the latter's own foreign policy goals and national strategies. For example, Rajagopal (2004, pp. 25–26) notes that when Britain signed the UN Charter, which proclaims self-determination, it was still fighting colonials wars (and particularly confrontational ones in places such as Kenya and Malaya); and continued to do so after having signed the Charter. The same question of respect of sovereignty of other countries arises in the very topical case of Russian–Ukrainian relations and the violation of Ukraine's territorial sovereignty by Russia, by the 'annexation' of Crimea.

Kant, as discussed below, made an important observation centuries ago – that the general perception of state sovereignty will have to change to enable effective addressing of cross-border crimes on an international level. The change should feature a shift from understanding sovereignty as states' right to govern themselves as they wish, to seeing sovereignty on similar terms as citizenship: essentially as an indication that the unit in question (state/person) is part of a larger community, to which it has rights and obligations:

> There is only one rational way in which states coexisting with other states can emerge from the lawless condition of pure warfare. Just like individual men, they must renounce their savage and lawless freedom, adapt themselves to public coercive laws, and thus form an international state (civitas gentium), which would necessarily continue to grow until it embraced all the peoples of the earth. But since this is not the will of the nations, according to their present conception of international right … [t]he positive idea of a world republic cannot be realised. If all is not to be lost, this can at best find a negative substitute in the shape of an enduring and gradually expanding federation likely to prevent war. The latter may check the current man's inclination to defy the law and antagonise his fellows, although there will always be a risk of it bursting forth anew.
> (Kant, 1795, cited in Crawford (2012, pp. 8–9))

Sovereignty is in this sense expressed by the delegation of decision-making authority to international organisations that are legitimised to legislate for their members, much like the concept of citizenship of a state. Member states must subsequently abide by these organisations' rules and decisions. Consequently, as a citizen is not allowed to pick and choose which laws are to apply to him, states should also only be able to influence and change the law-making bodies and the rules according to which these legislate, not individual decisions or rules made by the bodies. It is also worth noting that sovereignty encompasses not only the ability to make temporary decisions, but also long-term commitments.

Furthermore, the very moral basis for nation-state boundaries has been challenged. Authors such as Barry (1973) and O'Neill (1986) have stressed the rather arbitrary moral basis for nation-state boundaries in discussing issues of justice, noting that if one was to adopt a Rawlsian definition of justice, the premises of that would lead to arguments for redistribution of the world's wealth and resources in favour of those worst off, ignoring the boundaries of nation-states. Carens (1995, p. 230) argues that '[c]itizenship in Western liberal democracies is the modern equivalent of feudal privilege – an inherited status that greatly enhances one's life chances'.

5.3 International anti-corruption treaties and agreements

A plethora of multilateral instruments to prevent and combat corruption has been developed in the last two decades. This includes the fundamental UN convention – UNCAC – as well as, inter alia, the Inter-American Convention against Corruption, the Convention for the Fight against Corruption involving Officials of the European Communities or Officials of Member States of the European Union, the OECD Convention on Combating Bribery of Foreign Public Officials in International Business Transactions, CoE's Criminal Law Convention on Corruption, CoE's Civil Law Convention on Corruption as well as the African Union's Convention on Preventing and Combating Corruption. Other relevant initiatives include the Financial Action Task Force (FATF), the Extractive Industries Transparency Initiative (EITI) and the G20 Anti-Corruption Working Group.

Historical context – the FCPA

Posadas (2000, p. 347) traces the origins of corruption being addressed as a transnational issue to the investigations into corrupt transnational corporate payments, conducted in response to the Watergate scandal. The Watergate investigations generated significant public interest and revealed the, at times questionable, actions of political and business rulers; which, in turn, led to investigations into political campaign finances and the role of business therein (Posadas, 2000, p. 348). The Watergate investigation asked American companies to come forward with any questionable or illegal payments that they had made to the 1972 US Presidential campaign, which revealed that American corporations were also involved in political campaign financing in foreign countries and had transferred other suspicious payments to foreign government officials (ibid.).

The Securities and Exchange Commission (SEC) subsequently initiated investigations into four large companies: Gulf Oil Corporation, Phillips Petroleum Company, Northrop Corporation and Ashland Oil Inc.

It is worth noting that these initial SEC investigations into bribery of foreign government officials by American companies were due to the fact that these companies had failed to provide accurate financial statements, in violation of the US securities law. The SEC considered that such payments were materially relevant facts to be disclosed to the current shareholders and potential investors (United States Congress, 1973). Investigations were therefore initiated to increase transparency and to strengthen businesses' financial and corporate management systems as well as the public's confidence in businesses, rather than due to the consideration of moral and ethical issues. As put by Commissioner Loomis, the SEC was not aiming to be the 'guardian of corporate morality', but rather to ensure that companies disclose the information relevant for investors when making decisions in relation to the company (The Activities of American Multinational Corporations Abroad, supra note 5, at 36). Nevertheless, Posadas (2000, p. 351) notes:

> [i]llegal political contributions to foreign governments and transnational bribery were defined during the hearings as threats to not only the principles of democracy and a free market economy, but also to the conduct of U.S. foreign relations, including the lawful pursuit of American business interests abroad.

The SEC investigations revealed that considerable amounts were being transferred to foreign government officials and to support political campaigns. In the case of the Gulf Oil Corporation transferring four million US dollars to the then-ruling Democratic Party of the Republic of Korea for the 1966 and 1972 elections, this could have had a significant broader impact as the 1972 election was won by only a small margin. Northrop Corporation, a military aircraft manufacturer, was found to have paid almost half a million US dollars to two Saudi Arabian generals; and also had no oversight of its contractors' business dealings on behalf of Northrop (Multinational Corporations and United States Foreign Policy, supra note 3, at 112; and 151–58). The SEC's voluntary disclosure programme, which urged companies to come forward with noted instances of questionable payments to, and bribery of, foreign officials in return for diminished responsibility in front of the SEC, led to the organisation concluding that such practices were 'neither isolated nor rare' (Posadas, 2000, p. 355).

This led to the adoption of the Foreign Corrupt Practices Act in 1977, the first piece of legislation that criminalised not only the failure to adequately report and disclose facilitation payments to (i.e. the bribery of) foreign officials, but also the payments themselves. It is interesting to note that President Ford had suggested only criminalising the former, but the Senate opted for the stricter approach proposed by Senator Proxmire. The arguments that criminalising

American firm's corrupt practices abroad, when no other country was doing so, would significantly disadvantage American businesses competing internationally were also raised during the debates. Posadas (2000, p. 358) argues that 'it appears that Congress ultimately adopted sanctions because it simply considered the practice to be wrong'.

Previously, the US government departments' authority to investigate foreign payments was very limited, and further inhibited by difficulties obtaining information overseas and issues of cooperation with their counterparts in other countries. The act has since been amended twice: certain areas of the act were clarified in 1988 under the Omnibus Trade and Competitiveness Act; and in 1998 under the International Anti-Bribery and Fair Competition Act, to incorporate the US's international law obligations as part of the OECD.

Various international, regional and the most influential national legal instruments that have been put in place to combat corruption since the FCPA are explored in the subsequent sections.

UNCAC

The United Nations Convention against Corruption (UNCAC), the most comprehensive global legal instrument against corruption (see Low, 2006, p. 3), only entered into force in December 2005. The requirement for a dedicated UN convention on anti-corruption emerged in the discussions on the adoption of the UN Convention against Transnational and Organised Crime (UNCATOC) (see Vlassis, 2005, p. 127). UNCATOC itself touches upon corruption in the public sector and criminalises the supply and demand side of bribery-related offences (see Brunelle-Quraishi, 2011, p. 157). UNCATOC's focus on transnational organised crime, however, requires there to be a transnational element of the involvement of organised criminal groups in order for the convention to apply (ibid.).

The purpose of the UNCAC, as stated in art. 1 of the Convention, is:

a   To promote and strengthen measures to prevent and combat corruption more efficiently and effectively.
b   To promote, facilitate and support international cooperation and technical assistance in the prevention of, and fight against, corruption, including in asset recovery.
c   To promote integrity, accountability and proper management of public affairs and public property.

The Convention has four key pillars: prevention (art. 5–14), criminalisation (art. 15–42), asset recovery (art. 51–59) and international cooperation (art. 43–50). The concepts covered within the convention are discussed in more detail in section 2.2. UNCAC requires member states to adopt domestic legislation to comply with the requirements and recommendations set out in the Convention. As such, the convention is a means of standardising countries' domestic law and does not require states to give up significant amounts of sovereignty.

The UNCAC has particular relevance as the broadest convention, covering a large number of offences of corruption within the public and private spheres, with a detailed section on asset recovery and with 140 signatories and 178 parties (UNODC, 2016). This will be evidenced in the subsequent sections of this chapter. It does not, however, address some contentious issues that other treaties incorporate, such as the issue of political party financing, which is included in the African Union Convention on Preventing and Combating Corruption (AUCPCC).

UNCAC's requirements for states to adopt measures to prevent most types of corrupt behaviour are, however, somewhat caveated by the inclusion of the phrase 'in accordance with the fundamental principles of [the country's] legal system' when introducing a number of requirements (see Brunelle-Quraishi, 2011, p. 107). Obligations with such a caveat are seen by some as having no 'teeth' or being 'highly discretionary' (ibid.). The concepts of national sovereignty and non-intervention are further highlighted in art. 4 of the Convention, which reads:

1. States Parties shall carry out their obligations under this Convention in a manner consistent with the principles of sovereign equality and territorial integrity of States and that of non-intervention in the domestic affairs of other States.
2. Nothing in this Convention shall entitle a State Party to undertake in the territory of another State the exercise of jurisdiction and performance of functions that are reserved exclusively for the authorities of that other State by its domestic law.

Universal efforts to fight local issues can dilute and generalise the approaches to corruption to a level that is too abstract to be effective. Bribery, however, was the exception in the context of UNCAC. There are several reasons why it might have been easier to reach an agreement to include more demanding requirements in relation to bribery, compared to the other offences of corruption, discussed in section 2.2. These include the relative ease of defining bribery, as well as the ability for governments to be seen to take a strong stance against corruption by focusing their efforts on lower-level administrative corruption. As noted by Mendilow and Peleg (2014, pp. 5–6):

> If other forms of corruption proved too difficult to define, the accent fell on the offering or demanding of resources in return for policy decisions or, at the lower level (where the public officer comes in direct contact with the public), for such 'favors' as speeding up administrative treatment, or ignoring violations. The result was the impression that permeates the public discussion of corruption that the concept refers mainly to such behaviours, and hence to what could be called 'lower level' or 'administrative' corruption.

Furthermore, UNCAC's monitoring system has room to improve, compared to other multilateral agreements. Brunelle-Quraishi (2011, p. 165) notes that its peer review process 'is considered more rigorous than the self evaluation method, but more lenient than the expert review process' that has been adopted by a number of other treaties, as discussed below. UNCAC's monitoring process has been particularly criticised for not involving civil society in monitoring and evaluating countries' compliance with the Convention, and for evaluations being based on checklists and questionnaires rather than in-depth country analyses and visits (Brunelle-Quraishi, 2011, p. 158).

OECD anti-bribery convention

The 1997 OECD Convention on Combating Bribery of Foreign Public Officials in International Business Transactions, following negotiations between states, entered into force in 1999. Art. 1 of the convention sets out the offences of 'bribery of a foreign public official':

1. Each Party shall take such measures as may be necessary to establish that it is a criminal offence under its law for any person intentionally to offer, promise or give any undue pecuniary or other advantage, whether directly or through intermediaries, to a foreign public official, for that official or for a third party, in order that the official act or refrain from acting in relation to the performance of official duties, in order to obtain or retain business or other improper advantage in the conduct of international business.

2. Each Party shall take any measures necessary to establish that complicity in, including incitement, aiding and abetting, or authorisation of an act of bribery of a foreign public official shall be a criminal offence. Attempt and conspiracy to bribe a foreign public official shall be criminal offences to the same extent as attempt and conspiracy to bribe a public official of that Party.

The Convention has 38 Signatories: the OECD Members, as well as Argentina, Brazil, Bulgaria, Estonia, Slovenia and South Africa. All signatories have also adopted the 2009 Anti-Bribery Recommendation. Carrington (2010, p. 140) notes that the Convention 'marked the beginning of an international movement based on the premise that we all have a stake in the integrity of the global marketplace that deserves the protection of law'.

Brunelle-Quraishi (2011, pp. 150–151) outlines how the convention's agreement, as well as its drafting, was very much led by the United States. As the US at that time was the only OECD member state that had domestic laws criminalising bribery of foreign government officials by its businesses, naturally it felt it important that other states follow suit and adopt similar legislation. The OECD convention was thus modelled on the FCPA. As with the FCPA, the convention refers to bribery involving public officials and excludes bribery that occurs solely in the private sector.

The OECD Convention is primarily focused on the 'supply side' of bribery – individuals offering a bribe – and it does not address the issue of asset recovery (see Brunelle-Quraishi, 2011, pp. 151–152). This is in contrast to the UNCAC, as discussed previously. The Convention is also restricted to grand corruption as opposed to petty corruption, given that facilitation payments are explicitly excluded from the scope of the convention; the commentary on the Convention notes the following: 'Small "facilitation" payments do not constitute payments made "to obtain or retain business or other improper advantage" … and, accordingly, are … not an offence' (OECD, 2011, p. 15).

Nevertheless, given the damaging effects that corruption at all levels can have, the OECD (2011, p. 22) convention commentary provides the following recommendation:

> i) undertake to periodically review their policies and approach on small facilitation payments in order to effectively combat the phenomenon; ii) encourage companies to prohibit or discourage the use of small facilitation payments in internal company controls, ethics and compliance programmes or measures, recognising that such payments are generally illegal in the countries where they are made, and must in all cases be accurately accounted for in such companies' books and financial records.

Specific sanctions are not prescribed by the Convention; this is left to the discretion of the member states' individual legal systems (see Brunelle-Quraishi, 2011, p. 151).

A notable strength of the OECD Convention is its monitoring mechanism (see Brunelle-Quraishi, 2011, pp. 152–153; Low, 2003). Countries are subject to a four-phase peer review of their compliance with the requirements of the convention. Phase 1 consists of a peer review evaluating whether a country has adopted adequate national legislation to meet the OECD Anti-Bribery Convention's requirements. Phase 2 focuses on the state's application of the convention. Phase 3 focuses on enforcement of the Convention, the 2009 Anti-Bribery Recommendation and outstanding recommendations from Phase 2. Phase 4 is under development and due to start in 2016. The results of the review processes are made public (see, for example, OECD, 2010, 2014d), which, according to Brunelle-Quraishi (ibid.), is a key distinguishing feature of the Convention and contributes to its effectiveness.

The OECD also provides data on the enforcement measures that have been taken in response to foreign bribery by states parties to the OECD Convention (OECD, 2014, p. 1):

- 361 individuals and 126 entities have been sanctioned under criminal proceedings for foreign bribery in 17 Parties between the time the Convention entered into force in 1999 and the end of 2014.
- At least 95 of the sanctioned individuals were sentenced to prison for foreign bribery.

International law and development 159

- At least 110 individuals and 200 entities have been sanctioned in criminal, administrative and civil cases for other offences related to foreign bribery, such as money laundering or accounting, in 8 Parties.
- Approximately 393 investigations are ongoing in 25 Parties to the Anti-Bribery Convention. Prosecutions are ongoing against 142 individuals and 14 entities in 12 Parties for offences under the Convention.

Although the OECD countries that have conducted these investigations have done so under their domestic legislation and were also subject to a number of other international mechanisms discussed in this chapter, the reporting, oversight and follow-up of recommendation mechanisms with multiple peer review phases distinguishes the OECD Convention.

Regional initiatives

A number of regional anti-corruption conventions have been adopted. Regional fora can be particularly beneficial for smaller countries, providing them with a platform to present themselves as a coalition that carries more weight in international discussions and negotiations. This section discusses the major initiatives within three regions – the Americas, Europe and Africa.

1996 Inter-American Convention against Corruption (IACAC)

The Inter-American Convention against Corruption (IACAC) was the first regional convention that set out regional requirements in relation to anti-corruption (Brunelle-Quraishi, 2011, p. 153). The Convention was adopted by the Organisation of American States (OAS) and covers both the supply and demand sides of bribery. Pieth (1999, p. 538) describes the convention as 'a compromise between Latin-American interests in mutual legal assistance and extradition and the North American agenda in criminalizing active transnational commercial bribery'.

The IACAC criminalises corruption both in the public and the private sectors; and also the supply and demand side of corruption, in addition to illicit enrichment (Brunelle-Quraishi, 2011, p. 153). Brunelle-Quraishi (ibid., p. 154) also argues that the IACAC surpasses the UNCAC in that it does not include more lenient exceptions for facilitation payments and puts the burden of proof of the provenance of sudden increases of officials' assets on to the official rather than the prosecution (art. 20). The IACAC does not, however, consider asset recovery.

The IACAC did not initially include monitoring and compliance mechanisms; which was only addressed in an OAS General Assembly in 2001 (Brunelle-Quraishi, 2011, p. 155). This mechanism was modelled on the OECD Anti-Bribery convention and stipulates comparable peer-review-based procedures (ibid.) whereby a committee of experts reviews the implementation of the Convention by signatory states and the Conference of the States Parties to Convention subsequently reviews the performance of the committee. Although the state under review is allowed to change and appoint the reviewing experts, their investigations are complemented by reports and presentations submitted by the civil society. This ensures a more holistic overview of the situation as, as noted by De Michele (2003, p. 317), 'a third party – civil society – could play a role in providing alternative opinions that could help balance the information and avoid governments acting softly on each other'. The final reports of the committee are also published online for public scrutiny, which overall makes the IACAC monitoring mechanism more transparent and participatory than the UNCAC.

Council of Europe (CoE) conventions

The Council of Europe was established in 1949; it now has a membership of 47 states. The Council of Europe Criminal Law Convention on Corruption (CLCC) is wide-ranging, covering active and passive bribery of public officials, parliamentarians, civil servants and judges in one's home country and abroad; trading in influence; accounting offences in connection with crimes of corruption; and laundering the proceeds of funds gained as a result of corruption. When adopted in 1999, the Convention was considered 'the broadest among regional efforts to combat corruption' (Brunelle-Quraishi, 2011, p. 161; Pieth, 1999).

The Convention does not stipulate specific sanctions to be implemented by signatory states, but art. 19 of the Convention calls for 'effective, proportionate and dissuasive sanctions and measures, including, when committed by natural persons, penalties involving deprivation of liberty which can give rise to extradition', as well as legislation to be adopted to enable confiscation of the proceeds of crimes of corruption.

Art. 21–23 outline the need for effective collaboration between national law enforcement institutions, public authorities, public officials, financial institutions, and address the matter of the protection of whistleblowers; and chapter IV (art. 25–31) calls for efficient international cooperation, touching on the matters of mutual assistance, extradition, communication and information-sharing.

The implementation of the Convention is monitored by the 'Group of States against Corruption' (GRECO), of which states that ratify the CLCC automatically become members. GRECO undertakes monitoring of all member states' compliance with the CoE convention 'through a dynamic process of mutual evaluation and peer pressure' (CoE, 2016). The monitoring process is two-tiered – first of all, states' legislative and institutional structures are assessed and recommendations for improvement are provided. The second tier of evaluation looks at the states' implementation of the recommendations. This follow-up of the recommendations is a particularly important oversight factor, which incentivises countries to ensure strong anti-corruption legislation, institutions and implementation.

GRECO also monitors states' compliance with the 1999 Council of Europe Civil Law Convention on Corruption. This Convention requires signatory states to make provisions within their national laws 'for effective remedies for persons who have suffered damage as a result of acts of corruption, to enable them to defend their rights and interests, including the possibility of obtaining compensation for damage' (art. 1).

African Union Convention on Preventing and Combating Corruption (AUCPCC)

The AUCPCC was adopted in 2003, after five years of negotiations, and entered into force in 2006. The convention addresses corruption from both the supply and demand sides of corruption in the public and private spheres and does not provide any exceptions for facilitation payments (Brunelle-Quraishi, 2011, pp. 158–159). Art. 2 of the Convention states the objectives of AUCPCC with a very strong focus on development and the role that eradicating corruption can have:

1. Promote and strengthen the development in Africa by each State Party, of mechanisms required to prevent, detect, punish and eradicate corruption and related offences in the public and private sectors.
2. Promote, facilitate and regulate cooperation among the State Parties to ensure the effectiveness of measures and actions to prevent, detect, punish and eradicate corruption and related offences in Africa.
3. Coordinate and harmonize the policies and legislation between State Parties for the purposes of prevention, detection, punishment and eradication of corruption on the continent.
4. Promote socio-economic development by removing obstacles to the enjoyment of economic, social and cultural rights as well as civil and political rights.
5. Establish the necessary conditions to foster transparency and accountability in the management of public affairs.

Although the convention does not outline specific sanctions to be adopted by member states, it uses mandatory terms in relation to signatory states adopting the necessary legislation. Art. 5 of the Convention requires member states to 'undertake to' adopt the following measures in relation to the stated objectives of the Convention:

1. Adopt legislative and other measures that are required to establish as offences, the acts mentioned in art. 4 paragraph 1 of the present Convention.
2. Strengthen national control measures to ensure that the setting up and operations of foreign companies in the territory of a State Party shall be subject to the respect of the national legislation in force.
3. Establish, maintain and strengthen independent national anti-corruption authorities or agencies.

4   Adopt legislative and other measures to create, maintain and strengthen internal accounting, auditing and follow-up systems, in particular, in the public income, custom and tax receipts, expenditures and procedures for hiring, procurement and management of public goods and services.
5   Adopt legislative and other measures to protect informants and witnesses in corruption and related offences, including protection of their identities.
6   Adopt measures that ensure citizens report instances of corruption without fear of consequent reprisals.
7   Adopt national legislative measures in order to punish those who make false and malicious reports against innocent persons in corruption and related offences.
8   Adopt and strengthen mechanisms for promoting the education of populations to respect the public good and public interest, and awareness in the fight against corruption and related offences, including school educational programmes and sensitization of the media, and the promotion of an enabling environment for the respect of ethics.

The Convention's expansiveness had in fact been suggested to potentially have the effect of deterring countries from ratifying it (Webb, 2005, p. 203). By 2013, however, 34 had ratified and become parties of the Convention (AU, 2013).

AUCPCC's review process, similarly to the IACAC, is based on a peer review mechanism. Brunelle-Quraishi (2011, p. 160) notes that 'the AUCPCC's success is deemed quite low due to the reluctance of many African governments to criticize each other' as well as due to the financial challenges it has faced. Consequently, a global instrument such as the UNCAC can provide a useful advantage in that the states involved in the peer review process will not necessarily be neighbouring countries. A further involvement of the civil society in the monitoring process could also strengthen and increase the effectiveness of the Convention (ibid.).

Corporate and industry initiatives

There has, in recent years, been an increase in voluntary business initiatives making a stance against corruption and other behaviour perceived as unethical and immoral, such as the exploitation of workers in developing countries. This is in line with initiatives such as fair trade and a general increase in Western consumer interest in the nature in which businesses, which consumers support, operate.

United Nations Global Compact (UNGC)

The UNGC is the world's largest initiative on corporate sustainability, calling companies 'to align strategies and operations with universal principles on human rights, labour, environment and anti-corruption, and take actions that advance societal goals' (UNGC, 2016a). As of May 2016, 8610 companies in 163 countries had signed up to the initiative (ibid.).

The Global Compact was an initiative founded in 2000 by the United Nations to involve the private sector in international decision-making. UNGC provides a forum and an umbrella of the United Nations platform, to bring together businesses, governments and international institutions. The UNGC can be seen as the international community's effort to address the issue of corruption from a collective action perspective, by bringing together a range of actors to address corruption within their own organisations and institutions.

UNGC's mission is to use 'business as a force for good' (UNGC, 2016b). Companies pledge to abide by ten principles on human rights, labour, environment and anti-corruption, but are free to decide how the principles can be best implemented in practice within their context. Principle 10 on anti-corruption requires companies to adopt 'robust anti-corruption measures and practices to protect their reputations and the interests of their stakeholders' (UNGC, 2016c). This includes practices on risk assessment, reporting and supply chain management. The Global Compact requires signatory companies to adopt tangible measures to improve their performance in relation to the ten principles and report on their progress towards achieving them (Danish Federation of SMEs and Verner Kristiansen Kommunikation, 2016).

Although the Global Compact is a voluntary standard, and has been called 'a tiger without teeth' (Mueckenberger and Jastram, 2010, p. 231), there are significant incentives for companies to sign up to the initiative and to comply with its regulations. The non-legally binding nature of the ten principles 'does not necessarily rule out effectiveness' (ibid.). For example, firms bidding to deliver contracts for the Danish government are asked to sign a declaration such as 'We confirm that we will comply with the principles of the United Nations Global Compact if we are awarded the contract' (see, for example, Danida, 2016). Companies might also feel the incentives to sign up to the Global Compact due to a potential reputational impact, as, if a company's competitors sign up to the initiative, those companies that do not might be perceived as riskier to do business with or having something to hide. The more companies sign up to the initiative the more difficult it will be for others to avoid it.

Industry-specific initiatives

The Extractive Industries Transparency Initiative (EITI) aims to promote 'open and accountable management of natural resources' by strengthening government and company systems and informing public debate (EITI, 2016). EITI is supported by governments, companies and civil societies in implementing countries and is expanding beyond transparency standards for reporting on revenues, to other matters such as contracting and indeed becoming the industry standard-setting entity. The UK signed up to EITI in 2013. EITI, however, is focused on revenue flows within individual countries, ignoring transnational flows that may have more of an influence (see Shaxson, 2007).

The construction sector has followed suit and in 2012 established an equivalent transparency initiative – the Construction Sector Transparency Initiative (COST), 'to promote transparency and accountability in publicly financed construction' (COST, 2016).

FLEGT is an initiative of the European Commission, setting out measures to combat illegal logging and associated trade. Illegal exploitation of natural resources, such as timber, is closely associated with corruption and organised crime. Illegal logging also fuels corruption and organised crime. The initiative encourages greater transparency within the forestry sector. FLEGT, as a relatively recent initiative of the EC, has limited reach so far, particularly as the EU's role as global timber importers is low in comparison to other countries that are leading on timber imports – such as China, which is the destination for more than half of globally exported timber (WWF, 2017, p. 1). Consequently, working to influence others is of particular importance for such standards to have the desired effect at scale.

International Chamber of Commerce

The International Chamber of Commerce is a global business organisation. It has made a clear stance against corruption and has, since 1977, been publishing rules for enterprises to combat corruption and to comply with a number of international-level anti-corruption initiatives (ICC, 2011).

The International Chamber of Commerce has engaged businesses, governments and civil society organisations in a number of initiatives to tackle corruption. The Chamber, in partnership with TI, UNGC and the World Economic Forum's Partnering against Corruption Initiative, has produced a 'business case against corruption' guide, which sets out the rationale and imperative for businesses and corporations to actively engage in combatting corruption, as well as the risks associated with not engaging in anti-corruption activities.

5.4 Summary

This section presented an overview of the context that led to the proliferation of new international and regional conventions as well as domestic legislation covering offences of corruption in foreign jurisdictions in the last two decades. The different multilateral mechanisms discussed in this chapter have a development aim, which is why they are particularly relevant in the context of international development assistance. Given the relative recent adoption of the discussed conventions and treaties, their effectiveness is yet to be established.

Nevertheless, it is important to note the external pressures that are being exerted on domestic legislation from the multitude of international treaties and institutions, as well as the increasing transnational cooperation which requires harmonised regulatory and legal systems. These have also been influencing the behaviour of private entities (Hey, 2010). This is a feature not only of anti-corruption systems, but also those that concern the environment and other 'public goods' (see, for example, Morgera, 2012; Yang and Percival, 2009). The role of private actors, civil society and the media in challenging injustices and bringing perpetrators to account is also evolving. Private sector initiatives such as the UNGC, EITI and FLEGT are increasingly gaining significance.

The analysis of the international legal agreements on corruption also shows how the evolution of what is understood as corruption (discussed in Chapter 2) translates into different aspects of corruption being criminalised by domestic and international legislation. Notably, there has been a shift from seeing corruption as a misuse of power necessarily involving public officials, which was included in the TI definition initially and which is what the FCPA criminalises, to now also considering corruption within the private sector. TI has dropped the requirement of public officials' involvement for actions to be classified as corruption, as do the UNCAC as well as the UK Bribery Act in relation to what acts of bribery are covered by the legislation.

Drafting and enforcing universal laws, regulations and institutions poses significant challenges, such as ensuring that they are equitable, that their development is inclusive and that there are enough resources for monitoring and enforcing the requirements. Other issues to consider in relation to the effectiveness of international anti-corruption agreements are the incentives for states to comply, the costs of monitoring and enforcing the commitments as well as the implications on sovereignty. This is discussed in more detail in the following chapter.

Notes

1 Case Concerning the Gabčikovo-Nagymaros Project (Hungary/Slovakia), 1997 ICJ Rep. 7, separate opinion of Vice-President Weeramantry, at para. C(c).
2 This can include key provisions under human rights regimes, such as freedom from torture or persecution based on religious beliefs, as well as democratic rights.
3 Neo-liberal theory was primarily concerned with getting the prices right in the market and fiscal discipline, free trade and removing state-induced market distortions.
4 The movement started with the work of Sen (1999) and his influential book 'Development as Freedom', which ultimately influenced the reconsideration of the previous absolute domination of economics in the mainstream development discourse and literature.
5 See, for example, *R v. Jones* [2006] UKHL; *R (Gentle) v. Prime Minister* [2006] EWCA.
6 Both of which have a variety of schools of thought that analyse the nature of international law.

Bibliography

Ago, R., 1957. Positive Law and International Law. *Am J Intl L* 51, 691.
AU, 2013. African Union Advisory Board on Corruption: The 10th Anniversary of the AUCPCC Documents 7–9 December 2013.
Austin, J., 1832. *Province of Jurisprudence Determined: The First Part of a Series of Lectures on Jurisprudence, or, The Philosophy of Law*. John Murray, London.

Baker, B., 2010. The Future is Non-State, in: Sedra, M. (Ed.), *The Future of Security Sector Reform*. Waterloo, Ontario, Canada: The Centre for International Governance Innovation, pp. 208–228.

Barry, B.M., 1973. *The Liberal Theory of Justice*. Clarendon Press, Oxford.

Basu, K., 2003. Global Labor Standards and Local Freedoms. UNU World Institute for Development Economics Research. Available at: www.wider.unu.edu/publications/annual-lectures/en_GB/AL7/_files/78091862206319222/default/annual-lecture-2003.pdf (accessed 29 May 2014).

Bentham, J., 1789. *An Introduction to the Principles of Morals and Legislation*. Clarendon Press, Oxford.

Brunelle-Quraishi, O., 2011. Assessing the Relevancy and Efficacy of the United Nations Convention against Corruption: A Comparative Analysis. Notre Dame *Journal of International and Comparative Law* 2(1), 101–166.

Byers, M., 1997. Taking the Law out of International Law: A Critique of the Iterative Perspective. *Harvard International Law Journal* 38(1), 201.

Cappelletti, M., 1985. Who Watches the Watchmen? A Comparative Study on Judicial Responsibility, in: Shetreet, S., Deschenes, J. (Eds), *Judicial Independence*. Martinus Nijhoff, Dordrecht, p. 550.

Carens, J.H., 1995. Aliens and Citizens: The Case for Open Borders, in: Beiner, R. (Ed.), *Theorizing Citizenship*. State University of New York Press, New York, pp. 229–253.

Carfield, M., 2011. Participatory Law and Development: Remapping the Locus of Authority. *University of Colorado Law Review* 82, 739.

Carrington, P.D., 2010. Enforcing International Corrupt Practices Law. *Michigan Journal of International Law* 32, 129.

Chang, H.-J., 2007. Bad Samaritans: Rich Nations, Poor Policies, and the Threat to the Developing World. Random House Business, London.

Chirayath, L., Sage, C., Woolcock, M., 2005. *Customary Law and Policy Reform: Engaging with the Plurality of Justice Systems*. World Bank, Washington, DC.

CoE, 2016. Group of States against Corruption (GRECO). Available at: www.coe.int/t/dghl/monitoring/greco/general/4.%20How%20does%20GRECO%20work_en.asp (accessed 23 September 2016).

COST, 2016. CoST – Better Value from Public Infrastructure Investments. Construction Sector Transparency Initiative. Available at: www.constructiontransparency.org/the-initiative?forumboardid=1&forumtopicid=1 (accessed 23 September 2016).

Cotterrell, R.B., 1989. *The Politics of Jurisprudence: A Critical Introduction to Legal Philosophy*. Philadelphia, PA: University of Pennsylvania Press.

Crawford, J., 2012. *Brownlie's Principles of Public International Law*. Oxford University Press, Oxford.

Danida, 2016. Draft Terms of Reference: Scoping and Formulation of the EU Programme: Support to Combatting Corruption in Ukraine (2017–2019). Fine no. 403. Ukraine. 1–26/2016–14893.

Danish Federation of SMEs, Verner Kristiansen Kommunikation, 2016. Global Compact Small and Medium-Sized Enterprises on Their Way towards Global Responsibility: Ten Danish Case Stories on Human Rights, Labour Standards, Environment and Anti-Corruption in International Business Activities. Copenhagen: Ministry of Foreign Affairs of Denmark.

Davies, D., 1932. An International Police Force? *Royal Institute of International Affairs 1931–1939* 11(1), 76–99.

De Michele, R., 2003. Follow-up Mechanism of the Inter-American Convention against Corruption: A Preliminary Assessment: Is the Glass Half Empty? *The Southwestern Journal of Law and Trade in the Americas* 10, 295.

De Soto, H., 2003. *Mystery of Capital: Why Capitalism Triumphs in the West and Fails Everywhere Else*. Basic Books, New York.

De Soto, H., 2002. *The Other Path: The Economic Answer to Terrorism*. Basic Books, New York.

De Sousa Santos, B., 1987. Law: A Map of Misreading: Toward a Postmodern Conception of Law. *Journal of the Law Society* 14, 279.

De Visscher, C., 1957. *Theory and Reality in Public International Law*. Princeton University Press, Princeton, NJ.

Douglas, R.H., 1979. *Gödel, Escher, Bach: An Eternal Golden Braid*. Basic Books, New York.

EITI, 2016. Who We Are: Extractive Industries Transparency Initiative. Available at: https://eiti.org/about/who-we-are (accessed 23 September 2016).

Faundez, J., 2011. Legal Pluralism and International Development Agencies: State Building or Legal Reform? *Hague Journal on the Rule of Law* 3(1), 18–38. doi:10.1017/S1876404511100020.

Fitzmaurice, G., 1957. The General Principles of International Law Considered from the Standpoint of the Rule of Law. *Hague Academy of International Law* 92(1), 68.

Harper, E., 2011. *Working with Customary Justice Systems: Post-Conflict and Fragile States*. International Development Law Organization, Rome, Italy.

Hart, H.L.A., 1961. *The Concept of Law, Clarendon Law Series*. Oxford University Press (Clarendon), London.

Henkin, L., 1979. *How Nations Behave: Law and Foreign Policy*. Columbia University Press, New York.

Hey, E., 2010. Global Environmental Law and Global Institutions: A System Lacking 'Good Process', in: Pierik, R., Werner, W. (Eds), *Cosmopolitanism in Context: Perspectives from International Law and Political Theory*. Cambridge University Press, Cambridge, pp. 45–72.

Hill, D.W., 2010. Estimating the Effects of Human Rights Treaties on State Behavior. *Journal of Politics* 72(4), 1161–1174.

ICC, 2011. ICC Rules on Combating Corruption, prepared by the ICC Commission on Corporate Responsibility and Anti-corruption. Paris: ICC.

ICISS, 2001. *The Responsibility to Protect: Report of the International Commission on Intervention and State Sovereignty*. Ottawa, Canada: IDRC.

ICMT, 1945. International Conference on Military Trials : London, 1945. Available at: http://avalon.law.yale.edu/imt/jack17.asp (accessed 29 May 2014).

IMT Judgement, 2014. The Trial of German Major War Criminals: Proceedings of the International Military Tribunal Sitting at Nuremberg Germany. Available at: http://avalon.law.yale.edu/imt/judlawch.asp (accessed 29 May 2014).

International Commission of Jurists, 2014. Arab Charter on Human Rights Must Meet International Standards: ICJ. Available at: www.icj.org/arab-charter-on-human-rights-must-meet-international-standards/ (accessed 29 May 2014).

Janse, R., 2013. A Turn to Legal Pluralism in Rule of Law Promotion? *Erasmus Law Review* 6(3/4), 181–190.

Jessup, P.C., 1956. *Transnational Law*. Yale University Press, New Haven, CT.

Kelsen, H., 1945. *General Theory of Law and State*. The Lawbook Exchange Ltd, Clark, NJ.

Koskenniemi, M., 2009. Miserable Comforters: International Relations as New Natural Law. *European Journal of International Relations* 15(3), 395–422.

Lambert, H., Goodwin-Gill, G.S., 2010. *The Limits of Transnational Law: Refugee Law, Policy Harmonization and Judicial Dialogue in the European Union.* Cambridge University Press, Cambridge.

Low, L., 2006. *The United Nations Convention Against Corruption: The Globalization of Anti-Corruption Standards.* Steptoe and Johnson LLP, London.

Low, L., 2003. Milestones in Mutual Evaluation: The Phase 2 Review of the United States under the OECD Antibribery Convention, in: *International Law Forum*, pp. 106–118.

Lund, C., 2008. *Local Politics and the Dynamics of Property in Africa.* Cambridge University Press, Cambridge.

Manji, A., 2006. *The Politics of Land Reform in Africa: From Communal Tenure to Free Markets.* London and New York: Zed Books.

Marx, K., 1995. *Capital: An Abridged Edition.* Oxford University Press, Oxford.

Mendilow, J., Peleg, I., 2014. *Corruption in the Contemporary World: Theory, Practice, and Hotspots.* Lexington Books, Lanham, MD.

Menkel-Meadow, C., 2011. Why and How to Study Transnational Law. University of California, *Irvine Reviews* 1, 97.

Menski, W.F., 2006. *Comparative Law in a Global Context: The Legal Systems of Asia and Africa.* Cambridge University Press, Cambridge.

Morgera, E., 2012. Bilateralism at the Service of Community Interests? Non-judicial Enforcement of Global Public Goods in the Context of Global Environmental Law. *European Journal of International Law* 23(3), 743–767.

Mueckenberger, U., Jastram, S., 2010. Transnational Norm-Building Networks and the Legitimacy of Corporate Social Responsibility Standards. *Journal of Business Ethics* 97(2), 223–239. doi:10.1007/s10551-010-0506-1.

OECD, 2014. Working Group on Bribery: 2014 Data on Enforcement of the Anti-Bribery Convention. OECD. Available at: www.oecd.org/daf/anti-bribery/Working-Group-on-Bribery-Enforcement-Data-2014.pdf (accessed 23 September 2016).

OECD, 2011. Convention on Combating Bribery of Foreign Public Officials in International Business Transactions: and Related Documents. OECD Publishing. Available at: www.oecd.org/daf/anti-bribery/ConvCombatBribery_ENG.pdf (accessed 23 September 2016).

OECD, 2010. Working Group on Bribery in International Business Transaction: Compilation of Recommendations made in the Phase 2 Reports. OECD. Available at: www.oecd.org/daf/anti-bribery/anti-briberyconvention/38939143.pdf (accessed 23 September 2016).

OECD DAC, 2007. *OECD DAC Handbook on Security Sector Reform: Supporting Security and Justice.* OECD, Paris.

Olaniyan, K., 2014. *Corruption and Human Rights Law in Africa.* Bloomsbury Publishing, London.

O'Neill, O., 1986. *Faces of Hunger: An Essay on Poverty, Justice, and Development.* Harper Collins Publishers, London.

Otto, J.M., 2009. Rule of Law Promotion, Land Tenure and Poverty Alleviation: Questioning the Assumptions of Hernando de Soto. *Hague Journal on the Rule of Law* 1(1), 173–194.

Otto, J.M., Hoekema, A.J., 2012. *Fair Land Governance.* Leiden University Press, Leiden.

Pieth, M., 1999. Harmonization of Law Against Economic Crime. *European Journal of Law Reform* 1(4), 527.
Posadas, A., 2000. Combating Corruption under International Law. *Duke Journal of Comparative and International Law* 10.
Rajagopal, B., 2004. *International Law from Below: Development, Social Movements and Third World Resistance*. Cambridge University Press, Cambridge.
Rosenne, S., 1984. *Practice and Methods of International Law*. Oceana Publications, London.
Rostow, W.W., 1990. *The Stages of Economic Growth: A Non-communist Manifesto*. Cambridge University Press, Cambridge.
Rothwell, D.R., Kaye, S., 2011. International Law: Cases and Materials with Australian Perspectives. Available at: www.cambridge.org/gb/knowledge/isbn/item5562832/?site_locale=en_GB (accessed 28 May 2014).
Sen, A., 1999. *Development as Freedom*. Oxford University Press, Oxford.
Shaw, M.N., 2013. *International Law*. Cambridge University Press, Cambridge.
Shaxson, N., 2007. Oil, Corruption and the Resource Curse. *International Affairs* 83(6), 1123–1140. doi:10.1111/j.1468-2346.2007.00677.x.
Starke, J.G., 1936. Monism and Dualism in the Theory of International Law. *British Yearbook of International Law* 17, 66.
Summerton, N., 1996. Identity Crisis? The Nation-state, Nationality, Regionalism, Language and Religion. *Themelios* 21(3), 16–20.
Tamanaha, B.Z., 2009. *The Primacy of Society and the Failure of Law and Development (SSRN Scholarly Paper No. ID 1406999)*. Social Science Research Network, Rochester, NY.
Tamanaha, B.Z., 2008. Understanding Legal Pluralism: Past to Present, Local to Global. *Sydney Review* 30, 375.
Tamanaha, B.Z., Sage, C., Woolcock, M., 2012. *Legal Pluralism and Development: Scholars and Practitioners in Dialogue*. Cambridge University Press, Cambridge.
Teubner, G., 1988. And God Laughed...: Indeterminacy, Self-Reference, and Paradox in Law. Available at: www.jurauni-Frankfurtde42852676AndGodlaughedpdf (accessed 28 May 2014).
Triepel, H., 1899. *Völkerrecht und landesrecht*. C.L. Hirschfeld, Leipzig.
Trubek, D.M., Santos, A., 2006. Introduction: The Third Moment in Law and Development Theory and the Emergence of a New Critical Practice. Cambridge: Cambridge University Press, Cambridge, pp. 1–18.
Ubink, J.M., McInerney, T., 2011. *Customary Justice: Perspectives on Legal Empowerment*. International Development Law Organization, Rome.
UNGC, 2016a. What is the UN Global Compact? UN Global Compact. Available at: www.unglobalcompact.org/what-is-gc (accessed 23 September 2016).
UNGC, 2016b. Our Mission: UN Global Compact. Available at: www.unglobalcompact.org/what-is-gc/mission (accessed 23 September 2016).
UNGC, 2016c. Anti-Corruption: UN Global Compact. Available at: www.unglobalcompact.org/what-is-gc/our-work/governance/anti-corruption (accessed 23 September 2016).
United States Congress, 1973. Multinational Corporations and United States Foreign Policy Hearings Before the Subcommittee on Multinational Corporations of the Committee on Foreign Relations, United States Senate, Ninety-third – [Ninety-fourth] Congress. US Government Printing Office, Washington.

UNODC, 2016. Signatories to the United Nations Convention against Corruption. UNODC. Available at: www.unodc.org/unodc/en/treaties/CAC/signatories.html (accessed 17 September 2016).

Vlassis, D., 2005. United Nations Convention against Corruption Origins and Negotiation Process, in: Cornell, S. (Ed.), Annual Report for 2004 and Resource Material Series No. 66. Tokyo: UNAFEI, pp. 126–131.

Vreeland, J.R., 2008. Political Institutions and Human Rights: Why Dictatorships Enter into the United Nations Convention Against Torture. *International Organization* 62(1), 65–101.

Webb, P., 2005. The United Nations Convention Against Corruption: Global Achievement or Missed Opportunity? *Journal of International Economic Law* 8(1), 191–229.

Weber, M., 1978. *Economy and Society: An Outline of Interpretive Sociology*. University of California Press, Berkeley, CA.

Wojkowska, D., 2006. *How Informal Justice Systems Can Contribute*. UNDP Oslo Governance Centre, The Democratic Governance Fellowship Programme, Oslo.

WWF, 2017. *How China and its Timber Trade with the EU Can Influence the Flow of Illegal Timber in the Global Market*. WWF, Gland, Switzerland.

Yang, T., Percival, R.V., 2009. The Emergence of Global Environmental Law (October 15, 2009). *Ecology Law Quarterly*, Vol. 36; University of Maryland Legal Studies Research Paper No. 2009-36; Vermont Law School Research Paper No. 09-09. Available at: https://ssrn.com/abstract=1269157.

6 The UK government's use of multilateral and bilateral approaches to tackle corruption in developing countries

> The UK has significantly stepped up its work to fight corruption, and will continue to expand it. The government will reduce the opportunity for corruption; end impunity for those who commit it; and empower those who have suffered from it. It is only by making the international system hostile to illicit funds, creating disincentives and sanctions on corruption at all levels, and ensuring developing countries and their citizens have the tools to tackle it, that we can make progress.
>
> (UK Aid strategy (HMT and DFID, 2015))

The UK has made clear commitments to work on reducing corruption globally, as noted in the aid strategy quote above. A large majority of the UK's work on international development is delivered through other institutions. This is partly a result of the significant increases in the amount of funding DFID has been mandated to disburse without corresponding increases in staff numbers (see Figure 4.1).[1] As such, the first paragraph in the 2014–2015 annual report, which details DFID's operations and expenditure, immediately references the relatively low operating costs that have been even further reduced in 2014–2015:

> DFID's total expenditure was £9.8 billion, a slight reduction from £10.1 billion in 2013–14. This comprised £9.4 billion direct programme expenditure, £248 million total operating costs (including depreciation costs) and £109 million annually managed expenditure. This has been achieved within a lower total operating costs-to-total-budget ratio of 2.4% (previously around 3%).
>
> (DFID, 2015c)

Such reporting is likely to be partly in response to the high levels of scrutiny that DFID receives from the public, especially in relation to efficient use of resources in the context of general austerity and reductions in public sector expenditure. It is worth noting, however, that potentially a significant part of the operating costs that DFID 'saves' might be passed on to the organisations that implement the projects funded by DFID.

International development work inevitably involves a high number of parties that have to approve (both formally and/or informally) of a project for it to be able to take-off and to be likely to achieve the intended results. For DFID work this includes:

- DFID's leadership (Secretary of State and senior officials),
- The political party in power in the UK,
- UK citizens and the media,
- Developing country government leadership,
- Intended developing country recipient institution, as well as
- DFID staff at various levels.

This is a non-exhaustive list. One could also add, for example, recipient country citizens and media, and if a project is being implemented through another UK government department (for example, the NAO or HMRC), a charity (such as Oxfam, WfD or TI) or a multilateral organisation (WB, UN agencies, etc.), then these organisations' core mandates and strategies also have to align with the goals of a particular programme. The personal values and preferences of the individuals involved in planning, delivering and benefiting from programmes will also play a part in the shape and success of a programme.

This chapter will discuss the different delivery mechanisms that the UK uses in its anti-corruption programming, comparing their strengths and weaknesses. Particular attention will be paid to the impact of the interventions, for which, often, the scale of the intervention and mobilisation of other countries and organisations to take part in action can be key. The latter part of this chapter will therefore focus on methods that the UK uses to influence others to do more to tackle corruption.

6.1 Multilateral approaches

OECD DAC (2012) defines multilateral organisations as

> international institutions with governmental membership. They include organisations to which donors' contributions may be reported, in whole or in part, as multilateral Official Development Assistance as well as organisations that serve only as channels for bilateral ODA.

UK development spending through multilateral organisations has been rising in the past years, as can be seen from Table 6.1.

Table 6.1 shows that DFID spends almost two-thirds of its funds through multilateral organisations. This includes multilateral spending as well as bilateral spending through multilateral organisations (multi-bi). For ODA to count as a multilateral contribution under the OECD rules, it cannot be earmarked for particular programmes or purposes; as put by Gulrajani (2016, p. 7), the funding must 'lose its identity and become an integral part of the recipient institution's assets such that donors cannot track and pre-define its uses'. The particularities of multi-bi spending will be discussed in section 6.4.

Table 6.1 UK ODA by delivery channel

Type of ODA	2010		2013		2014	
Total bilateral ODA	**£5.2b**	**60.8%**	**£6.7b**	**59.0%**	**£6.8b**	**58.3%**
Of which multi-bi	£1.9b	22.5%	£2.3b	20.5%	£2.1b	18.3%
Total multilateral ODA	**£3.3b**	**39.2%**	**£4.7b**	**41.0%**	**£4.9b**	**41.7%**
Total ODA	**£8.5b**	**100%**	**£11.4b**	**100%**	**£11.7b**	**100%**

Source: DFID (2015b, p. 14).[1]

Note
1 The figures are rounded therefore might not add up exactly when aggregated.

It is worth mentioning, however, that the balance between multilateral and bilateral aid allocation does not appear to be deliberately chosen. The House of Commons International Development Committee (IDC) noted that 'it is not clear to us how DFID precisely determines its balance between multilateral and bilateral spending', urging the agency to clearly set out the criteria used (IDC, 2016, p. 3). Mark Lowcock, Permanent Secretary of DFID, however, argued in an oral evidence session at the IDC that the decision to use multilateral or bilateral aid delivery channels is 'driven by competition':

> Our strategy to drive value for money is to have competition between the different choices. If we know we want a project to put another million girls in northern Nigeria into education, we get propositions from a variety of service deliverers and choose the one that is going to do it best with the best value for money. With that approach, the outcome of which sort of organisation delivers what for us is driven by value for money and competition, rather than an a priori view. That is the approach that we are keen to sustain.
> (Quoted in IDC, 2016, p. 12)

ICAI, however, argued that 'DFID's choice of multilaterals as a delivery partner is not always evidence based' and that 'DFID does not always consider alternatives to multilaterals in-country, making it hard to ensure transparency and value for money' (ICAI, 2015a, p. 25). It has to be noted, however, that alternatives to channelling funding through multilateral organisations might be lacking due to staffing constraints. As mentioned in this chapter, designing, procuring and overseeing bilateral programmes directly can require significant staff inputs. In offices that have high spending targets and low numbers of staff, direct programme design might not be feasible. It does not, however, preclude spending through other channels such as NGOs or providing direct budget support.

DFID's work with multilateral organisations

ICAI has identified 47 multilateral organisations with which DFID engages (ICAI, 2015a, p. 2). These include UN agencies and international development banks (such as the WB, the European Commission, African Development Bank (AfDB), European Bank for Reconstruction and Development (EBRD), etc.). Expenditure through multilateral organisations consists of the UK's core (and membership) contributions to these organisations' budgets (£4 billion or 42.5 per cent of its total spend in 2014–2015 (DFID, 2015c, p. 60)) as well as individual project, country, region or appeal support through these organisations (multi-bi spending). DFID contributed most to the following organisations' core activities in 2014–2015, as shown in Table 6.2.

The OECD determines what percentage of countries' core contributions to multilateral organisations' budgets qualifies as ODA (ICAI, 2016b, p. 14). For example, only 76 per cent of the core contribution of the UK to the World Health Organization counts as ODA, whereas 60 per cent to the ILO assessed contributions and 100 per cent of contributions to the World Food Programme are ODA-eligible (OECD, 2016). Non-DFID core contributions to multilateral organisations were from the budgets of the organisations responsible for the thematic area (see Table 6.3).

Working through multilateral organisations can have numerous benefits, including coordinating with other donors, avoiding duplication of programmes and providing the possibility for more efficient delivery chains as well as delivering programmes at scale (DFID, 2015b, p. 47). Multilaterals can also provide suitable entry points to deliver programmes as well as perceived neutrality to a variety of interventions abroad (Gulrajani, 2016). This can be necessary in politically sensitive contexts.[2] ICAI also noted that DFID uses multilaterals 'as a mechanism to deliver aid where the security of the delivery chain is vital and where the risk of corruption is high' (ICAI, 2015a, p. 22).

Table 6.2 DFID's contributions to multilateral organisations' core activities

Rank	Organisation	DFID funding in 2014–2015
1	The International Development Association (part of the World Bank Group)	£1.4 billion
2	The European Commission – development share of the budget	£416 million
3	Gavi, the Vaccine Alliance (including the International Finance Facility for Immunisation)	£342.7 million
4	The European Development Fund	£327.3 million
5	The Strategic Climate Fund	£291 million
6	The Global Fund to Fight AIDS, Tuberculosis and Malaria (GATFM)	£285 million
7	The Africa Development Fund (AfDF, including contributions to the African Development Bank)	£217.8 million
8	The Central Emergency Response Fund (CERF)	£94 million
9	The Private Infrastructure Development Group (PIDG)	£72.5 million
10	The Asian Development Fund (AsDF, including contributions to the Asian Development Bank)	£58.3 million

Source: DFID (2015c, p. 60).

Table 6.3 Non-DFID core multilateral contributions

Multilateral agency	Contributing department or fund	£m
European Union (non-DFID share)	–	442
Peacekeeping contributions	Conflict Pool	67
Council of Europe	FCO	25
World Health Organization	Health	11
United Nations	FCO	14
International Labour Organization	DWP	8
Montreal Protocol Multilateral Fund	DEFRA	7
International Atomic Energy Agency	DECC	5
Organisation for Security and Co-operation in Europe	FCO	3
UN Environment Program	DEFRA	3
Commonwealth Foundation	FCO	1
International Organisation for Migration	Home Office	1
International Telecommunications Union	DCMS	0.4
Commonwealth Secretariat	DCMS	0.4
Total		588

Source: ICAI (2016b, p. 15).

The Multilateral Aid Review (MAR) was established in 2010 by the UK government to assess the effectiveness and value for money of channelling the funding for development through the different multilateral organisations (DFID, 2011). An update to the MAR was undertaken in 2013 and a new MAR was due to be released in the first half of 2016. In light of the UK having voted in a referendum to leave the European Union, this has been delayed and will most likely be revised. The 2011 and 2013 MARs have indicated some concerns about the transparency and accountability for the funds channelled through the organisations. ICAI suggested that '[t]ransparency, as opposed to process scrutiny, should be the priority for DFID' (ICAI, 2015a, p. 1).

ICAI has reviewed DFID's engagement with multilateral institutions, concluding that overall DFID's impact on multilateral organisations is significant, not least as it is the largest donor for many key organisations (ICAI, 2015a). The report, however, noted that DFID does not have a clear strategy for its engagement with multilateral organisations. ICAI noted that 'DFID's focus on improving agencies' management processes has often been at the expense of strategic dialogue on what multilaterals do and how they do it' (ICAI, 2015a, p. 1). This chapter subsequently discusses in more detail the main multilateral organisations that the UK works with in the sphere of anti-corruption.

The need for a multilateral approach to combat corruption

The leak of more than 11.5 million confidential documents from the Mossack Fonseca law firm in early 2016, called the 'Panama Papers', brought issues of tax avoidance and evasion to the public's attention (BBC News, 2016). The documents detailed how 214,000 offshore companies were being used by officials, celebrities, criminals, businessmen and their associates, to hide wealth from public scrutiny.

Senior officials ranking as high as heads of state from a number of countries, including Argentina, Iceland, Saudi Arabia, Ukraine and the United Arab Emirates, were implicated, and this resulted in the resignation of some, including the Icelandic Prime Minister Sigmundur Davíð Gunnlaugsson (Castle et al., 2016). The Panama Papers also touched upon the UK, as they revealed that the former Prime Minister (PM) David Cameron's father was a client of the firm (Hamilton, 2016). In response, the British PM announced measures to make offshore jurisdictions more transparent (ibid.). This included pushing for new rules to allow authorities to prosecute corporate entities for facilitating tax evasion. The PM also announced that most of the United Kingdom's dependencies, including the British Virgin Islands and the Cayman Islands, agreed to provide law enforcement agencies and tax authorities full access to information about the beneficial owners of offshore companies (ibid.).

While the use of offshore companies based in tax havens is, in itself, not illegal, these can be used for a variety of criminal purposes, such as tax evasion and laundering the proceeds of criminally obtained funds (from, for example, theft, drugs or arms dealings). Offshore companies will also in many cases be used for tax avoidance – which is not illegal in itself (as opposed to tax evasion), but raises moral and ethical questions and has negative implications on a country's ability to collect tax, as does tax evasion, which is a major source of a government's income, necessary for the delivery of public services and infrastructure. Whereas in 2005 tax collection constituted 35 per cent of developed countries' GDP, in developing countries it constituted only 15 per cent, and 12 per cent of GDP in the poorest developing countries (Fuest and Riedel, 2009, p. 1).

Fuest and Riedel (2009, pp. 4–5) note that most studies distinguish between domestic and international levels of tax avoidance and evasion practices, and elaborate on examples of each:

> The domestic component of tax evasion and avoidance would include, for instance, non-declared or under-reported income from work or domestic business activities. The international component of tax avoidance and evasion includes practices like transfer price manipulation by multinational firms or the holding of financial assets in offshore bank accounts by private individuals with the purpose of concealing capital income.

Examples of tax avoidance would include setting up private foundations to channel money, in jurisdictions where the law prevents registered agents from revealing the true owners of the foundations, using escrow (third party offshore companies) to pay bribes, or bearer shares[3] which can be used to conceal the real identity of the owners of companies (see, for example, de Willebois et al., 2011). In the EU, under the 2005 European Savings Directive, banks are legally obliged to withhold taxes on the interest from the accounts of European customers; this, however, applies to individuals and not corporations, which means that creating an offshore company could facilitate tax evasion.

As such, the domestic and international aspects are interlinked, as the former could lead to the latter if assets are transferred out of the country. Sections 3.5 and 4.2 discussed the increased damage that international tax dodging can cause, as money is taken out of the economy rather than being reinvested within it and supporting local businesses and workers.

The Panama papers provide evidence that when one jurisdiction changes its laws to reduce the scope for secrecy, those seeking to hide their assets can, in many cases, simply transfer their funds to other jurisdictions. Analysis undertaken by the International Consortium of Investigative Journalists (ICIJ), on the changes in the location of Mossack Fonseca's clients' bearer shares, clearly shows that when the British Virgin Islands (BVI) toughened their legislation on bearer shares in 2005 (under BVI Companies Act 2004), Mossack Fonseca moved a significant number of its bearer share clients to Panama (ICIJ, 2016).

Such movements of money across borders, to where the regulations are more permitting, point to the pressing need for the coordinating of global action and regulation. Those attempting to hide the proceeds of corruption, or to evade paying tax, will naturally seek the least regulated environments. An analysis of panel data following a number of G20 countries signing bilateral treaties with tax havens to increase transparency in the banking sector found that 'tax evaders shifted deposits to havens not covered by a treaty with their home country' (Johannesen and Zucman, 2014, p. 65). Coordination globally, which can include working with and through multilateral organisations and international legal instruments, is therefore an important element in ensuring that the proceeds of illicit activity will not be easy to deposit in secretive environments and that benefits from such activity will not be easily enjoyed.

Furthermore, international cooperation between law enforcement agencies is necessary to facilitate prosecutions and the recovery of assets that are moved across borders. This relates to inter-state assistance tracing financial flows across jurisdictions to link assets to a particular offence, as well as gathering evidence within a different jurisdiction to substantiate a case (Zinkernagel et al., 2014, p. 21).

This chapter further discusses a few examples of multinational initiatives that the UK government supports.

StAR and ICAR

ICAR is a not-for-profit 'centre of excellence' in asset recovery, highly regarded as a training and capacity-building provider for developing country institutions working in asset recovery. ICAR's core funding is provided by Liechtenstein, the Swiss Agency for Development and Cooperation and DFID, as well as through project-specific grants. The organisation provides training, casework, legal and policy analysis and IT tools assistance to facilitate asset recovery.

Capacity-building work is useful for asset recovery cases, as these are particularly complex and require a range of financial, accounting, investigatory, forensics and international cooperation skills. Zinkernagel et al. (2014, p. 18) note that capacity-building is particularly important so that:

> (i) law enforcement officials and prosecutors understand and correctly apply the available tools and (ii) partner countries see the added value of conducting their asset recovery investigations and prosecutions through a multi-disciplinary approach. Law enforcement officials, prosecutors, and courts also need to understand how their legal systems interact with foreign ones through mutual legal assistance.

ICAR, however, does not have the mandate to get involved in operational work. Such involvement could breach confidentiality measures if intelligence that is only intended for sharing among state/law enforcement officials with appropriate clearances is viewed by ICAR who are not authorised to see it (due to lack of clearances or the information being shared on a government to government basis). This could hinder and complicate investigation procedures.

StAR is a partnership between the World Bank Group and UNODC 'that supports international efforts to end safe havens for corrupt funds' and works to facilitate the timely return of stolen assets to developing countries (StAR, 2016). It provides a platform for collaboration of different law enforcement agencies as well as expertise in developing legal frameworks and training that could facilitate asset recovery.

Zinkernagel et al. (2014, p. 30) argue that greater donor involvement in the issue of asset recovery is desirable for a number of reasons, including the large impact that it can have on developing countries, and that the stolen assets are often held in financial centres in developed donor countries, stating:

> (i) asset recovery is undoubtedly a development problem; (ii) as a bridge between requesting and requested countries, donor agencies are uniquely positioned to help address it; and (iii) donor agencies can fill a significant gap and prove essential in addressing some of the challenges related to recovering and repatriating stolen assets.

DFID supports StAR and ICAR, which were also discussed in sections on asset recovery – see sections 3.5 and 4.2.

International Organisation of Supreme Audit Institutions (INTOSAI)

Working with regional and multilateral institutions can permit governments to transfer skills to multiple countries while building institutional knowledge. As staff rotations or turnover can be quite high in public sector institutions, the transfer of skills via international and regional mechanisms could prove to be of value (Olson et al., 2016).

The International Organisation of Supreme Audit Institutions (INTOSAI) is 'an umbrella organisation for the external government audit community', founded in 1953 (Intosai, 2016a). It provides 'an institutionalised framework for supreme audit institutions to promote development and transfer of knowledge, improve government auditing worldwide and enhance professional capacities, standing and influence of member SAIs [Supreme Audit Institutions] in their respective countries' (ibid.). Seven regional INTOSAI institutions promote the organisation's work, including the African Organization of Supreme Audit Institutions, which has its branches for English-speaking and French-speaking African countries, respectively – AFROSAI-E and AFROSAI-F (Intosai, 2016b).

INTOSAI's institutions provide audit manuals and guidance on how to apply certain international standards within developing country audit institutions. In particular, AFROSAI-E uses an Institutional Capacity Building Framework to situate the maturity and development of an institution within five levels, considering the following criteria (AFROSAI-E, 2016):

- Independence and Legal Framework
- Organisation and Management
- Human Resources
- Audit Standards and Methodology
- Communication and Stakeholder Management

African Tax Administration Forum (ATAF)

The African Tax Administration Forum (ATAF) works to improve the capacity and revenue collection processes of African states' tax administration institutions. The organisation also aims to 'advance the role of taxation in African governance and state building' and to develop strong partnerships between regional tax administration institutions (ATAF, 2016). ATAF could potentially play a significant role in coordinating anti-money laundering and tracking illicit financial flows regionally; for which the UK's technical support could be valuable.

Commonwealth Secretariat

The Commonwealth Secretariat provides technical advice and guidance to policymakers in Commonwealth countries, to facilitate sustainable and inclusive development, the rule of law, human rights and good governance, among other goals (Commonwealth, 2016). The organisation leverages the members' shared history and institutional structures, to facilitate peer-to-peer cooperation and lesson learning. The Secretariat has been hosting international conferences to bring the stakeholders together. The conferences enhance practitioner's networks, communities of practice and research to improve the efficiency and accountability of public service institutions.

6.2 Bilateral approaches

Bilateral ODA spending is defined, by DFID (2015b, p. 26), as 'all spend that does not take the form of a core contribution to a multilateral organisation as defined on the OECD DAC's list of ODA-eligible international organisations'. This includes money allocated for specific calls or programmes implemented by multilateral agencies, bilateral aid which is not assigned to a particular country or region, debt relief, support to NGOs active in development as well as 'administrative costs and spending on development awareness' (Gulrajani, 2016, p. 7). In 2014, 33.1 per cent of UK's bilateral aid was not assigned to a particular country or region. This included contributions to multilateral agencies' programming where the benefiting country is not known at the outset of the programme (which can be the case with demand-led programmes) (34.3 per cent), core contributions to NGOs and other private institutions (17.8 per cent), DFID projects in multiple regions or countries (25.6 per cent), as well as funds spent supporting international development work in the UK or supporting refugees in the UK (17.8 per cent) (DFID, 2015b, pp. 38–39). Figure 6.1 shows the breakdown allocation of UK's bilateral aid in 2014.

This section will discuss bilateral spending that is not directed via multilateral agencies (bilateral aid excluding multi-bi), which is discussed in more detail in section 6.4.

Bilateral international development assistance delivery mechanisms have the benefit of enabling development agencies to direct funds exactly towards the issues and delivery actors that the institution chooses. Most of the UK's bilateral ODA is spent in its priority countries, as discussed in section 4.1. The OECD peer review of the UK's ODA has noted that '[t]his tight geographical

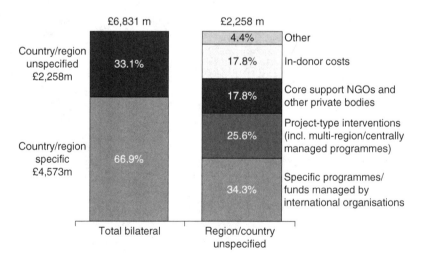

Figure 6.1 Breakdown of UK bilateral aid in 2014.
Source: DFID (2015b, p. 39).

concentration is undermined, to some extent, by the decline in the share of UK bilateral assistance programmed at country level' (OECD, 2014, p. 17).

A distinction can be made between bilateral international development assistance programmes planned and executed from DFID centrally, which are often multi-country programmes, and those designed at a DFID country office. Regarding the former, the OECD (2014b, p. 17) notes that 'DFID's country offices are not systematically consulted about these programmes, which makes it difficult for them to have a comprehensive view of the department's overall actions in country'. An additional complication with centrally managed programmes relates to the number of programmes touching upon some key offices. Some countries can have more than one hundred centrally managed programmes operating in the country (Olson *et al.*, 2016, p. 32). This means that DFID country advisors are often unable to fully engage with and support all the DFID programmes operating in their country due to their large number, and as the country advisors also have a portfolio of local programmes to manage. This also creates issues of coordination.

Country level programmes, however, often do have the benefit of enabling cross-country learning and knowledge dissemination across different DFID country offices. This is particularly useful for research-focused programmes, or those that have a research element.

Bilateral mechanisms also have significant drawbacks. In particular, they require more oversight and management time from the donor agency (which was discussed in section 6.2), they increase the risks of duplication of efforts between different agencies, and some bilateral programming in particular contexts might be perceived as intrusive regarding a country's sovereignty (see section 6.3; this can include anti-corruption in politically volatile and sensitive contexts).

Working with private contractors

The UK is increasingly delivering its international development programmes using private sub-contractors (OECD, 2014, p. 19). While such an approach can facilitate contracting specialists to work on specific programmes, concern has been voiced by a number of DFID's partners about the extent to which 'long-term development of national capacities' is supported when working through private contractors (ibid.).

Fund management

As mentioned at the beginning of the chapter, the wider pressures within the civil service to reduce departments' own administration and running costs (in favour of project costs) has resulted in an increased recourse to large programmes, including challenge funds being tendered by DFID and the FCO. Suppliers that manage funds on behalf of the UK government are required, depending on the programme and working with the UK government department, to undertake the following responsibilities:

- put together the documentation for and advertise calls for tenders to address a particular issue identified to be financed by the fund;
- propose a panel to evaluate the received proposals;
- carry out due diligence checks on selected grantees;
- provide programme support and training;
- oversee grantees' compliance with reporting and monitoring requirements and collate these for the entire fund; and
- compile and disseminate the lessons learned from the programme.

By tendering out fund management programmes to private sector suppliers the UK government substantially reduces its own project running and monitoring burden. In some cases, or for certain components, there is a clear advantage to commissioning the private sector to undertake the activities. For example, the due diligence requirements can be very effectively done by private sector institutions that have large databases, experience and expertise in such work. Other programme elements, however, might be just as easily undertaken by the international development organisations themselves.

Contracting

In its programme documents and reports DFID has been putting a lot of emphasis on getting value for money for its funding (DFID, 2016c). Section 4.1 discussed in detail the scrutiny that DFID is subject to by various institutions and civil society groups, and some of the approaches that the organisation takes to increase its value for money. This includes largely moving to payment by results (PBR) contracting: output-based and milestone contracting, whereby it pays its contractors for the delivery of a report or a project, rather than for the level of input.[4] The IDC (2016a) argues that the positive effects of PBR have not been sufficiently proven, particularly in light of the adverse incentives for programmes to focus on easily achievable short-term goals rather than on tackling the root causes of problems in difficult environments (IDC, 2016, p. 22). Furthermore, PBR can complicate DFID's other goals of ensuring flexibility and adaptiveness of its multi-year programming.

DFID's increased focus on demand-led rather than supply-led programmes, and for these to correspond with the needs and priorities of the aid recipient developing countries, further complicates its ability to set milestones for programmes at the outset of large multi-year programmes, as it can be difficult to foresee demand before starting and marketing a programme.

Following the same value for money reasoning, DFID tries to reduce the risk that falls on it by various means, such as having its contracts set to be paid in British pounds. This can, however, become a particular issue for DFID beneficiaries if the value of the pound falls, as when it happened following the referendum in Britain on whether Britain should remain an EU member state.

Working with national governments

DFID has largely moved away from direct general budget support for developing countries to more targeted forms of financing, and has committed to end general budget support (HMT and DFID, 2015, p. 21; IDC, 2016a, p. 3). This could partly be explained by allegations of corruption within the programmes and the difficulties associated with donors tracking and ensuring value for money of funds that are being spent by governments in developing countries. Section 4.1 elaborated on the example of Uganda, which had funding suspended due to allegations of international development funds not being used for the purposes they were intended, and instead being syphoned off to government officials' private accounts.

As such, while DFID rarely channels money through national developing country governments, numerous programmes offer technical assistance to governments. Nevertheless, the IDC has noted that traditional budget support, if done in the presence of anti-corruption controls and a favourable environment, can have the significant benefit of giving aid recipient governments ownership and control of their development work (IDC, 2016a, p. 3). It can also help prevent duplication of service provision as well as an erosion of the social contract between the citizens of a country, who give legitimacy to a government, in return for the provision of basic services such as security, education and healthcare. Furthermore, the approach is low in transaction costs and provides a predictable source of income to developing countries, and will be more appropriate as an aid delivery mechanism in well-governed countries (IDC, 2016a, p. 13). As such, the IDC (2016, p. 4) 'recommend therefore that consideration ... be given as to the case for an option to give general budget support in exceptional circumstances, where systems are in place to effectively monitor transparency and accountability'.

Working with other UK government departments

The UK government has committed to increasingly channelling its ODA through UK government departments other than DFID (HMT, 2015, p. 29). This will significantly increase the level and number of UK government departments that will spend ODA (see figures in Table 6.4 for current levels of ODA spending by HMG's departments).

DFID's Statistics on International Development 2015 report also notes the geographical differences in allocation of DFID and non-DFID funding. Whereas DFID spent most of its funds in the priority countries it had selected (see section 4.1 on this), in 2014 DFID supported 66 countries; and the UK as a whole provided ODA to 131 countries (DFID, 2015b, p. 31). See Figure 6.2 for a breakdown of DFID and non-DFID spending. More than 80 per cent of the UK's ODA was, however, spent in 20 countries (DFID, 2015b, p. 31).

It is also interesting to note the differences between DFID and non-DFID allocations of ODA to countries of different levels of income. As shown by Table 6.5,

Table 6.4 ODA spending by UK government departments other than DFID[1]

	2013		2014	
	£m	% UK ODA	£m	% UK ODA
Department for International Development	10,016	87.7	10,084	86.0
Of which:				
EU attribution	689	6.0	374	3.2
Total non-DFID	1,409	12.3	1,642	14.0
Of which:				
Foreign & Commonwealth Office	295	2.6	366	3.1
Department of Energy and Climate Change	408	3.6	192	1.6
Home Office	33	0.3	136	1.2
Department for Business, Innovation and Skills	49	0.4	79	0.7
Department for Environment Food and Rural Affairs	40	0.4	57	0.5
Scottish Government	11	0.1	12	0.1
Department of Health	12	0.1	11	0.1
Department for Work and Pensions	10	0.1	8	0.1
Export Credits Guarantee Department	30	0.3	3	0.0
Ministry of Defence	3	0.0	2	0.0
Welsh Government	1	0.0	1	0.0
Department for Culture, Media and Sports	1	0.0	0	0.0
Other sources of UK ODA				
EU Attribution (non-DFID)	124	1.1	442	3.8
Conflict Pool	198	1.7	180	1.5
Gift Aid	91	0.8	106	0.9
CDC Capital Partners PLC	100	0.9	42	0.4
BBC World Service	0	0.0	2	0.0
Colonial Pensions administered by DFID	2	0.0	2	0.0
Total UK Net ODA	**11,424**	**100.0**	**11,726**	**100.0**

Source: DFID (2015b) data annex, table 3.

Note

1 It is worth noting a few changes in the calculations of ODA contributions between 2013 and 2014. First of all, EU contributions, 85 per cent of which had been allocated to DFID prior to 2014, have now been reduced to 46 per cent (DFID, 2015b, p. 15). This is to reflect that other HMG departments lead on programmes such as 'European Neighbourhood' and the 'Pre-Accession' EU funding. Furthermore, DFID's funding to the Conflict Pool (the predecessor to the Conflict, Security and Stability Fund) had until 2014 been calculated within DFID's total ODA spending, and was only separated in 2014 (DFID, 2015b, p. 19).

DFID allocated the majority of its funding to least developed countries (LDCs), whereas only 20.8 per cent of non-DFID ODA was allocated to LDCs.

Verdier (2008, p. 467) argues that as the recipient country's wealth increases, the marginal political gains to the donor increase, whereas developmental gains to the recipient country that are realised, with each dollar spent on aid in a country, decrease (see Figure 6.3).

Multilateral and bilateral approaches 185

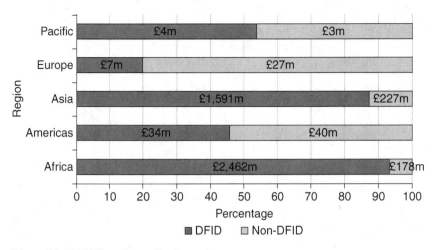

Figure 6.2 2014 bilateral spending by regions.
Source: DFID (2015b, p. 36).

While it is worth keeping in mind that the majority of poor people currently live in middle-income countries such as China and India (Sumner, 2012), such discrepancies raise the question of whether ODA spent by departments other than DFID have the same primary focus of poverty reduction as DFID is bound to by law. The 2015 UK Aid Strategy cites 'tackling extreme poverty and helping the world's most vulnerable' as the fourth out of the four objectives of UK ODA (HMT and DFID, 2015, p. 9).

To avoid sending the wrong message regarding the primary objective of ODA to HMG departments other than DFID, the House of Commons International Development Committee (IDC), in their 2016 interim report on the allocation of UK aid resources, argues that

> The Government should make reducing poverty a legal obligation for the spending of all ODA, regardless of which department is spending it and

Table 6.5 Breakdown of UK bilateral net ODA by income group in 2014

	DFID		Non-DFID	
	£m	%	£m	%
Least Developed Countries	2,224	62	88	21
Other Low-Income Countries	228	6	31	7
Low Middle-Income Countries	1,013	28	249	59
Upper-Middle-Income Countries	144	4	57	13
Total	**3,609**	**100**	**425**	**100**

Source: DFID (2015b, p. 33).

which legal power it is being spent under, which should be made explicit in all ODA programming.

(IDC, 2016, p. 3)

This section looks at the ODA spent on tackling corruption by the different HMG departments and agencies.

FCO

The FCO is playing a major role in interdepartmental funds, such as the Prosperity Fund and the Conflict, Security and Stability Fund (HMT and DFID, 2015). The Conflict, Security and Stability Fund is a joint fund of DFID, the FCO and the Ministry of Defence, managed by the National Security Council (NSC). The 2015 spending review noted that it is expected to grow by 19 per cent in real terms by 2019–2020, from £1 billion in 2015–2016 to over £1.3 billion by 2019–2020 (HMT, 2015).

The Prosperity Fund is a £1.3 billion fund, intended to run for 5 years (2015–2020), and managed by a secretariat within the FCO and overseen by a cross-ministerial board (ibid.). The fund aims to support growth in ODA-eligible countries, by investing in infrastructure, education, healthcare as well as governance. Anti-corruption features as one of the key themes as well. The fund does not have specific allocations intended for certain regions, countries, sectors or departments, but aims to strategically allocate money to the best opportunities that different HMG departments put forward. While the fund's primary purpose

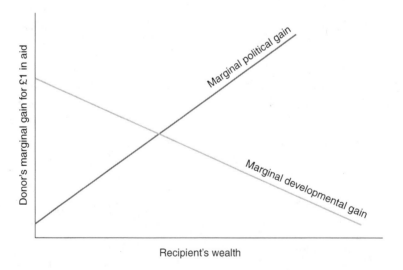

Figure 6.3 Donors' marginal gains as a function of the recipient country's wealth.
Source: Verdier (2008, p. 467).

is poverty reduction, it takes the view that the best way of achieving poverty reduction is economic activity. The secondary purpose of the fund is to increase the links and trade opportunities for UK companies between the UK and countries where the fund operates.

The House of Commons International Development Committee noted concerns over the Conflict, Security and Stability Fund being 'led by the National Security Council (NSC), which also raises particular issues over its accountability and transparency' (IDC, 2016, p. 15). This is particularly due to the mandate of the NSC being primarily concentrated on the UK's national interests and the associated lack of transparency and accountability towards the public. Civil society raised concerns to the IDC about 'whether it will prioritise poverty reduction over a narrow definition of the national interest' (IDC, 2016, p. 16).

HMRC

HMRC has for the last five years been involved in long- and short-term assistance programmes with developing countries' tax institutions: the HMRC Tax Expert Unit (£1.8 million, 2015–2018) and the HMRC Capacity Building Unit (£22.9 million, 2014–2024) (ICAI, 2016a). The latter programme provides short-term on-request tax assistance to developing countries.

HMRC also provides secondments to developing country tax institutions for one to two years, and has established mentoring arrangements for staff at senior levels at HMRC and its counterparts in developing countries. ICAI noted that DFID is the largest donor in the international tax sphere, however its tax programmes are still at an early stage and HMRC has not yet reached half the planned deployment capacity (ICAI, 2016a). The review further raised the question of the effectiveness of short-term specialised expert assistance, as opposed to long-term engagement with the developing country agencies.

Law enforcement agencies

Three law enforcement institutions in the UK primarily engage in anti-corruption internationally: the National Crime Agency (NCA), Crown Prosecution Services (CPS) and the Serious Fraud Office (SFO). The agencies do undertake international anti-corruption work, on cases of (mostly grand) corruption that have a UK element: either because the perpetrators are UK citizens or companies, or the money passes through the UK.

The International Corruption Unit (ICU) within the NCA, which investigates international bribery, corruption and related offences and supports foreign law enforcement agencies with international anti-corruption investigations, has received significant funding from DFID (NCA, 2016a). The Unit has absorbed the work that the London Metropolitan Police Proceeds of Corruption Unit did previously on investigations of money laundering in the UK by foreign politicians and officials, and the City of London Overseas Anti-Corruption Unit's investigations of UK citizens and companies accused of involvement in overseas corruption.

The ICU has worked and continues to work alongside their counterparts in developing countries, to assist them in drafting Mutual Legal Assistance (MLA) requests and to gather evidence on corrupt activities that would later be used in court. This work builds the capacity of the local institutions and also facilitates the work of UK law enforcement institutions, namely by improving the quality of evidence supplied by developing countries for prosecuting the crimes. Similarly, the CPS posts criminal justice advisors in developing countries, usually based in high commissions or embassies. The NCA also deploys International Liaison Officers (ILOs) to developing countries, to facilitate collaboration and long-term partnerships between the UK and local or regional law enforcement institutions.

The international division of the CPS and the NCA also works with the wider legislative, court and administration of justice systems in developing countries to improve the overall justice environment and the chances of the corrupt being prosecuted for their crimes domestically. The CPS's proceeds of crime unit works with the NCA to pursue corruption cases that can be prosecuted in the UK.

The SFO works to tackle the most complex and serious cases of fraud, corruption and bribery in England and Wales. As such, the high profile and large cases that the SFO works on can send powerful messages against impunity to corrupt officials and businessmen in developing countries. SFO's work is case driven, and as a much smaller organisation than the NCA or the CPS, it has to invest its capacity-building resources strategically. It nevertheless could offer support and training to its counterparts in developing countries with which it works on cases or is likely to collaborate with in the future (Olson *et al.*, 2016).

Coordination

Issues of coordination have been noted by the IDC of the House of Commons, which has suggested that 'a lack of clarity may exist as to which department may be leading and coordinating delivery of ODA, where a number of different departments are involved in the same region or area of work' (IDC, 2016, p. 27).

As the 2015 Aid Strategy stipulates that going forward more ODA will be spent through government departments other than DFID (HMT and DFID, 2015, p. 10), coordination is a particularly important factor to consider. DFID, however, does not have a mandate to oversee and coordinate ODA spent by other UK government departments (ICAI, 2015b, p. 1). As discussed in the previous section, DFID funds work on anti-corruption through other government agencies, including HMRC, CPS, SFO, FCO and the NAO. This multiplicity of agencies working towards the same goal, the differences in political economies of developing countries as well as various institutions' individual structures, cultures and leadership arrangements, in addition to a number of donors and international organisations working on these same issues, require significant coordination efforts.

Furthermore, there is a need to keep in mind the institutional priorities of the different government departments that might be engaging in anti-corruption work within a development context. For example, the UK's law enforcement agencies, including the CPS and the NCA, have been working in developing countries and contributing to the UK's ODA work. The work that they do thus has to fit within their institutional mandate (countering UK-related crime), as well as the ODA requirements of being spent primarily for developmental purposes. There might also be an issue of the availability of staff within other HMG institutions to carry out work that is not seen as part of the institution's core mandate. With the majority of HMG institutions having undergone significant funding cuts, departments might find it difficult to release staff, particularly those specialising in areas of high demand, as they would struggle to have their regular responsibilities covered.

Interdepartmental coordination and policy consistency is important in the context of mutual legal assistance and asset recovery, as noted by Zinkernagel et al. (2014, p. 21),

> if a donor country fails to respond to MLA requests from a developing country or does not apply domestic policies aimed at curbing money laundering, this may completely undermine efforts to build that developing country's capacity to investigate and prosecute asset recovery cases.

The work of the different government departments abroad also has to be closely coordinated, to ensure a 'one HMG' approach. This can take the form of, for example, requiring missions or programmes to be co-funded by different government departments to ensure buy-in and coordination, or within DFID's centrally funded programmes, for interventions to be partially funded by the local DFID country offices. This does ensure coordination (as country offices would not be likely to contribute to funding work they do not see as a priority), however it also increases the administrative burden on country offices and other government departments and complicates country office budget planning processes.

Certain risks to sending audit or law enforcement practitioners to developing states to share experience and lessons learnt should be kept in mind. Technologies and systems being used in donor and recipient countries can differ vastly. Technical barriers to interdepartmental cooperation and information-sharing, such as incompatible IT systems within different departments as well as different staff reporting and responsibility lines, can also be an issue. Anecdotes can be heard about, for example, developing country intelligence officers delivering training sessions on investigations in fragile and low-income countries, sharing 'best practice' but having no experience or suggestions on how to work in an environment where social security numbers are not used and criminals' identification documents are often forged.

6.3 Key strengths and weaknesses of different implementation channels

To date, analysis of the strengths and weaknesses of different programme implementation channels has been primarily directed towards 'the range of options within each channel, rather than calculated consideration *across* the bilateral and multilateral spectrum', as put by Gulrajani (2016, p. 6). Opinions about the benefits and drawbacks of the different aid channels, however, can be strong; as noted by the former chair of the OECD DAC: 'in many donor countries there is almost a built-in notion (in governments and perhaps still more in legislatures) that "bilateral is best"' (OECD, 2015, p. 82). This section, building on the work of Gulrajani (2016), discusses the relative effectiveness of the two programme implementation channels.

Institutionalist literature suggests that multilateral approaches are more effective than bilateral approaches in bargaining and coordination of approaches (see Oye, 1986; Snidal, 1991; Verdier, 2008). This, in turn, permits operating on a larger scale and using standardised approaches that permit the reduction of transaction costs (Verdier, 2008, p. 440). While working through multilateral organisations clearly presents benefits, not least of which is also of cutting down on the UK government's own administrative costs, it can also present significant drawbacks. Different transparency measures within multilateral organisations can make tracing the impact of the money the UK has allocated to causes and projects via these organisations, and ensuring effectiveness in the use of funds, challenging.

Indeed, individual governments are directly accountable to their citizens for their expenditure, and monitoring of DFID's expenditure is substantial, as discussed in section 4.1. This creates incentives for DFID itself to ensure that the money it spends is used appropriately and purposefully. Furthermore, bilateral assistance can create the foundations for long-term partnerships and a direct exchange of expertise (Sippel and Neuhoff, 2009).

The strengths of bilateral approaches within international relations institutionalist literature are considered to primarily be 'in areas involving enforcement through retaliation', as put by Verdier (2008, p. 440). Authors such as Wright and Winters (2010, p. 73) go so far as to say that

> bilateral aid during the Cold War was ineffective in promoting reform because donors could not credibly commit to withdrawing aid from strategically important recipients even when reform was not forthcoming, but in the post–Cold War era, donors can make more credible threats to withdraw aid.

Bilateral approaches to international development, however, are generally considered less effective than multilateral approaches (Gulrajani, 2016). This section will discuss the factors that might render a particular implementation channel more effective.

Political capture

A growing evidence base suggests that bilateral approaches are more susceptible to political capture, which can skew the aid allocation process to primarily consider the donor's rather than the recipient's interests (see Gulrajani, 2016; Verdier, 2008).

Cremer (2008, p. 3) notes that the issue of politics and diplomatic ties between countries has for a long time meant that countries were reluctant to engage with issues of corruption on a bilateral basis. Corruption was perceived as an issue of purely domestic affairs.[5] Accusations of corruption are indeed often being used as a political tool to bring down or damage political opponents, or, as put by Widmalm (2008, p. 213), 'corruption ... is a favourite stick with which to beat political opponents'. Nye (1970, p. 566) argues that '[o]ne of the first charges levelled at the previous regime by the leaders of the coup of the less developed country is "corruption". And generally the charge is accurate.' Widmalm (2008, p. 122) notes that '[r]egardless of whether it is true or not, the effects of an allegation of corruption are truly hard to dodge'.

Gulrajani (2016, p. 10) suggests that multilateral approaches are seen to be more autonomous and neutral than bilateral ones, as '[b]eing at arm's length from major shareholders is, in most people's minds, indicative of greater objectivity in decision-making regarding the aims and modalities of development cooperation, minimising the exploitation of aid for the purposes of securing the national interest'. Reinsberg (2015, p. 46) notes that multilateral organisations such as the World Bank are 'remote from electoral pressure' and accountability to voters, thus reducing political pressures. International law and multilateral organisations, however, are also susceptible to political capture, particularly due to the influence of their largest shareholders (Gulrajani, 2016, p. 11). Plato's writings thousands of years ago illustrate one of the most important issues to be considered when discussing international approaches to issues such as corruption – who sets the rules and for whose advantage:

> And each ruling group sets down laws for its own advantage; a democracy sets down democratic laws, a tyranny tyrannic laws; and the others do the same. And they declare that what they have set down – their own advantage – is just for the ruled, and the man who departs from it they punish as a breaker of the law and a doer of unjust deeds. This, best of men, is what I mean: in every city the same thing is just, the advantage of the established ruling body. It surely is master; so the man who reasons rightly concludes that everywhere justice is the same thing, the advantage of the stronger.
> (Plato, 1991, p. 16)

An important question to consider is that of who is, or has been included in, making laws. In the context of a nation-state and a democracy in particular, people are delegated to make laws for the benefit of the entire population. In an international context, however, states come together with their own values and national interests in mind first and foremost, which are also considered when tackling issues that are a threat to all states (such as climate change, spread of diseases or terrorism) and when working together to increase the well-being of all states (for example, in trade). This section considers the extent to which international law and policies advantage states at different stages of development, states of different sizes and those states that came out victors of certain conflicts.

A key issue that often arises from multilateral agreements is the difference in the individual country or region's social, political, economic, historical and cultural circumstances. As put by Rider (1997, p. 4),

> [w]hilst states can and should learn from each other, this must be a cooperative exercise, characterized by mutual respect and sensitivity. It is remarkable in certain areas of the law, such as financial services regulation, how some have supposed that rules of law that have been fashioned over many years to address the circumstances in a particular environment can be simply picked up and planted, with any hope of success, in an entirely foreign situation. Markets are a result of the economic, social and political factors that operate within a given society; the laws which regulate and reinforce them should be specific to that particular environment.

Addressing grand corruption requires compatible global structures. The manner in which they are introduced and designed, however, may need to be adapted to reduce disproportionate financial and other burdens on lower-income and small states.

Small and micro states, particularly those that have been traditionally viewed as 'tax havens' have a disproportionate burden as a result of these (Grynberg et al., 2004). Following the 2008 crisis, compliance with regulations such as the Financial Action Task Force (FATF) rules can be seen as a necessary step in an attempt to safeguard the integrity of the international financial system by combatting money laundering and terrorist financing. The expertise, technology and manpower required to comply with the regulations and submit the required information within the required timeframe, however, can place a disproportionately heavy burden on small and micro states. Failure to comply with such regulations would complicate these countries' (for example, Caribbean islands) participation in the international markets, which is something that such countries can often not afford. Money therefore can be diverted from nationally identified priorities such as disaster prevention and resilience to financial reporting (Sharman and Mistry, 2008).

Issues of leadership within international fora and organisations can pose difficulties. Most donors and international organisations acknowledge the merits of a coordinated and unified approach to matters of development. Agreeing on who will ultimately be taking the lead on shaping the agenda and decision-making, however, might be problematic if more states want to 'coordinate' rather than 'be coordinated'.

Key financial contributors do get more standing regarding shaping the agenda, as they can match funds that others contribute, or pilot programmes they want to see happening on a larger scale. As such, DFID has been proudly stressing that it upholds its commitment to 0.7 per cent of GNI spending on international development. The OECD peer review of the UK's ODA spending notes that reaching the 0.7 per cent target in 2013 is a 'commendable, well planned achievement [which] adds weight to the UK's internationally recognised leading role. Maintaining that level of support until 2015/2016 and beyond will reinforce the UK's legitimacy with respect to the global development agenda' (OECD, 2014, p. 17). One of the factors that DFID considers when evaluating the success and value for money of its international development assistance via multilateral organisations is the degree to which it was able to influence the agenda and activities of the multilateral institution (see, for example, ICAI, 2015a). Some argue, this can result in resource inefficiencies and interfere with the setting of long-term and coherent agendas by multilateral agencies (Gulrajani, 2016).

Nevertheless, it is worth noting that the 'veneer of neutrality' that multilateral agencies possess can be useful when negotiating recipient governments' policy concessions, regardless of the actual pressures that bilateral donors exert within the structures of the multilateral institutions (Gulrajani, 2016, p. 11). As put by Rodrik (1996, p. 177), it allows 'sovereign governments to swallow a bitter pill without appearing to cave-in to either another sovereign government or a private entity'.

Monitoring, enforcement and policing

Thucydides, in the History of the Peloponnesian War, presents a dialogue between an Athenian general who conquers the small and politically neutral island of Melos, and a policeman of the island (see Lanni, 2008, p. 469), where the Athenian claims the following:

> we both alike know that in the question of human affairs the question of justice only enters where there is equal power to enforce it, and that the powerful exact what they can, and the weak grant what they must.

Issues of enforcement are central to theoretical discussions on the effectiveness and the nature of law. If we are to move away from the unit of a nation-state towards a more international or transnational approach to law, the deliverability of rights and privileges, and economic and social rights in particular, becomes very difficult to ensure as it has traditionally been the responsibility of individual nation-states. Global procedural regularity and uniformity is almost impossible to ensure; and law is largely dependent on the will of states to enforce it in other jurisdictions. Even if states are willing to enforce international law in other jurisdictions, the methods of doing so remain problematic. There is an issue of immediacy, where international justice systems often are rather slow at responding to violations, as well as the relevance and proportionality of sanctions. Economic sanctions are often resorted to in cases of violations of international law. These, however, take a while to have an effect. Furthermore, in terms of proportionality and relevance, sanctions are either on an entire state, in which case their effect is not necessarily most harshly felt by the perpetrators, but rather the ordinary citizens of a country; or it is on a small group of individuals related to the state apparatus, in which case it could be argued that freezing their assets or seizing their properties abroad is not on the same scale as widespread and serious violations of law or human rights that they might have engaged in. Humanitarian interventions are extremely politically controversial, costly and only methods of last resort in a select number of cases.

Universal enforcement of international law is an inherently problematic concept, as it would imply that independent states are willing to surrender part of their sovereignty to an acknowledged 'superior' authority (which would then be able to enforce international law). This authority would also have to have the material resources, in addition to an acknowledged theoretical superiority, necessary to carry out judgments. The International Court of Justice (ICJ) can only adjudicate when both parties involved in a case agree to abide by its decision (art. 36 of the Statute of the ICJ). The International Criminal Court (ICC) operates under the principle of complementarity, where it only investigates and prosecutes cases when 'the State is unwilling or unable genuinely to carry out the investigation or prosecution' (art. 17 of the Rome Statute). This effectively translates into international courts addressing cases in developing and less politically and economically powerful states, and results in criticism of international legal institutions as being a tool of the Western countries to judge the politically and economically weaker nations. For example, the ICC's cases' geographical concentration (see ICC, 2014) in one continent has led to the court being criticised as a 'court for Africa'.[6]

Other explanations for the geographical concentration of the cases have been put forward. First of all, the financial aspect of investigating cases on an international level inevitably requires great selectivity of cases and trial of only the most serious offenders; which can easily lead to (perceived or actual) politicisation of international courts. Human Rights Watch (2008, pp. 44–45) points out that the Rome Statute, the treaty that established the ICC and delimits its functions, jurisdiction and structure, delimits the jurisdiction of the court to crimes that occurred after the 1 July 2002, and requires the elements of gravity and complementarity for a case to be admissible. This effectively excludes many situations from the court's jurisdiction. Moreover, the ICC can only investigate cases implicating states that are parties to the Rome Statute, those referred by the UNSC, or non-state parties that voluntarily submit to the ICC's jurisdiction.[7]

Traditionally, inter-state legal agreements and commitments have been of a largely bilateral and reciprocal nature, rather than international and/or seeking to become universal. The Vienna Convention on the Law of Treaties (VCLT) codifies the role of reciprocity in the law of treaties, establishing the requirement of a mutual relationship for a treaty provision to be relevant. Subsequently, only a state that can prove it has been directly affected by the non-abidance to a treaty of another state can successfully invoke the treaty obligations of the latter state in court.

Paulus (2012, p. 90) discusses this as being

> the 'tit for tat' of classical international law, which, in a positive sense, can lead to a virtuous cycle of law abidance, but also, in a negative sense, to a downward spiral in which one violation follows the next and obligation and violation become indistinguishable from each other.

This would manifest in the form of a 'race to the bottom' in the sphere of bilateral financial regulation, in destroying rather than protecting the environment, and in legalising rather than abolishing torture. The author further argues that the system of reciprocity to enforce international law should be transformed rather than abandoned, as central institutions 'remain under-developed to [unilaterally] implement community interests and values at the international level' (Paulus, 2012, p. 91).

Shaw (2013, pp. 7–8) speaks of reciprocity (for example, in the case of states protecting the diplomatic immunity of foreign officials on duty, expecting their diplomats to receive the same treatment) and of states' consideration of the advantages and rewards for observing international law (such as the possibility of one state's observance of international law swaying an otherwise neutral state, as well as reassuring friendly states, to support them in the case of an international conflict). Bilateralism, however, is not applicable in human rights, humanitarian and related law. The Vienna Convention (VCLT, art. 60(5)) recognises the particularity of human rights treaties in comparison to other inter-state agreements, stating that paragraphs 1 to 3 of art. 60 are not valid in the context of treaties of humanitarian character. These paragraphs refer to material breaches of bilateral treaties by one of the parties entitling the other to invoke the breach as grounds for terminating the treaty or for suspending its operation.

The lack of bilateralism in a large number of multilateral treaties means that monitoring bodies are very important in ensuring the upholding of the treaties, as other 'State parties can hardly be counted upon to exercise the kind of horizontal control which, in usual treaties, provides the required disciplining function' (De Schutter, 2010, p. 96). This is evidenced, according to De Schutter (ibid.), by a 'striking underuse by States of mechanisms allowing for inter-State complaints', both at global and regional levels. Individual states would need to have both the resources and the interest required to monitor other states' compliance with international law, especially when they are not directly affected by particular states' behaviour (for example, in relation to human rights violations of other countries' citizens or asylum seekers on foreign territory). Also, some states may be reluctant to confront their trade partners, allies or countries of strategic interest in other areas in relation to what can be perceived as domestic policies (such as the aforementioned human rights issues).

Organisations tasked with monitoring compliance are often severely under-resourced. For example, the UN Working Group on Arbitrary Detention (UNWGAD), which is mandated to 'investigate cases of deprivation of liberty imposed arbitrarily or otherwise inconsistently with the relevant international standards set forth in the Universal Declaration of Human Rights or in the relevant international legal instruments accepted by the States concerned' (OHCHR, 2013), consists of voluntary members who simultaneously hold various other positions and has no policing or sanctioning power. It is not surprising that enforcement and monitoring agencies are not strongly supported or funded by the large, politically and economically powerful states, as some of the monitoring agencies' decisions and acts (if these were entirely independent) would not always serve the funding states' interests. International and independent monitoring of state compliance with treaties and declarations would be a very costly undertaking. Therefore, for many treaties and agreements, a system of self-monitoring is in place, whereby 'states submit reports on human rights violations taking place within their borders and the measures they are taking to eliminate them' (see Hill (2010, p. 1162) also Hafner-Burton and Tsutsui (2005)). However, trusting non-democratic countries with a dubious track record to honestly report on the progress of the state in ensuring its citizens' social and political rights seems a little too optimistic.

Furthermore, the international courts do not possess an international policing system that they could call upon to arrest criminals and surrender them to international courts for trial. Individual states' police forces therefore have to be relied upon. This is problematic for two reasons – in non-democratic states, the police may not have the autonomy, or be willing, to challenge potentially corrupt/violent leaders; and when the police force of another state is brought in (which is an increasingly common phenomenon), the values that they are defending may differ from the prevalent value in their host state. Huggins (1998) argues that the United States has used its police assistance programmes in other states as a means to establish intelligence and other social control structures in host states.

Authors such as Shaw (2013, p. 6), however, insist that despite the lack of strict enforcement and monitoring mechanisms, '[c]ontrary to popular belief, states do observe international law, and violations are comparatively rare'. The author refers to 'a common frame of reference' and 'a common language' that international law provides states in dispute or disagreement: '[i]t can constitute a mutually understandable vocabulary book and suggest possible solutions which follow from a study of its principles' (Shaw, 2013, p. 7). Such a claim, however, can be challenged by pointing to the fact that the official and binding legal documents are usually in English; and while translations of these exist, the translations are often not officially binding, and can in fact contain inaccuracies or connotations not present in other languages, which could lead to misunderstandings and further disagreements.

Accountability and efficiency

As discussed in section 4.1, DFID is scrutinised by a number of official bodies, including the parliamentary committee on international development and ICAI, and perhaps most intently by the public and the media, who are interested in how efficiently the UK's taxpayers' money is spent. This section has discussed how this distance from the electorate permits multilateral organisations to reduce popular political pressures on the focus of the organisation's work (Reinsberg, 2015). This can result in reduced scrutiny of the effectiveness of international development assistance spending, and render bilateral channels better at 'controlling how resources are spent and apportioning blame and credit' (Gulrajani, 2016, p. 15).

Such scrutiny of bilateral donors translates into intense reporting requirements for aid recipients and multilateral organisations that receive earmarked funds. The World Bank (2004, p. 207) noted:

> Tanzanian government officials have to prepare about 2,000 reports of different kinds to donors and receive more than 1,000 donor delegations each year. These requirements tax rather than build provider organizations' limited capacities, diverting efforts toward satisfying donor obligations rather than reporting to domestic policymakers.

Furthermore, donors often expect to meet with high-ranking officials and policymakers during their visits, which creates a significant administrative burden on the leadership of local institutions. Multilateral organisations can play a significant role in streamlining reporting requirements and subsequently reducing the burden on recipient country governments. Furthermore, Palagashvili and Williamson (2016) suggest that bilateral donors are more fragmented sectorally and geographically.

Effectively targeted aid has been argued to signify aid spent either in the poorest countries (see Alesina and Dollar, 2000; Dreher *et al.*, 2009; Wright and Winters, 2010) or in well-governed countries (see Hout, 2007; Winters and Martinez, 2015). Multilateral agencies are observed to be spending more aid in poorer countries (Gulrajani, 2016, p. 12) and bilateral agencies in better-governed countries (Dollar and Levin, 2006; Palagashvili and Williamson, 2016). Bilateral agencies have been noted to give 19 per cent of their aid to low-income countries overall, whereas multilateral agencies on average spend 55 per cent in low-income countries (Gulrajani, 2016, p. 12). Nevertheless, bilateral donors are better placed to provide peer-to-peer support to government officials and share experience and operational skills, which could be very useful to support, for example, asset recovery. Solely considering a country's level of income to determine whether aid flows are directed towards the poor, however, does not take into account the fact that now the majority of poor people live in middle-income countries. As such, aid strategically directed towards making countries' income work for the poor could have a great positive effect on poor people (see Sumner, 2012).

Nunnenkamp and Thiele (2006) suggest that donors with colonial history or particular export-related interests accord less significance to the quality of governance in recipient countries. Schudel (2008) argues that donors with lower levels of corruption are less tolerant of corruption in recipient countries and are therefore more selective of aid recipients based on governance criteria. It is important to note, however, that the least well-governed countries are perhaps in most need of technical assistance to improve their governance structures. Assistance, of course, has to be directed strategically and with appropriate safeguards in place to avoid funds being misappropriated. Dietrich (2013) notes that in countries where governance is poor, donors tend to use non-state actors such as NGOs and private sector partners for programme implementation, rather than recipient country structures, to increase the likelihood of programmes achieving their intended aims. Winters and Martinez (2015) note that bilateral donors tend to be more responsive towards the level of governance in a country, adapting their assistance from programmatic aid to technical assistance. The authors found 'less evidence' that considerations of governance affect multilateral aid flows (Winters and Martinez, 2015, p. 518).

Schudel also makes a distinction between allocating aid for 'more strategic (e.g. political and/or economic) goals' (Schudel, 2008, p. 2) and 'primarily for developmental purposes' (Schudel, 2008, p. 4) and accordingly characterises donors that appear to be more inclined towards the former as 'corrupt donors' and the latter – as 'not corrupt'. The dichotomy between strategic aid allocation (in the donor country's national interest) and developmental aid, as argued by Schudel (2008), is interesting to consider in the context of the UK's 2015 Aid Strategy, which explicitly situates the UK's ODA spending in the donor country's interest (HMT and DFID, 2015). Most of the UK's ODA, being spent by DFID, which is bound by the 2002 International Development Act, is set to have poverty reduction as the primary purpose of spending. Spending ODA in both developmental and poverty reduction aims, as well as with a view to contributing to the donor's national interests, is therefore not seen by the major donors as necessarily incompatible. Accountability for the effectiveness of aid spent is demanded by civil society and taxpayers in relation to both of these aims (see Chapter 4).

Furthermore, donors and researchers consider thorough and up-to-date knowledge of the local political economy to be essential in order for interventions to be successful (see Fisher and Marquette, 2013; Manuel, 2015). This is particularly necessary and costly (due to security and access concerns as well as frequently evolving and complex environments) in fragile state environments (see, for example, IDC, 2016). Multilateral approaches, as discussed by Verdier (2008), can make use of economies of scale. This could be particularly useful in relation to political economy analyses and continuous monitoring of political, social and economic developments within a donor country, and adapting programming accordingly.

Summary

This section discussed how bilateral approaches have the benefits of increased scrutiny from the public and therefore more demands for aid to be accountable, and have the benefit of reciprocal relationships in order to monitor the enforcement of international regulations and laws. Multilateral approaches, on the other hand, appear to be less politicised and can therefore be better placed to introduce or demand necessary reforms; they can harness economies of scale that can be beneficial in reducing overall costs of international development work and the administrative burden for the recipient country institutions.

6.4 Combining the key strengths of different approaches

Significant proportions of ODA do not fall neatly within the bilateral or multilateral categories. This section discusses bilateral funding through multilateral organisations and the 'coalitions of the committed' approach, for lack of a better term, where countries that are committed to a certain cause create a regime and work in small groups to enforce it and to influence other countries to join.

Multi-bi

The UK allocates a considerable proportion of its ODA funding for particular earmarked projects and programmes of multilateral agencies, which is referred to as 'bilateral ODA through a multilateral' (DFID, 2015b) or 'multi-bi' (Gulrajani, 2016). Although the proportion of DFID multi-bi spending has been gradually decreasing as a percentage of DFID expenditure over the past several years, as shown in Table 6.1 it remains roughly around 20 per cent of total UK aid expenditure. Multi-bi represents 35 per cent of the UK's ODA to the multilateral system (Gulrajani, 2016, p. 18). DAC donors that spent a higher proportion of multilateral assistance as multi-bi than the UK were: Iceland (65 per cent), Australia (57 per cent), the United States (49 per cent), Norway (48 per cent), Canada (48 per cent), Switzerland (44 per cent), Denmark (37 per cent) and Japan (36 per cent) (ibid.).

While voluntary contributions to UN development funds and programmes originated in the 1960s as a way for donors to exert influence over the institutions, earmarking, as argued by Gulrajani (2016, p. 17), 'though also relating to the desire for political influence, stemmed from frustrations with the slow pace of governance reforms, the desire to engage non-state actors and the emergence of new global challenges'. Tortora and Steensen (2014, p. 16) argue that the reasons why donors use earmarked funding via multilateral organisations are not specifically outlined in policy documents or strategies, noting that 'most DAC members make earmarked contributions on a case-by-case basis, and decision-making about core and earmarked resources is often made by different parts of the administration'.

Tortora and Steensen single out the UK, together with Australia, for having started developing a strategy on selecting aid delivery mechanisms, namely the Strategy for World Bank trust funds (Tortora and Steensen, 2014, p. 16):

> This strategy introduced a set of principles that programme officers are expected to take into account before deciding to provide earmarked funding. One of the principles is to consult with the Department for International Development (DFID) lead department when making any decisions on

supporting a new trust fund. In principle, this should allow the lead department to assess, for example, whether Umbrella Facilities – rather than a new trust fund mechanism – would provide an appropriate framework in a particular case. It would also ensure, in principle, that all funding decisions align to the prioritisations made by the Bank's Board.

Gulrajani (2016, p. 18), however, argues that 'scattered decision-making on multi-bi flows within donor countries ... makes coherence and coordination difficult for a donor seeking a holistic picture of total investment in a multilateral institution'. Consequently, consultations with various thematic leads within a donor government could increase policy coherence, however they require significant resources to ensure coordination. Furthermore, the House of Commons International Development Committee interim report on the allocation of resources notes that DFID does not appear to have a clear strategy of how it determines the split between the multilateral and bilateral aid it disburses; it attempts to determine the most appropriate funding mechanism for individual interventions (IDC, 2016, pp. 12–13).

Multi-bi aid has received substantial amounts of criticism for being 'used by wealthy donors to bilateralise international institutions with their pet projects' thus deepening democratic deficits within multilateral institutions (Gulrajani, 2016, p. 17), and named 'trojan multilateralism' (Sridhar and Woods, 2013). As such, Gulrajani (2016, p. 6) argues that multi-bi aid can 'destabilis[e] the performance, credibility and governance of multilateral institutions' and developmentally focused multilateral programmes. Gulrajani (2016, p. 17) subsequently argues that this would be opposite to the intended empowerment of aid recipient countries to take ownership and control of their countries' development course, as intended by the Paris principles of aid effectiveness; which ultimately makes multi-bi aid 'a supply-driven instrument'.

Multi-bi aid can also involve high transaction costs (OECD, 2015). In particular, oversight of multi-bi spending can create a significant burden on the multilateral institutions that are implementing the programmes. OECD notes that in 2012–2014, 205 assessments of multi-bi spending were carried out by DAC members alone (OECD, 2015). DFID also commissions reviews for its own monitoring and evaluation purposes of how effectively its funding is spent via multilateral organisations. The OECD peer review of the UK's international development assistance noted:

> DFID's oversight requirements for non-core funding are becoming heavy and time consuming for all its multilateral partners. Requests for reporting are not always consistent across countries and are not harmonised with other donors. This puts the quality of partnerships at risk.
>
> (OECD, 2014, p. 17)

Gulrajani (2016, p. 19) presents the evidence on the attributes of multilateral, bilateral and multi-bi aid channels, summarised in Table 6.6.

Table 6.6 Attributes of multilateral, bilateral and multi-bi channels

	Multilateral	Bilateral	Multi-bi
Politicised	–	X	–
Demand-driven	–		
Selective	X	X	–
Promotes Global Public Goods	X		–
Efficient		–	
Fragmented		X	–

Source: Gulrajani (2016, p. 19).

Note
Key: X = strongly linked; – = weakly linked.

This analysis of strengths and weaknesses is not exhaustive, as important factors such as the ability to leverage other donors' involvement, as well as ensuring that aid continues to be supported domestically, are not explicitly considered.

Nevertheless, in political environments where aid is explicitly noted to be spent in the UK's national interest and there are significant requirements and public expectations to report vis-à-vis the results of the assistance, multi-bi aid presents a good alternative to harness some of the benefits of multilateral aid while keeping the visibility and control over aid that a bilateral approach allows for.

'Coalitions of the committed'

'Coalitions of the committed', as the UK government opted for in 2016 at its Prime Ministerial anti-corruption summit, can have distinct advantages, including ensuring that the agenda is not 'watered down' due to a compromise being required. This has been observed in a number of negotiations for global conventions and agreements, for example in relation to including provisions on political party financing within the UNCAC (Brunelle-Quraishi, 2011).

Also, a 'coalitions of the committed' approach can result in change on a larger scale than bilateral work. Economies of scale can be realised by using existing multilateral structures with complementary aims, such as the OECD, but offering a more inclusive approach than regional or other mechanisms. Such approaches can also facilitate best practice approaches being tried and adapted elsewhere.

This approach, of course, does not come without its risks and challenges. Fora such as the 2016 London anti-corruption summit, aimed to create and foster 'coalitions of the committed', will inevitably be selective. Putting together the guest list, however, poses considerable challenges.

First of all, it is difficult to accurately judge a country's or its leaders' commitment to tackling corruption, or to evaluate progress towards eradicating corruption. Reasons for this have been discussed in Chapter 2 and include the varying definitions, the clandestine nature of the phenomenon and the associated difficulties measuring the extent of it. This can mean that countries and leaders that are committed to the cause can go unrecognised and unsupported internationally, thus making their efforts to eradicate corruption more difficult to achieve. Recognising corrupt leaders as anti-corruption champions, on the other hand, could also complicate the work of domestic actors to expose and eradicate corruption within their government, as these leaders will be given international support and more opportunities to implement their own agendas.

A pertinent example to consider in this respect would be Kenya in the early 2000s. Wrong (2009) in *It's our turn to eat* eloquently describes the situation in Kenya when the presidency was handed over from Moi to Kibaki. After decades of authoritarian rule with rampant patronage systems and corruption, there was a general feeling that corruption will no longer be tolerated within Kenya, and this feeling of a general rejection of corruption permeated within all levels of society. Wrong (2009, pp. 6–7) notes:

> Newspapers recounted with glee how irate passengers were refusing to allow *matatu* [mini bus] touts to hand over the usual *kitu kidogu* – that ubiquitous 'little something' – to the fat-bellied police manning the roadblocks, lecturing officers that a new era had dawned. ... And the new president kept hitting the right notes. When the country's biggest companies took out fawning newspaper advertisements congratulating him, Kibaki reproved them for wasting money. He had no intention, he said, of following his predecessor's example by putting his face on the national currency, streets and buildings.

Soon, however, it became apparent that Kibaki and his entourage were engaged in some of the same type of corrupt practices that the former government had been practising (Wrong, 2009).

Second, there is a balance to be struck between welcoming those countries that are doing a lot to tackle corruption, but might not be in an influential position globally, and those that might appear to be doing less, but whose actions will have significant positive repercussions within global arenas. For example, the Cayman Islands and the British Virgin Islands not being invited to the conference has meant that they were unable to participate in shaping the agenda and will therefore be less likely to buy into a regime and rules that they did not take part in creating.

Third, although a coalition of the committed approach can help with some of the challenges that more inclusive international initiatives face, such as commitment of resources and watering down of specific commitments, there is still a significant issue of enforcement and monitoring to be considered. Political will within the countries that initiate such works needs to be sustained and follow-up events and monitoring bodies need to be set up for the initiative to deliver results.

It is still very early days of the 2016 Summit initiative. Follow-up and monitoring of commitments will be required for the initiative to make a difference.

Multilateral and bilateral approaches 203

Nevertheless, parallels can be made between the global concern about corruption and other issues, such as nuclear proliferation. Verdier (2008, p. 439) discusses how 'superpower bilateral diplomacy' was combined with a multilateral approach when setting up the Nuclear Proliferation Treaty (NPT):

> The United States and the Soviet Union did more than negotiate a text that was agreeable to other countries; they also bribed and threatened some of their respective clients into signing the NPT … the NPT regime, along with several other important regimes, is neither bilateral nor multi-lateral, but a combination of both.

Verdier argues that different states will incur varying costs of compliance to multilateral regimes; and those that will incur low costs do not need particular bilateral arrangements (involving incentives or sanctions), as opposed to those that are likely to incur high compliance costs (Verdier, 2008, pp. 440–441).

It is worth noting that the Anti-Corruption summit is not the first such attempt to achieve multilateral ambitions using bilateral means that the OECD has undertaken. Johannesen and Zucman (2014, p. 66) note:

> At the summit held in April 2009, G20 countries urged each tax haven to sign at least 12 information exchange treaties under the threat of economic sanctions. Between the summit and the end of 2009, the world's tax havens signed a total of more than 300 treaties.

These treaties have been argued to raise the probability of detecting wrongdoing (ibid.). As discussed in section 6.1, countries that do not have such treaties to share information with other states about the provenance of funds deposited in their jurisdictions, or permit the use of highly anonymous instruments such as bearer shares, will give those that engage in corruption a better chance to keep their wealth hidden.

Civil society and media can play a crucial role in monitoring compliance with the law and regulations, and bringing to the law enforcement and public's attention cases of misconduct and violations. As noted by the example put forward by Johannesen and Zucman (2014, p. 66), following an amended tax treaty between Switzerland and France in 2009 to exchange information necessary for tax enforcement, which had previously been classified under banking secrecy laws in Switzerland, the media has played a role in increasing the effectiveness of the treaty:

> one of France's richest persons and her wealth manager were taped discussing what to do with two undeclared Swiss bank accounts, worth $160 million. After a visit to Switzerland, the wealth manager concluded that keeping the funds in Swiss banks or bringing them back to France would be too risky. He suggested that the funds be transferred to Hong Kong, Singapore, or Uruguay, three tax havens which had not committed to

exchanging information with France. After the tapes were made public, they received extensive newspaper coverage and eventually the funds were repatriated to France.

Cooperation with businesses can facilitate setting more adequate laws to ensure that the burden of compliance on businesses is proportionate to the risks. It can also encourage collaboration between the business and relevant authorities when cases of potential misconduct come to light. An example of such collaboration is the Joint Money Laundering Intelligence Taskforce (JMLIT), set up by the NCA in partnership with the UK government and the UK's financial sector (the British Bankers' Association and more than 20 major UK and international banks) to combat high-end money laundering (NCA, 2016b). JMLIT was initially set up as a one-year pilot, to share expertise in analysing the methods used by money launderers to exploit the UK's financial system, thus facilitating a better collective understanding of new and emerging money laundering threats; more efficient targeting of law enforcement agencies' efforts by bringing them up to speed with the latest industry developments; and more informed prioritisation of risks by banks (ibid.).

Expanding such an approach to a multilateral/regional level could facilitate cooperation in addressing corruption globally. The JMLIT model has already been replicated by a number of countries.

6.5 Summary

Section 6.1 presented the case for a joint approach and international collaboration to address corruption. Significant legislatory and enforcement changes in just one country might not have the intended effect on corruption if other jurisdictions do not adopt the same measures. Nevertheless, it is worth noting that even initiatives in individual states have a positive impact. The introduction of the FCPA in the US, for example, was the basis on which subsequently comparable legislation in other countries, such as the UK's Bribery Act, as well as international instruments such as the UNCAC, were modelled. Even though prosecutions for acts of corruption that take place in developing countries with proceeds of crime passing through the jurisdictions with such legislation have so far been relatively few, the message it can send is strong. It can create a sense among the rich that their money can no longer easily be hidden away in Western Europe and other foreign financial centres. This creates the incentives for people to keep their wealth, especially if gained illicitly, within their country of origin. This, in turn, can mean investment within the local economy, job creation and an overall smaller negative effect of corruption on the local economy (see section 3.5).

The Panama Papers elicited a significant response from the UK Government. One month after the leak of the papers, HMRC was already investigating 700 leads that had a link with the Panama Papers, and the Government announced that it would be allocating up to 10 million GBP to an inter-agency taskforce to analyse the papers (HMT, 2016). The task force, jointly led by HMRC and NCA, would also be drawing on specialists from the SFO and the Financial Conduct Authority (FCA). There is significant commitment from the UK to address the crimes unveiled by the Panama Papers, however, the transnational nature of the crimes will only make this possible if other states cooperate and join in the endeavour. The Anti-Corruption Summit, hosted by the UK's Prime Minister in May 2016, provided the forum required to discuss such multilateral cooperation, to agree on specific commitments by groups of countries that sign up to undertake specific actions in order to contribute to combatting corruption globally, or to form 'coalitions of the committed'.

This chapter has looked at a number of different types of organisations that international development agencies enter into partnerships with. The partners delivering programmes on anti-corruption or parts thereof will be a significant determinant of the success of the programmes. Gulrajani (2016, p. 6) sums up the overall existing evidence on the advantages of the different programme implementation channels as follows: 'the advantages of multilateral channels derive from their ability to collectively organise, pool and advance common global causes, while bilateral channels are conduits for donor control, visibility and preferences', suggesting that donors' motivations for giving aid should play a large role in determining the delivery channel.

This chapter has also discussed two approaches to combining the benefits of bilateral and multilateral aid delivery channels – multi-bi – and forming 'coalitions of the committed' based on inter-state partnerships on issues of strategic priority.

Multi-bi offers possibilities to harness some of the benefits of multilateral aid, such as easier approaches to leveraging other donors' support and involvement in particular issues, reducing aid fragmentation, working in fragile and harder to access environments and realising economies of scale. It does not come without drawbacks, in particular as multilateral channels appear to be more politicised and influenced by the major donors, and it increases administrative and monitoring burdens on the multilateral institutions.

The 'coalitions of the committed' approach could well accommodate the development of partnership rather than top-down aid approaches to international development. Partnerships within the anti-corruption sphere do not have to match organisations with their direct counterparts (NGOs with NGOs, NAOs with NAOs, ministries of justice with ministries of justice, etc.) to deliver results. The skills and expertise that some organisations may require may at times be best provided by other types of organisations, for example, assistance in drafting legal and operational frameworks for a National Audit Office could well be provided by a Ministry of Justice; or public outreach and dissemination of Audit findings could be best advised upon by marketing agencies.

A 'coalitions of the committed' approach can therefore work well to treat aid recipients as equal partners in development, thus increasing country ownership of reforms; it can also work well to involve a range of actors, businesses, civil society and media in particular, in its work, empowering people to use multilateral systems and international law to challenge corruption and injustice.

Notes

1 DFID currently employs 2700 staff in London, East Kilbride and globally (DFID, 2016e).
2 For example, DFID was able to continue its support to Zimbabwe through the UN when the UK's political relations were tense (ICAI, 2015a, p. 22).
3 Using bearer shares for a company means that the name of the owner of the company does not have to be disclosed as ownership is determined by whoever holds the share certificates.
4 As mentioned in section 4.1, PBR was followed for nearly 80 per cent of contracts that DFID procured centrally between April and October 2015 (IDC, 2016, p. 22).
5 This, however, is also applicable to international institutions including multilateral development banks. As mentioned in section 4.2, however, international organisations' access to operate and assist people in the country may ultimately be weighed up as being more impactful than an attempt to solve all the political issues within the country operating on a zero-tolerance of corruption.
6 The ICC has tried individuals from the Democratic Republic of Congo, Central African Republic, Uganda, Sudan, Kenya, Libya and Côte d'Ivoire.
7 The question then arises, if the cases addressed by courts, as well as their decisions, were to be regarded as legal precedents, could they be more accurately characterised as political settlements – as the court only considers crimes that were committed in a particular place and time frame? The crimes would also need to be considered of sufficient enough gravity to be brought to the courts by the UNSC or the (mostly likely new) government of the perpetrators' state.

Bibliography

AFROSAI-E, 2016. Institutional Capacity Building Framework. Available at: https://afrosai-e.org.za/about/institutional-capacity-building-framework (accessed 24 September 2016).

Alesina, A., Dollar, D., 2000. Who Gives Foreign Aid to Whom and Why? *Journal of Economic Growth* 5(1), 33–63.

ATAF, 2016. Overview. Available at: www.ataftax.org/en/about/Pages/Overview.aspx (accessed 24 September 2016).

BBC News, 2016. Panama Papers: What the Documents Reveal. Available at: www.bbc.co.uk/news/world-35956055 (accessed 24 September 2016).

Brunelle-Quraishi, O., 2011. Assessing the Relevancy and Efficacy of the United Nations Convention against Corruption: A Comparative Analysis. Notre Dame *Journal of International and Comparative Law* 2(1), 101–166.

Castle, S., Erlanger, S., Gladstone Stephen, R., 2016. Iceland's Prime Minister steps down amid Panama Papers scandal. *NY Times*.

Commonwealth, 2016. About Us. Available at: http://thecommonwealth.org/about-us (accessed 24 September 2016).

Cremer, G., 2008. *Corruption and Development Aid: Confronting the Challenges*, translated by Elisabeth Schuth. Lynne Rienner Publishers, Boulder, CO.

De Schutter, O., 2010. *International Human Rights Law: Cases, Materials, Commentary*. Cambridge University Press, Cambridge.

de Willebois, E. van der D., Sharman, J.C., Harrison, R., Park, J.W., Halter, E., 2011. *The Puppet Masters: How the Corrupt Use Legal Structures to Hide Stolen Assets and What To Do About It*. World Bank Publications, Washington, DC.

DFID, 2016a. About – Department for International Development. Available at: www.gov.uk/government/organisations/department-for-international-development/about#who-we-are (accessed 23 September 2016).
DFID, 2016b. DFID Procurement: SME Action Plan. Available at: www.gov.uk/government/uploads/system/uploads/attachment_data/file/521005/SME-Action-Plan-April2016.pdf (accessed 24 September 2016).
DFID, 2016c DFID Procurement: SME Action Plan. April 2016. Available at: www.gov.uk/government/uploads/system/uploads/attachment_data/file/521005/SME-Action-Plan-April2016.pdf (accessed 24 September 2016).
DFID, 2015a. DFID Annual Report and Accounts 2014–2015. Williams Lea Group on behalf of the Controller of Her Majesty's Stationery Office, London.
DFID, 2015b. Statistics on International Development 2015 – Publications. DFID, London.
DFID, 2015c. DFID Annual Report and Accounts 2014–2015. Williams Lea Group on behalf of the Controller of Her Majesty's Stationery Office, London.
DFID, 2011. Multilateral Aid Review: Ensuring Maximum Value for Money for UK Aid Through Multilateral Organisations. Available at: www.gov.uk/government/publications/multilateral-aid-review (accessed 24 September 2016).
Dietrich, S., 2013. Bypass or Engage? Explaining Donor Delivery Tactics in Foreign Aid Allocation. *International Studies Quarterly* 57(4), 698–712. doi:10.1111/isqu.12041.
Dollar, D., Levin, V., 2006. The Increasing Selectivity of Foreign Aid, 1984–2003. *World Development* 34(12), 2034–2046.
Dreher, A., Sturm, J.-E., Vreeland, J.R., 2009. Development Aid and International Politics: Does Membership on the UN Security Council Influence World Bank Decisions? *Journal of Development Economics* 88(1), 1–18.
Fisher, J., Marquette, H., 2013. Donors Doing Political Economy Analysis: From Process to Product (and Back Again?). ISA Annual Convention panel on 'Politicising or Depoliticising Aid? The Political Economy of Political Economy Analysis', San Francisco, 3–6 April 2013. Available at: https://ssrn.com/abstract=2206474 or http://dx.doi.org/10.2139/ssrn.2206474.
Fuest, C., Riedel, N., 2009. Tax Evasion, Tax Avoidance and Tax Expenditures in Developing Countries: A Review of the Literature. Report prepared for the UK Department for International Development (DFID).
Grynberg, R., Silva, S., Remy, J.Y., 2004. Plurilateral Financial Standards and Their Regulation at the WTO: The Experience of Small Developing States. *Journal of World Invest. Trade* 5, 509–554.
Gulrajani, N., 2016. Bilateral versus Multilateral Aid Channels. ODI Rep. Available at: www.odi.org/sites/odi.org.uk/files/resource-documents/10393.pdf.
Hafner-Burton, E.M., Tsutsui, K., 2005. Human Rights in a Globalizing World: The Paradox of Empty Promises. *American Journal of Sociology* 110(5), 1373–1411.
Hamilton, M.M., 2016. British PM Announces New Transparency Measures Following Panama Papers Revelations. Available at: https://panamapapers.icij.org/20160411-cameron-parliament-reform.html (accessed 24 September 2016).
Hill, D.W., 2010. Estimating the Effects of Human Rights Treaties on State Behavior. *Journal of Politics* 72(4), 1161–1174.
HMT, 2016. UK launches cross-government taskforce on the 'Panama Papers' – News Stories. Available at: www.gov.uk/government/news/uk-launches-cross-government-taskforce-on-the-panama-papers (accessed 24 September 2016).
HMT, 2015. Spending Review and Autumn Statement 2015, Cm. Her Majesty's Treasury, London.

HMT, DFID, 2015. UK Aid: Tackling Global Challenges in the National Interest. Paper. Available at: www.gov.uk/government/uploads/system/uploads/attachment_data/file/478834/ODA_strategy_final_web_0905.pdf.

Hout, W., 2007. *The Politics of Aid Selectivity: Good Governance Criteria in World Bank, US and Dutch Development Assistance.* Routledge, Abingdon, Oxon.

Human Rights Watch, 2008. *Courting History: The Landmark International Criminal Court's First Years.* Human Rights Watch.

ICAI, 2016a. ICAI Annual Report 2015 to 2016 Report to Parliament's International Development Committee. Available at: http://icai.independent.gov.uk/wp-content/uploads/ICAI-Annual-Report-2015-to-2016.pdf (accessed 24 September 2016).

ICAI, 2016b. UK Aid's Contribution to Tackling Tax Avoidance and Evasion. Available at: http://icai.independent.gov.uk/report/tax/ (accessed 27 September 2016).

ICAI, 2015a. How DFID Works with Multilateral Agencies to Achieve Impact (No. 44). Available at: http://icai.independent.gov.uk/wp-content/uploads/ICAI-Report-How-DFID-works-with-multilateral-agencies-to-achieve-impact.pdf (accessed 27 September 2016).

ICAI, 2015b. A Preliminary Investigation of Official Development Assistance (ODA) Spent by Departments other than DFID (No. 41). Available at: http://icai.independent.gov.uk/wp-content/uploads/A-preliminary-investigation-of-Official-Development-Assistance-ODA-spe...pdf (accessed 24 September 2016).

ICC, 2014. All Cases. Available at: www.icc-cpi.int/en_menus/icc/situations%20and%20cases/cases/pages/cases%20index.aspx (accessed 30 May 2014).

ICIJ, 2016. The Panama Papers: Explore the Panama Papers Key Figures. Available at: https://panamapapers.icij.org/graphs/ (accessed 24 September 2016).

IDC, 2016. UK Aid: Allocation of Resources: Interim Report, Third Report of Session 2015–2016. Available at: www.publications.parliament.uk/pa/cm201516/cmselect/cmintdev/927/927.pdf (accessed 4 April 2016).

Intosai, 2016a. About Us. Available at: www.intosai.org/about-us.html (accessed 24 September 2016).

Intosai, 2016b. Regional Organizations. Available at: www.intosai.org/regional-organizations.html (accessed 24 September 2016).

Johannesen, N., Zucman, G., 2014. The End of Bank Secrecy? An Evaluation of the G20 Tax Haven Crackdown. *American Economic Journal of Economic Policy* 6(1), 65–91.

Lanni, A., 2008. The Laws of War in Ancient Greece. *Law and History Review* 26(3), 469–489. doi:10.1017/S0738248000002534.

Manuel, C., 2015. Investment Climate Reform Doing it Differently: What, Why, and How. First Synth. Pap. Available at: www.bdsknowledge.org/dyn/be/docs/298/LASER2015DoingICRdifferentlyMay15.pdf (accessed 27 September 2016).

NCA, 2016a. International Corruption Unit (ICU). Available at: www.nationalcrimeagency.gov.uk/about-us/what-we-do/economic-crime/international-corruption-unit-icu (accessed 24 September 2016).

NCA, 2016b. Joint Money Laundering Intelligence Taskforce (JMLIT). Available at: www.nationalcrimeagency.gov.uk/about-us/what-we-do/economic-crime/joint-money-laundering-intelligence-taskforce-jmlit (accessed 24 September 2016).

Nunnenkamp, P., Thiele, R., 2006. Targeting Aid to the Needy and Deserving: Nothing but Promises? *World Economy* 29(9), 1177–1201.

Nye, J.S., 1970. Corruption and Political Development: A Cost–Benefit Analysis, in: Heidenheimer, A.J., Johnston, M., LeVine, V.T. (Eds), *Political Corruption: Readings in Comparative Analysis.* Transaction Books, New Brunswick, NJ, pp. 564–578.

OECD, 2016. Development Finance Statistics Annex 2 List of ODA-Eligible International Organisations – OECD. Available at: www.oecd.org/dac/stats/annex2.htm (accessed 24 September 2016).

OECD, 2015. *Multilateral Aid 2015: Better Partnerships for a Post-2015 World*. OECD, Paris.

OECD, 2014. *OECD Development Co-operation Peer Reviews: United Kingdom 2014*. OECD Publishing.

OECD DAC, 2012. Multilateral Aid Report. Available at: www.oecd.org/dac/aid-architecture/DCD_DAC(2012)33_FINAL.pdf (accessed 24 September 2016).

OHCHR, 2013. Working Group on Arbitrary Detention. Available at: www.ohchr.org/EN/Issues/Detention/Pages/WGADIndex.aspx (accessed 30 May 2014).

Olson, J., Kerusauskaite, I., Clarke, J., Francino, M., 2016. Financial Accountability and Anti-Corruption Partnerships Programme Scoping Report.

Oye, K.A., 1986. *Cooperation under Anarchy*. Princeton University Press, Princeton, NJ.

Palagashvili, L., Williamson, C.R., 2016. Ranking Foreign Aid Agency Best Practices: New Donors, New Findings. Available at: www.claudiawilliamson.com/yahoo_site_admin/assets/docs/Palagashvili_and_Williamson_Manuscript_1_6_2016.38113927.pdf (accessed 24 September 2016).

Paulus, A., 2012. Whether Universal Values Can Prevail over Bilateralism and Reciprocity, in: Cassese, A. (Ed.), *Realising Utopia: The Future of International Law*. Oxford University Press, Oxford, pp. 89–104.

Plato, 1991. *The Republic of Plato*. Basic Books, New York.

Reinsberg, B., 2015. Foreign Aid Responses to Political Liberalization. *World Development, Political Conditionality and EU Foreign Aid* 75(November), 46–61. doi:10.1016/j.worlddev.2014.11.006.

Rider, B.A.K. (Ed.), 1997. *Corruption: The Enemy Within*. Kluwer Law International, The Hague; Boston.

Rodrik, D., 1996. Why is there Multilateral Lending?' Annual World Bank Conference on Development Economics, in: Bruno, M., Pleskovic, B. (Eds), *IBRD*, Washington, DC, pp. 167–205.

Schudel, C.J.W., 2008. Corruption and Bilateral Aid: A Dyadic Approach. *Journal of Conflict Resolution* 52(4).

Sharman, J.C., Mistry, P.S., 2008. *Considering the Consequences: The Development Implications of Initiatives on Taxation, Anti-money Laundering and Combating the Financing of Terrorism*. Commonwealth Secretariat, London.

Shaw, M.N., 2013. *International Law*. Cambridge University Press, Cambridge.

Sippel, M., Neuhoff, K., 2009. A History of Conditionality: Lessons for International Cooperation on Climate Policy. *Climate Policy* 9, 481–494. doi:10.3763/cpol.2009.0634.

Snidal, D., 1991. Relative Gains and the Pattern of International Cooperation. *American Political Science Review* 85(3), 701–726.

Sridhar, D., Woods, N., 2013. Trojan Multilateralism: Global Cooperation in Health. *Global Policy* 4(4), 325–335. doi:10.1111/1758-5899.12066.

StAR, 2016. Stolen Asset Recovery Initiative (StAR). Available at: http://star.worldbank.org/star/ (accessed 24 September 2016).

Sumner, A., 2012. Global Poverty and the 'New Bottom Billion' Revisited: Exploring the Paradox That Most of the World's Extreme Poor No Longer Live in the World's Poorest Countries. IDS, Working Papers.

Tortora, P., Steensen, S., 2014. Making Earmarked Funding more Effective: Current Practices and a Way Forward (No. 1). OECD Development Co-operation Directorate.

Verdier, D., 2008. Multilateralism, Bilateralism, and Exclusion in the Nuclear Proliferation Regime. *International Organization* 62(3), 439–476.

Widmalm, S., 2008. *Decentralisation, Corruption and Social Capital: From India to the West*. Sage Publications, India.

Winters, M.S., Martinez, G., 2015. The Role of Governance in Determining Foreign Aid Flow Composition. *World Development* 66(February), 516–531. doi:10.1016/j.worlddev.2014.09.020.

World Bank, 2004. World Development Report 2004: Making Services Work for Poor People. Available at: https://openknowledge.worldbank.org/bitstream/handle/10986/5986/WDR%202004%20-%20English.pdf?sequence=1&isAllowed=y (accessed 28 May 2014) Washington DC. Co-publication of World Bank and OUP.

Wright, J., Winters, M., 2010. The Politics of Effective Foreign Aid. *Annual Review of Political Science* 13, 61–80. doi:10.1146/annurev.polisci.032708.143524.

Wrong, M., 2009. *It's Our Turn To Eat: The Story of a Kenyan Whistle Blower*. Fourth Estate, London.

Zinkernagel, G.F., Pereira, P.G., De Simone, F., 2014. *The Role of Donors in the Recovery of Stolen Assets, U4 Issue*. Chr. Michelsen Institute, Bergen.

7 Conclusions and wider implications

> Euclid is supposed to have told Ptolemy: 'There is no "royal road" to geometry.' It is not clear that there is any royal road to evaluation of economic or social policies either.
>
> (Sen, 1999, p. 85)

As noted above, Sen (1999, p. 85) stresses the wide range of considerations that are to be taken into account when designing and evaluating economic and social policies. Policies can have different effects in different environments, due to a number of influencing factors; and their effectiveness will also depend on one's definition and understanding of the key aims they are meant to contribute towards. For example, one programme to alleviate poverty might help a small number of the poorest people to turn their lives around, whereas another one, costing the same amount, might contribute to ensuring that people living on the verge of poverty do not cross that line. Assessing which one is more effective can be a difficult decision. Similarly, with anti-corruption programming, judging the success of a programme or the effectiveness of an approach can be a difficult undertaking. This is due to a number of reasons, such as the definitions and measurement of corruption, as discussed in the previous chapters, the chosen methods of programme delivery, as well as other competing policy goals.

Due to its numerous devastating consequences, corruption has become an issue that is increasingly addressed by international development programming – both multilateral and bilateral. Corruption, however, is not a monolithic entity that is easily defined, quantified and measured, as discussed in Chapter 2. Agreement on the definition of the phenomenon and evidence on the scale, levels and circumstances under which it can cause most damage to wider development indicators would help direct efforts to where they can make most difference. Whereas international development agencies use a working definition of corruption, the phenomenon is often not defined in legal instruments, which instead address specific offences of corruption, such as bribery, embezzlement or fraud.

The causes, motivations and effects of corruption, and the subsequent means that may be effective in tackling it, are equally numerous, as demonstrated in

212 Conclusions and wider implications

Chapter 3. The theories that have been dominant in the literature and international development organisations' approaches have historically largely focused on economic analyses of individuals' behaviour. In turn, this led to an increased focus of anti-corruption efforts on petty corruption, rather than high-level political corruption. Furthermore, petty corruption has been a topic that managed to get sufficient attention in policy, due to the awareness and personal experience of ordinary citizens of the subject, as well as the often-perceived politically non-threatening nature of crusades against petty corruption.

Chapter 4 discussed the UK's work on anti-corruption in developing countries. The UK and DFID are often seen as leaders in international development programming (OECD, 2014) – innovating, leveraging support from other organisations and being responsive to the latest thinking about anti-corruption interventions and 'best practice' in conducting development work more generally. It is worth considering, however, that whereas previously DFID was being seen as setting its own agenda and therefore highly regarded in the academic literature and by its peers (Barder, 2005), the UK's domestic political agenda and considerations of the UK's national interest seem to more strongly than ever permeate the latest ODA strategy published in November 2015 (HMT and DFID, 2015).

A coherent UK government's approach to corruption in developing countries, however, can be a significant determinant of the effectiveness of its efforts. Coordination is necessary between DFID, the FCO, law enforcement, audit and taxation agencies, among others. For example, currently if a UK agency provides training to developing country governments on submitting MLAs, other agencies might not be able to release information requested by the country if it is considered by the FCO to have the potential to endanger individuals in the requesting country in ways that the UK government would find unacceptable (for example, lead to imprisonment due to political views). As such, in this example, it is crucial that government agencies' capacity-building and support work (such as writing MLA requests) is coordinated with the FCO's security analysis as well as DFID's poverty reduction agenda, in order to have the desired effect.

The increasing global interconnectedness and the transnational nature of corruption requires global cooperation to tackle large-scale corruption. International cooperation is required to disrupt the cross-border flows of funds intended for corruption and proceeds of corruption, as well as the transnational networks that facilitate and engage in corruption. This can, in turn, have ripple effects on disrupting other criminal activities and networks. Chapter 5 discussed the significant proliferation of legal agreements and multilateral conventions on anti-corruption during the last two decades, building on the international legal framework that has been rapidly developing since the 1950s. There is now a significant number of frameworks and regulations that also requires States to adopt domestic legislation to comply with their international requirements. While this is a useful start, the reach and effectiveness of the agreements could be increased by involving all the stakeholders, including the private sector and civil society (for example, by using public consultations and publishing audits and financial information online).

Civil society, media and their public scrutiny are key to addressing corruption. They can significantly complement the work of law enforcement institutions in detecting and reporting suspicious behaviour and use information about corrupt practices to 'shame' people into avoiding them and organising against corruption. Although civil society is increasingly being included in multilateral arrangements, there is, however, a lot more to be done in this regard to enable citizens and civil society groups to challenge corrupt practices.

The extent to which individuals are empowered to challenge corrupt behaviour within their governments and institutions is increasing, however it is still almost negligible. As demonstrated in section 5.3, the majority of international anti-corruption mechanisms that include reviews of countries' compliance with their obligations under the mechanisms do not adequately involve the civil society and do not publish all their findings for public scrutiny. Domestic audit systems, as discussed in section 4.2, also often have such shortcomings. Furthermore, in order to challenge corruption, civil society has to be relatively established and strong, which is often not the case in DFID's target countries (Van Rooy, 2013).

Multilateral approaches can play a significant role in leveraging support and contributions from other countries, coordinating and generating economies of scale to facilitate change on a large scale, as discussed in Chapter 6. There are, however, issues surrounding the monitoring, accountability and enforcement of international agreements. Furthermore, internationally there seem to be more donors that appear to 'want to coordinate rather than be coordinated'. DFID often judges the success of operating through multilateral organisations by the extent to which it influences other (particularly multilateral) organisations to work towards DFID's priorities (see ICAI, 2015). The value for money requirements and scrutiny that is currently placed on the UK's international development assistance funding means that DFID tracks and monitors the efficiency of its spending via multilateral organisations, particularly multi-bi aid, thus creating significant reporting pressures on the multilateral institutions.

Regional and industry initiatives were discussed in section 5.3, including UNGC and EITI, and regional anti-corruption instruments. Such initiatives might be more culturally and historically appropriate for particular contexts and also provide a platform for smaller countries to present themselves as a coalition with more weight in international fora. As discussed in section 5, however, peer review mechanisms might be weaker within regional agreements and initiatives as states have been reported to be less willing to criticise their neighbours.

Development programmes need to more systematically take into account the complex and varied nature of corruption. This includes taking realistic approaches to corruption within the countries they operate in; adapting the choice of programme delivery agents; and considering the longer-term effects and the reputational issues potentially associated with tolerating corruption.

Furthermore, the complexity of tackling corruption at high levels of government, which often involves transnational flows of proceeds of corruption, demonstrates that a traditional development agency such as DFID might not have the required technical skills in-house to address such issues. This points to the need for increased interdepartment and inter-agency collaboration.

The UK is taking a significant step towards channelling more of its ODA via government departments other than DFID. This can create significant opportunities to leverage these organisations' particular skill sets and, with DFID advising on the 'soft skills' international development programme delivery side, result in more effective and targeted programmes. The international development assistance provided by law enforcement agencies within the UK (CPS, NCA, SFO) are good examples of concentrating resources where they can have the most influence – these organisations' financial investigators, lawyers and prosecutors go to developing countries to form relationships and work alongside their developing country colleagues on particular cases, thus sharing practical knowledge and on-the-job know-how. Certainly, the motivations for engaging in such work are two-fold – both to assist the country but also their own investigations (subsequently to meet their own performance measure targets). The alignment of such interests creates a win–win situation for the developing country and its institutions as well as for the agency that is providing the assistance.

At the same time, there would be value in mainstreaming considerations of corruption within international development programming, just as has been done with gender and environment concerns. This would develop an increased awareness of the phenomenon and the need to adjust international development programme delivery channels according to the likelihood of leakage of funds in the recipient country. This is particularly important, as accountability to the UK's taxpayers is a key demand on ODA spending.

Effectiveness of aid should also be kept in mind in order to ensure that funding for international development continues to be accepted and supported by the general public in donor countries, given the public nature of the funds that are being invested for international development initiatives. This is particularly important within the wider context of the UK government's public spending cuts. In the context of the UK increasingly spending ODA funds through departments other than DFID, coordination between different UK government departments and the HMG agenda is an area that merits further exploration. Current UK legislation only requires DFID to have poverty reduction as the primary focus of its ODA spending (IDC, 2016). Other HMG departments will naturally have to ensure that their spending meets the ODA requirements and falls within the remit of their institutional mandates, as well as HMG's overall agenda and the needs of the developing countries, as depicted by the intersecting circles in Figure 7.1.

Setting out this interrelationship between institutional mandates, wider political agendas and local needs highlights the necessity for explicit consideration of whose priorities and preferences are being considered when allocating ODA spending.

The emergence of new donors in international development is creating an interest in the effectiveness of established donors' practices (Gulrajani, 2016, p. 5). New donors, particularly large ones, entering the international development scene will influence the types of assistance that is on offer to developing

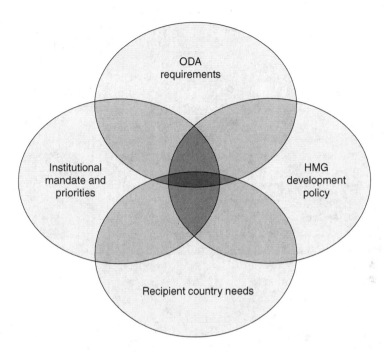

Figure 7.1 The requirements of various policy alignments for successful programmes.

countries. Burke-White (2014) discusses the emergence of a multi-hub international legal system, where alliances are based on thematic issues and the leaders of these alliances might not necessarily be the traditional North American and Western European countries, but also emerging powers such as BRICS. As such, China clearly offers an alternative approach to international development that is becoming a rival to the traditional development agencies that have dominated the sphere in the twentieth century. China's leadership in establishing the 'New Development Bank' (NDB) in Shanghai and the Asian Infrastructure Investment Bank (AIIB) in Beijing shows that China is starting to provide alternative institutions to the Washington-based International Monetary Fund and the World Bank (see Chin, 2014; Lim, 2015). As a result, developing states are presented with more of a choice as to what types of interventions, aid and trade relationships they would like to engage in with foreign countries.

The approaches of China and the UK to addressing corruption within the context of development are in some ways at opposite sides of the spectrum. In order to more successfully address corruption in developing states, there appears to be an argument for bringing the two countries' approaches closer together, namely, by focusing the assistance on where it is more likely to make a real difference and by considering a broad range of factors before providing

216 *Conclusions and wider implications*

development assistance or engaging in substantial commercial relations with other developing countries. Asset recovery and grand corruption appear to be areas where international assistance can bring particular value in tackling corruption.

The plurality of legal mechanisms at the national, regional and global levels, and the intricate interrelationships between these, adds to the complexity of international development programming in the sphere of anti-corruption (see, for example, Francioni, 2012; Morgera, 2012, p. 744). Programme delivery partners, as well as the institutions to be supported, should be carefully chosen for programmes to have the intended and maximum possible effect on eradicating corruption. Furthermore, the mission and purpose of institutions working on corruption should be clearly defined and enforced.[1]

Multilateral and bilateral aid delivery channels each have their own strengths and weaknesses, as discussed in Chapter 6. In light of the UK's focus on value for money and large-scale impacts, as well as its willingness to influence how its ODA funds are spent by multilateral organisations, two approaches to combining the benefits of multilateral and bilateral aid delivery channels were discussed. Multi-bi aid can leverage multilateral organisations' economies of scale, facilitate coordination with other donors and provide assistance from a source that is perceived as more neutral than bilateral development agencies (Gulrajani, 2016). The UK's 'coalitions of the committed' approach to leveraging the support of other countries to join it in the fight against corruption globally is an innovative and potentially strong approach. Civil society, media and the private sector, however, should not be excluded from programming and decision-making, which involves and affects their countries directly.

This book highlighted numerous difficulties in relation to tackling corruption globally, including entrenched practices, lacking laws, inefficient institutions and the lack of enforcement capabilities of multilateral organisations and international instruments. Nevertheless, there has been recent progress. Chapter 5 discussed the limited extent to which individuals have been empowered to use international legal mechanisms and access multilateral organisations' institutional mechanisms to seek justice on the one hand, and on the other hand to be sanctioned by such mechanisms. However, there has been a significant shift within international conceptions of justice mechanisms towards considering individuals' personal responsibility for wrongdoing. The shift towards personal responsibility for high-level officials within key international legal cases is reducing the opportunities for impunity and sending a clear message that corruption will not be tolerated even at the highest levels of government. For example, Noriega claimed immunity as the head of the Panamanian government in *United States of America v. Noriega* (1990). Referring to *Hatch v. Baez* (1876) and *Underhill v. Hernandez* (1897), the court argued, at pp. 1521–1522:

> In order for the act of state doctrine to apply, the defendant must establish that his activities are 'acts of state', i.e. that they were taken on behalf of the state and not, as private acts, on behalf of the actor himself ... That the acts

must be *public* acts of the *sovereign* has been repeatedly affirmed ... Though the distinction between the public and private acts of government officials may prove elusive, this difficulty has not prevented courts from scrutinising the character of the conduct in question.

As Noriega's drug trafficking was clearly not linked to his public duties as the head of state, the court ruled that Noriega was not privy to immunity as a result of his official role. The Pinochet case, *Regina v. Bartle and the Commissioner of Police for the Metropolis and Others Ex Parte Pinochet* (1999), prosecuted in the UK, further and significantly limited the immunity that former heads of state can enjoy for crimes committed during their time in office (Wedgwood, 1999). Prosecuting high-level officials for crimes of corruption sends a clear signal that people at all levels of government and business can be brought to account for their actions.

For high-level prosecutions to take place and be successful, however, significant levels of international cooperation, including capacity-building, data-sharing and compatibility of legal systems and procedures is needed. The UK's and other Western states' ODA budgets can be utilised to ensure that the preconditions for such collaboration are in place, and that the necessary resources are provided for the investigations, prosecutions and asset recovery relating to high-level corruption cases.

Clearly articulating the benefits of different channels of international development assistance, including of partnerships with developing countries and joining 'coalitions of the committed' to address particular issues in international development, such as anti-corruption, will help countries to select the methods of assistance that align most closely with their priorities and are likely to have the intended consequences.

The UK has made direct statements in relation to delivering international development assistance in its own interest: to increase prosperity in developing countries, which will open new markets for UK companies; to increase stability globally, which will reduce the risks of terrorism affecting the UK; and to eradicate, contain and develop effective medication against diseases, which will reduce the likelihood of them spreading to the UK (HMT and DFID, 2015). While this might lead some to question the altruistic nature of the UK's programmes and willingness to get involved in shaping more politically sensitive and governance-related systems in some countries, it might have a positive effect on the fight against corruption globally. This is because of the, now universally perceived, devastating consequences of corruption on economic growth, stability and other indicators of development, and the resulting increase in the UK government's efforts to combat it globally.

Furthermore, assistance in the form of international partnerships, knowledge-sharing and transnational networks of cooperation rather than a top-down provision of aid could improve the effectiveness and sustainability of anti-corruption efforts. While developing countries are likely to gain more from the knowledge and experience of the Global West, such relationships will be mutually

218 *Conclusions and wider implications*

beneficial: for example, the FCA could learn from Kenya's experience in regulating the mobile banking market; and the law enforcement agencies' work in the UK can be significantly assisted by efficient work and collaboration with their developing country counterparts on cases that touch upon multiple jurisdictions.

In conclusion, while there are many challenges to tackling corruption globally, it is an endeavour worth undertaking; and the recent focus on anti-corruption as well as the progress made offers promising signs of the possibility of lasting change in the prevalence and attitudes towards corruption. The fight against corruption will, without doubt, be a long and challenging undertaking. However, as noted by Weber (2004, p. 93),

> It is absolutely true, and our entire historical experience confirms it, that what is possible could never have been achieved unless people had tried again and again to achieve the impossible in this world.

Note

1 This relates to institutions not carrying out their mandate in full (in relation to monitoring party financing mechanisms in a number of countries, see, for example, Wardle (2016)) as well as institutions extending their reach to operate in contexts and manners for which they do not have the required authorisations (see an example about mandates in section 6.1).

Bibliography

Barder, O.M., 2005. Reforming Development Assistance: Lessons from the UK Experience. Center for Global Development, Working Paper No. 70. Available at: https://ssrn.com/abstract=984062 or http://dx.doi.org/10.2139/ssrn.984062.

Burke-White, W.W., 2014. Power Shifts in International Law: Structural Realignment and Substantive Pluralism. U Penn Law Sch. Public Law Res. Pap.

Chin, G.T., 2014. The BRICS-led Development Bank: Purpose and Politics beyond the G20. *Global Policy* 5(3), 366–373. doi:10.1111/1758-5899.12167.

Francioni, F., 2012. Public and Private in the International Protection of Global Cultural Goods. *European Journal of International Law* 23(3).

Gulrajani, N., 2016. Bilateral versus Multilateral Aid Channels. ODI Rep. Available at: www.odi.org/sites/odi.org.uk/files/resource-documents/10393.pdf.

HMT, DFID, 2015. UK Aid: Tackling Global Challenges in the National Interest. Paper. Available at Available at: www.gov.uk/government/uploads/system/uploads/attachment_data/file/478834/ODA_strategy_final_web_0905.pdf.

ICAI, 2015. How DFID Works with Multilateral Agencies to Achieve Impact (No. 44). ICAI. Available at: http://icai.independent.gov.uk/wp-content/uploads/ICAI-Report-How-DFID-works-with-multilateral-agencies-to-achieve-impact.pdf (accessed 24 September 2016).

IDC, 2016. UK Aid: Allocation of Resources: Interim Report, Third Report of Session 2015–2016. Available at: www.publications.parliament.uk/pa/cm201516/cmselect/cmintdev/927/927.pdf.

Lim, A.C.H. (2015, April 19). The US, China and the AIIB: From Zero-sum Competition to Win–Win Cooperation? *Eurasia Review.* Available at: www.eurasiareview.com/19042015-the-us-china-and-the-aiib-from-zero-sum-competition-to-win-win-cooperation-analysis/.

Morgera, E., 2012. Bilateralism at the Service of Community Interests? Non-judicial Enforcement of Global Public Goods in the Context of Global Environmental Law. *European Journal of International Law* 23(3), 743–767.

OECD, 2014. *OECD Development Co-operation Peer Reviews: United Kingdom 2014, OECD Development Co-operation Peer Reviews.* OECD Publishing.

Sen, A., 1999. *Development as Freedom.* Oxford University Press, Oxford.

Van Rooy, A., 2013. *Civil Society and the Aid Industry.* Routledge, London.

Wardle, P., 2016. Cost of Politics: Synthesis Report. Westminster Foundation for Democracy. Available at: www.wfd.org/wp-content/uploads/2016/07/Cost-of-Politics-Synthesis-Report-1.pdf (accessed 26 September 2016).

Weber, M., 2004. *The Vocation Lectures: 'Science as a Vocation' 'Politics as a Vocation'.* Hackett Publishing Company, Indianapolis.

Wedgwood, R., 1999. International Criminal Law and Augusto Pinochet. *Virginia Journal of International Law* 40, 829.

Index

Page numbers in **bold** denote figures, those in *italics* denote tables.

administrative corruption *see* petty corruption
African Union Convention on Preventing and Combatting Corruption (AUCPCC) 14, **99**, 156, 161–162
AFROSAI 179
Angola 126
anti-corruption agencies 105–107, 161
Anti-Corruption Plan (UK) 91–92, 121
anti-corruption strategies 92–93, 95
Arab Spring 1
asset recovery 76, 120–123, 177, 216
ATAF (African Tax Administration Forum) 179
audit **110**, 110–112, 178–179, 189, 205, 212

Ban Ki-Moon 120
bankruptcy *17*
Basel Institute for Governance 121
Bayley, D. 13, 24
behaviour change 92, 115
bilateral aid **90**, **180**, 180–189, 216
Bilateral Aid Review (BAR) 88
bilateral approaches to combatting corruption 180–189, 190–199
Brazil 112
bribery *19*, 64, 154, 156–159
Bribery Act (UK) 107–108, 165, 204
British Virgin Islands (BVI) 177, 202

'capability' approach 43–44
capacity building 95, 121, 178–179, 187
China 25, 125–127, 215
civil society 97, 112–117, 127, 160, 162, 203, 213
citizen engagement 66–67

clan politics 30
'coalitions of the committed' 201–204, 216
Coase, R.H. 52
COE (Council of Europe) Convention **99**, 160–161
collective action theory 3, 58–60, **60**, 74, 95
colonial legacies 27–28, 197
Commonwealth Secretariat 179
Conflict, Security and Stability Fund (CSSF) 91, 186–187
Confucianism 25–26, *116*
consequences of corruption 63–71, **71**; on the economy 63–66; on the efficiency of bureaucratic institutions 66–67; on the environment 69–70; on inequalities 67–68; on stability 68–69
contractors 181–182
corporate misconduct *17*, 18
Corruption Perception Index (CPI) 33, 48–50, 97, **98**, 106–107, 118
Corruption Summit (2016; UK) 7, 9, 92, 96, 100, 201–205
COST (Construction Sector Transparency Initiative) 164
cost of interventions 130–131
cost–benefit calculations 56
'cultural differences' argument 27
customary rules 149, 142
Cremer, G. 2, 16, 124, 191
cross-departmental collaboration 90, 160, 188–189, 212, 214

de Soto, H. 142
decentralisation 55, 63, 71, 111, 142
definitions of corruption 12–24, 211

Index 221

democracy 28, 120, 126, 154, 191
democratisation 55
devtracker 6, 94, 97
direct budget support 86, 94, 183
direct anti-corruption programme support 6, 96
Dodd Frank Act 118
dualism (international law context) 143–144

education 61, 66, 91, **104**, 117, 162
effectiveness of anti-corruption interventions 127–129, 131, 214, 217
effectiveness of international law 146, 193, 196–198
embezzlement 20, 120
enforcement 18, *19*, 53, 95, 102, 142–143, 146, 158, 193–196, 216
European Commission (EC) *15*, 164, 174
European Savings Directive 176
Extractive Industries Transparency Initiative (EITI) 70, **99**, 163

facilitative crime 23
FATF (Financial Action Task Force) **99**, 153, 192
FCPA (Foreign Corrupt Practices Act) 107, 153–155, 157, 165, 204
fiduciary risk 93
Forest Law Enforcement, Governance and Trade (FLEGT) 70, 164
fragile states 32, 69, 91, 94, 100–102, 117, 119–120, 189, 198, 205
fund management 181–182

Georgia 105
gift-giving 23, 26, 29, 115
globalisation 3
grand corruption 74–75, 104, 119, 192
GRECO (Group of States against Corruption) 160–161

Hegel, G.W.F. 28
Hong Kong 105–106
human rights 105, 139, 141, 144, 146–147, 149–152, 195–196

IACAC (Inter-American Convention against Corruption) **99**, 159–160, 162
IATI 6, 7, 101
Ibori 3–4, 122–123
ICAC (Independent Commission against Corruption, Hong Kong) 105–106
ICAR 177–178

ICC (International Chamber of Commerce) 164
illicit financial flows *17*, 75–77, 108
incentives 3, 50–53, 56–58, 60–61, 64, 70, 73, 86, 102, 104–107, 118–119, 132, 163, 165, 171, 182, 190, 203–204
Independent Commission on Anti-Corruption (ICAI) 6–7, 75, 78, **99**, 101, 173–175, 196
India 27, 55, 114
indirect anti-corruption programme support 6, 96–97
Indonesia 45, 51, 66, 73
inequalities 38, 41–44, 67–68, 143
informal justice 142–143
informal sector 68, 142
information: asymmetries 52; sharing 155
interdependencies 4, 100, 107, **109–110**, 129, 132, **215**
international cooperation 18, 177, 204, 212, 217
International Criminal Court (ICC) 194, 206
International Court of Justice (ICJ) 149, 194
International Development Act of 2002 87
International Development Committee (IDC) 101–102, 173, 182–183, 188, 200
International Development (Official Development Assistance Target) Act of 2015 87
International Development (Reporting and Transparency) Act of 2006 93
International Monetary Fund (IMF) 2, 57, 111, 124, 126, 215
INTOSAI 179
investment 64, 69, 73, 125, 142

Johnson, J. 8, 14, 50–51, 94, 112
Joint Anti-Corruption Unit (JACU) 91
Joint Money Laundering Intelligence Taskforce (JACU) 204
justice 39–45, 77, 151, 153

Kenya 45, 74, 96, 108–110, 132, 202, 218
Klitgaard, R.E. 56–57, 61–62, 70
Kuczynski, P. 46–**47**

laundering proceeds of crime 21, 23–25, 121, 123, 159–160, 179, 187, 192, 204
law and development 140–141
Least Developed Countries (LDCs) 125, 184–**185**
Leff, N. 13, 64

legal pluralism 9, 142–145
Libertarianism 40–42
LIBOR 107
lobbying 22–23, 30, 131
Lowcock, Mark 173

mandate 16, 87, 101, 106, 109–110, 124, 171–172, 187–189, 195, 214–**215**, 218
Mandela, Nelson 27
measurement of corruption 48–50, 123
media 93, 97, 100–102, 112, 117–120, 119, 129, 203, 213
meritocratic 30, 72
Migdal, J.S. 60–61, 63
migration 39, 46, 77, 89, 91, 145, 180
misappropriation 20
money laundering *see* laundering proceeds of crime
monism (international law context) 143–144
monitoring 24, 51, 94–75, 111–112, 156–160, 162, 165, 182, 190, 195–198, 200, 202–203, 213
morality 1, 29–30, 38, 52, 146, 151, 154
motivation (for corruption) 23–24, 45–47
MPesa 132
multi-bi 180, 199–201, 205, 216
Multilateral Aid Review (MAR) 175
multilateral approaches to combatting corruption 172–179, 190–199, 216
multilateral organisations 105, 153–165
Mutual Legal Assistance (MLA) 159, 188–189, 212

national interest 88–90, 187, 191, 198, 201, 217
national security 89
neoliberal school 70, 140–141, 165
neopatrimonialism 30
nepotism 22, 30, 32, 68
New Institutional Economics (NIE) 52–53
Nigeria 4, 55, 75, 96, 108, 112, 132
NORAD *15*
North, D. 52
Nozick, R. 39–45
Nussbaum, M. 43–44
Nye, J.S. 13, 49, 75, 191

obstruction of justice 21
OECD *15*, 95, **99**, 101, 118, 155, 157–159, 172, 174, 180, 203
OECD ODA peer review 6, 88, 90, 91, 159, 200

Official Development Assistance (ODA) 5, 9, **87**, 172, 180, 189
offshore *17*, 120, 176–177

Panama Papers 25, 119, 175–177, 204–205
parliaments **104**, 110–112
patronage 29–30, 68–69, 101, 202
Payment by Results (PBR) 102, 182, 206
Peru 129
petty corruption *15*, 50, 53, 74–75, 156, 158–159, 161, 212
Philippines 105
Plato 28–29, 191
pluralistic socio-conscious approach 55
police 49, 52, 58–59, **104**, 104–108, 121, 187, 196, 202
policy implications 61–63
political economy approach 53–55
political funding 22
predictability 72–73
principal–agent theory 3, 52, 56–59, **60**, 61
proceeds of corruption 24–25, 75–76, 120–123, 160, 176–177, 187–188, 204, 212–213
proceeds of crime *see* proceeds of corruption
procurement 6, *17*, 18, 22, 53, 68, 111, *128*, 162
Prosperity Fund 91, 186–187
property rights 40, 52–53, 142
public choice theory 50
public expenditure tracking 111
public financial management (PFM) **104**, 111, *128*
public versus private interests 13–16, 22, 28–30, 32, 56, 65

Rawls, J. 39–42, 78, 153
reforms 4, 30–31, 49, 51, 55, 57, 61, 86, 98, 106–107, 111–112, 126–127, 140–141, 199, 205
refugee *see* migration
regional initiatives 159–164
religion *115*, 115–117, 132, 142
rent seeking 50–53, **54**, 55, 65, 70, 72, 78
Responsibility to Protect (R2P) 152
rights 39–45, 141, 151
Rose-Ackerman, S. 24, 52–53, 56, 113
Rostow, W.W. 140
Rothstein, B. 30–31, 38, 57–58

scandals 30, 48, 86, 106, 118, 153
SEC (Securities and Exchange Commission) 119, 154

Sen, Amartya 39–45, 165, 211
SIDA (Swedish International Development Cooperation Agency) 3, *15*, 16
Smith, A. 44
social capital 68, 114
social norms 68, 86, 141
soft skills 30, 214
sources of international law 142, 148–151
South Korea 54, 65, 72–73, 75–76, 120
sovereignty 123, 151–153, 155
stakeholder engagement 26, 101
STAR **99**, 120, 178
state capture 18, 22, **54**, 71
strengthening legal systems 107–110, 114
Structural Adjustment Programmes (SAPs) 70–71
Switzerland 120, 203

tax 16–17, 72–73, 111–112, 176–177, 187, 203; tax evasion 23, 176–177; tax avoidance 23, 176–177
terrorism 89, 192, 217
tied aid 91
trade *17*, 70, 89, 91, 125–126, 151, 162, 164–165, 187, 192, 215
tragedy of the commons 69–70
transaction costs 50, 52–53, 141, 183, 190, 200
transparency 16, 22, 97, **104**, 154, 160–161, 187, 190
Transparency International *15*, 16, 33, 48, 68, 92, 114
Transparency International Bribe Payers' Index 50
trust *15*, 16, 20, 46, 49, 58, **67**, 68, 113–114

Uganda 92–93

UK aid strategy 7, 88, 91, 171, 188, 198
Ukraine 152
UNCAC (United Nations Convention Against Corruption) 2, 18–20, 48, 77, **99**, 155–158
UNCATOC (United Nations Convention against Transnational and Organised Crime) 155
UNDP (United Nations Development Programme) *15*, 57
UNGC (United Nations Global Compact) **99**, 162–165
United States **5**, 65, 123, 154, 157, 199, 203
USAID *15*, 67, 114, 118
utilitarianism 39–40, 42

value for money 77, 88, 102, 110, 131, 173, 175, 182–183, 193, 213, 216
values 4, 23, **104**, 107, 113, 115, 117, 148–151, 172, 191, 195–196
Vienna Convention (VCLT) 194–195
violence 1, 3, 68–69

Watergate 153–154
whistleblower protection 4, 93, 114, 118–119
white collar and blue collar crimes (differences), 25
Wolfensohn, James 2, 124
World Bank *15*, 57, 70, 121, 123–125, 130, 145, 174, 191, 199–200, 215
World Bank Business Environment Survey 49
World Bank Control of Corruption Index 50

zero tolerance (of corruption) 94

Taylor & Francis eBooks

Helping you to choose the right eBooks for your Library

Add Routledge titles to your library's digital collection today. Taylor and Francis ebooks contains over 50,000 titles in the Humanities, Social Sciences, Behavioural Sciences, Built Environment and Law.

Choose from a range of subject packages or create your own!

Benefits for you
- Free MARC records
- COUNTER-compliant usage statistics
- Flexible purchase and pricing options
- All titles DRM-free.

Benefits for your user
- Off-site, anytime access via Athens or referring URL
- Print or copy pages or chapters
- Full content search
- Bookmark, highlight and annotate text
- Access to thousands of pages of quality research at the click of a button.

REQUEST YOUR FREE INSTITUTIONAL TRIAL TODAY

Free Trials Available
We offer free trials to qualifying academic, corporate and government customers.

eCollections – Choose from over 30 subject eCollections, including:

Archaeology	Language Learning
Architecture	Law
Asian Studies	Literature
Business & Management	Media & Communication
Classical Studies	Middle East Studies
Construction	Music
Creative & Media Arts	Philosophy
Criminology & Criminal Justice	Planning
Economics	Politics
Education	Psychology & Mental Health
Energy	Religion
Engineering	Security
English Language & Linguistics	Social Work
Environment & Sustainability	Sociology
Geography	Sport
Health Studies	Theatre & Performance
History	Tourism, Hospitality & Events

For more information, pricing enquiries or to order a free trial, please contact your local sales team: www.tandfebooks.com/page/sales

The home of Routledge books

www.tandfebooks.com